OUT OF PLACE

ASIAN AMERICAN SOCIOLOGY SERIES
General Editor: Anthony Christian Ocampo

Brown and Gay in LA: The Lives of Immigrant Sons
Anthony C. Ocampo

Japanese Americans and the Racial Uniform: Citizenship, Belonging, and the Limits of Assimilation
Dana Y. Nakano

Out of Place: The Lives of Korean Adoptee Immigrants
SunAh M Laybourn

Out of Place

The Lives of Korean Adoptee Immigrants

SunAh M Laybourn

I'm so glad our paths crossed. Keep shining!

SunAh

NEW YORK UNIVERSITY PRESS

New York

NEW YORK UNIVERSITY PRESS
New York

www.nyupress.org

Cataloging-in-Publication data is available from the publisher.

This book is printed on acid-free paper, and its binding materials are chosen for strength and durability. We strive to use environmentally responsible suppliers and materials to the greatest extent possible in publishing our books.

Manufactured in the United States of America

10 9 8 7 6 5 4 3 2 1

Also available as an ebook

CONTENTS

Introduction

Exceptional Belonging

An unexpected, unfortunate event brought me to the US. It was the fall of 1983. I was only a few months old and recently adopted from Korea. My parents, a White couple in their mid-30s, and I were living in Japan, where my dad was stationed as a US Marine. Although we had no plans to go to the US so soon, news of my paternal grandfather's passing led the three of us to fly back home to Markesan, Wisconsin. As we made our way through the customs and immigration checkpoint, we were stopped by an immigration officer.

My parents had my Korean passport, but they didn't have a visa for me to enter the country. As my dad recalls, there was a lot of back and forth between him and the immigration officer. "I told him that we were coming home on emergency leave to attend my father's funeral and that I didn't know that I needed a visa to get you into the USA. Of course, I had your adoption papers, my emergency leave papers, and the communication from the American Red Cross, which was the organization that notified my commanding officer of my father's death."

After much discussion between my dad and the immigration officer, the immigration officer and his supervisor, and the supervisor and my dad, the agent stamped my passport, and I was allowed into the US. We stayed for a month before flying back to Japan.

Even after the airport incident, once we moved back to the US for my dad's final military assignment, my parents assumed, as most American parents of internationally adopted children do, that I had US citizenship. After all, citizenship is a family matter. Even if the child of US parents is born abroad, they still acquire US citizenship. However, international adoption does not adhere to the citizenship rules governing biological kinship. At that time, international adoption and naturalization were separate processes despite early lobbying by adoption agencies and adoptive parents for federal-level policy changes to expedite adoptee naturalization.[1]

It would be several years later that my parents finally understood my citizenship status. By then we had been living in the US for about six years; my dad had since retired from the military. While updating their life insurance policies, they became unavoidably aware that I was not a citizen. My dad promised my mom he would do whatever was necessary to secure my citizenship, and in the fall of 1993, my father began the application process.

After obtaining the forms to Petition for Naturalization on Behalf of Child[2] for US citizen parents of an internationally adopted child and not the initial form he was given for Application for Certificate of Citizenship for the child of "alien parents who were later naturalized,"[3] completing and submitting the correct forms, proactively following up at each stage of the process, having incorrect fees returned, resubmitting correct fees, and waiting for correspondence on a date for my naturalization interview—only to have to reschedule—a year and a half later, on Lincoln's birthday, I became a naturalized citizen. I was 12 years old.

I was one of the lucky ones. Others were not so lucky.

In early 2015, Immigration and Customs Enforcement (ICE) agents were at Adam Crapser's front door in Vancouver, Washington, serving him deportation paperwork.[4] Adam was adopted as a toddler from Korea to the US, but neither the Wrights, his first adoptive family, nor the Crapsers, who adopted him after the Wrights relinquished him to the state, took the necessary steps to naturalize him.[5] He was now in his late 30s with a wife and young children of his own. When Adam reapplied for a green card, the standard background check was flagged.[6] Responding to his case, Rose M. Richeson, spokeswoman for ICE's Seattle field office, noted that ICE prioritizes deportation of "individuals who pose a threat to national security, public safety, and border security."[7] Adam's criminal record began with a burglary of the first degree conviction, a charge for breaking into the Crapsers' home to retrieve personal belongings, including a Korean-language Bible from when he was in a Korean orphanage as a child.[8] Later he was convicted of felony gun possession, assault, and theft.[9]

The news of "Adam Crapser's Bizarre Deportation Odyssey," as the *New York Times Magazine*[10] headline described it, sent shockwaves through its readership—those intimately touched by adoption and those personally unfamiliar with it alike. Adam's deportation proceedings exposed the enduring loopholes in the Child Citizenship Act of 2000 (CCA).[11] The CCA granted automatic US citizenship to internationally adopted children who were under the age of 18 at the time of the legislation and to future international adoptees adopted under the appropriate visas.[12] However, because Adam was already over 18 years of age when the CCA passed, his citizenship status and that of others in the earliest international adoption cohorts remained unchanged. Instead, he fell under existing rules for the immigration and naturalization process.

Although Adam entered the US legally when he was adopted as a toddler, it was incumbent upon his adoptive parents to ensure his naturalization.

They did not.

If the Crapsers would have given Adam his adoption paperwork, he would have been able to reapply for his green card earlier.

They would not.[13]

By the time the Crapsers provided Adam with his adoption paperwork and he submitted the green card application in 2012, he was living in the US without authorization and, given his previous criminal activity,[14] eligible for deportation. He joined the three dozen other international adoptees who have faced deportation charges.[15] While the number of deported adoptees pales in comparison to the more than quarter million immigrants who have been deported on average annually in the past two decades,[16] adoptee citizenship disputes are a stark illustration of the precarity of belonging.

Counsel argued it was a mere technicality that Adam did not have citizenship. After all, Adam was brought to the US as a child, adopted by American parents, and as such should have the rights and responsibilities like any other child of US citizens. That much had already been confirmed through previous adoptive parent organizing and codified through the CCA.[17] Supporters—adoptees, Asian Americans, and allies—pressed for an administrative closure of his case. Immigration judges and the Board of Immigration Appeals can use this procedural tool to temporarily pause removal proceedings under appropriate circumstances, giving individuals the opportunity to pursue other forms of relief. Critics—most notably adoptees—took the hard line that if Adam hadn't committed the crimes, then he would not have been flagged for deportation, though ignoring that his citizenship status would still be in limbo.

By the end of his nearly nine-month stay in an Immigration and Customs detention facility while he awaited trial, Adam was ready for the denouement. In late October, Judge John C. O'Dell ordered Adam's deportation. Before the 2016 holiday season, Adam said goodbye to his pregnant wife, two children, and the only country he ever knew and boarded a plane to Korea: his first trip back since his adoption 38 years earlier.

* * *

How does one go from adoptable orphan to deportable immigrant, desirable yet discardable, in one lifetime—from special laws, policies, and even individual exceptions facilitating adopted Korean children's immigration to the US to being omitted from conventional immigration narratives until being deported as an adult? What ideas of race, family, and citizenship do adoptable orphans and deportable immigrants represent? What does the Korean adoptee story tell us about becoming and belonging?

In unraveling these questions, I demonstrate how adoptable orphan and deportable immigrant are not happenstance constructions. Rather, they are racialized classifications intentionally crafted to advance beliefs about national belonging. Considered separately, they represent age-specific investments in kinship, citizenship, and race. Adoptable orphans are vulnerable children, typically from the Global South, whose family ties are portrayed as wholly replaceable through adoption by citizens in the Global North. Deportable immigrants are expendable adults, who were never seen as fully belonging to the US and therefore easily disposable. By examining these constructions together, I aim to outline a continuum of inclusion and exclusion. In doing so, my goal is to investigate how racialization processes and assimilation expectations converge throughout individuals' lives—here creating adoptable orphans and deportable immigrants—and to assess what the Korean adoptee case tells us about how belonging and becoming are created across time and one's life, informally and formally, structurally and affectively.

My focus on the Korean adoptee case becomes particularly compelling for several reasons. First, adoption from Korea set the foundation for the contemporary international adoption industry. Although there were previous instances of transnational adoption, Korean adoption institutionalized the process with impacts on policy, both foreign and domestic, and beliefs about family and race.[18] Second, Korean adoption began at a unique time in the Asian American race-making process when Asian Americans' racial status was being actively contested from the top down and the bottom up in response to changing racial ideologies and geopolitics.[19] Finally, although Korean adoptees are not the only undocumented adoptees who have been deported or who are vulnerable to deportation, they have positioned themselves as the most visible impacted adoptee contingency. Staking citizenship claims on members of a racial group, who have historically been constructed as foreigners, definitively outside of the American family, presents unique challenges with implications for the strategies adoptee advocates, elected officials, and other stakeholders use in adoptee citizenship rights advocacy.

Asian Americans, Race, and the Feeling of Belonging

The intertwining of kinship, citizenship, and race as a feature of US national belonging was formally established in 1790 when Congress restricted naturalization to "free white persons."[20] While the law did not explicitly mention gender, by 1855, a woman's naturalization was conferred through her husband's citizenship. Although this Naturalization Act provided a pathway to citizenship for immigrant women, it was only available to those who met the racial requirements of citizenship. Citizenship was beholden to beliefs about race and belonging, and the family produced the nation-state.

Throughout subsequent decades, women would continue to slip in and out of citizenship based on their husband's status. Almost 50 years later, the Expatriation Act mandated that "any American woman who marries a foreigner shall take the nationality of her husband," revoking the citizenship of women married to non-citizens.[21] A woman could regain citizenship upon her husband's naturalization if he chose to naturalize and as long as he was not deemed ineligible for naturalization. Eventually the Cable Act would repeal the previous law, but it included one major caveat—the citizenship of female American citizens married to non-citizens of Asian descent could still be revoked.[22] Asians were so firmly located outside of the national body that a White woman's position in the nation could be revoked by proximity.

Eventually the 1952 McCarran-Walter Act eliminated race as a basis for citizenship eligibility. However, prior to that, how individuals sought to prove their Whiteness to attain citizenship encompassed a variety of capricious and contradictory factors based in a mixture of popular beliefs and "science."[23] This is illustrated by the courts' approach to immigrants from western and southern Asia, who in early "scientific" racial classifications were categorized as Caucasian but seen by the average man as not White. Petitioners argued for their naturalization eligibility drawing upon ideas of Whiteness that were biological, cultural, and social, the definitions of which were often at odds with one another, but ultimately enforced by those in power to uphold White domination.[24] This process simultaneously created boundaries around Whiteness and non-Whiteness, dictating who was legible as a person suitable for becoming a member of the national family.

Accordingly, a large body of research argues that the construction of Asians as foreigners is central to the US citizenship project. Scholars identify how Asians have been framed as racial and foreign "Others" to White Americans through the racialization of Asian physical features and cultural differences.[25] Because of this, even once Asians were legally permitted within the US they could never be seen as "real" Americans.[26] In this view, Asians are firmly planted outside of the national family even as they are allowed within its geopolitical borders. Lisa Lowe, commenting on Asians' insider and outsider positions, calls out the "contradictions of Asian immigration, which at different moments in the last century and a half of Asian entry into the United States have placed Asians "within" the US nation-state, its workplaces, and its markets, yet linguistically, culturally, and racially marked Asians as "foreign" and "outside" the national polity.[27]

Racialized stereotypes about Asian Americans' culture exist along a continuum of assimilation and exclusion, acting as a mechanism defining a White collective identity.[28] From the late 1800s to early 1900s, US industries recruited Asian male workers as cheap, expendable labor while media, government, and everyday people construed them as a threatening Yellow Peril encroaching upon White American culture and prosperity.[29] By the mid-20th century, the same entities that vilified

Asians in America lauded them as an exemplary model minority for their socioeconomic success, crediting their cultural values, work ethic, and family structure.[30]

Asian Americans' simultaneous inclusion and exclusion creates boundaries around belonging upholding the racial hierarchy. Claire Jean Kim illustrates how Asian Americans, Black Americans, and White Americans are "racially triangulated" between and across one another through processes of cultural valorization and civic ostracism that uphold White domination.[31] While Asian Americans are culturally valorized in comparison to Black Americans, in this model, Asian Americans' presumed foreignness becomes a justification for their exclusion from civic membership. In a field of racialized positions, all racial groups are constantly evaluated against one another along multiple dimensions, constraining how they experience the full rights and privileges of citizenship. Nadia Y. Kim extends racial triangulation theory by arguing that America's general lack of familiarity with Asian Americans contributes to their foreignness. Thus, invisibility complements visibility in establishing Asian Americans' misrecognition within the national body.

My approach builds upon scholarship on Asian Americans and the citizenship project to examine how racialization processes and assimilation expectations take distinct shape throughout Korean adoptees' lives, acting as initiation rites into their racial place as Asian Americans, who are racialized as "Others." Korean adoptees are a unique case to investigate these race-making processes because of their intimacy with Whiteness. To conduct this examination, I explore the refusals of belonging shaping adoptees' position as adoptable orphans and deportable immigrants. To do so, I offer the concept of "exceptional belonging." I define "exceptional belonging" as the condition of being extraordinarily equipped for inclusion through culturally constructed narratives of deservedness while also being routinely identified for exclusion whether through formal policies, informal practices, or interpersonal interactions. Thus, exceptional belonging is organized throughout the various realms of society in distinct yet mutually reinforcing ways. Patricia Hill Collins's domains of power framework becomes instructive here.[32] As a power analytic, it offers an organizing tool for examining how power relations, such as those that create a racialized citizenship and the rights and privileges thereof, are enacted and resisted across the structural, disciplinary, interpersonal, and cultural domains of society.

Through this lens, "adoptable orphan" and "deportable immigrant" are ideological framings and legal constructions that uphold the status quo. "Adoptable orphan" holds the promises of assimilation, as unattainable as they may be; "deportable immigrant" performs the promises of protections inherent in belonging, to the detriment of those deemed outside the national ideal. These positions engender affective dispositions shaping one's feelings of belonging and non-belonging. In other words, exceptional belonging is not only about the practices and policies of legality, or lack thereof, but also about how one is made to *feel* part of or apart from the nation. These feelings have power. Shared feelings move people to act on behalf of themselves and others they identify with or in ways to exclude those they see as different from themselves. These feelings can lead an immigration officer to allow a White military couple's child into the country without proper documentation or an immigration judge to deport an undocumented criminal immigrant.

Emotions are not merely feelings but rather social and cultural practices that establish oneself, a sense of we-ness, and the distinction between "us" and "them." Thus, the cultural politics of emotions act as one of the structuring mechanisms of the nation-state.[33] Asian Americanists' analysis of Asians' racialization as "foreigners within" is an example of the emotional component of national borders.[34] Public feelings shape and are shaped by emotional investments in a racialized national identity. Paula Ioanide details how racialized fears of those who are unlike the national "us" (e.g., racial minorities, immigrants) can be mobilized in support of racial violence carried out through policing, the military, immigration policies, and welfare programs.[35] Consequently, the emotional investments in national membership reinforce structural racism. In a racialized social structure, members are socialized into an emotional subjectivity reflecting their location in the racial hierarchy, what Eduardo Bonilla-Silva refers to as "racialized emotions."[36]

While group members never unitarily experience racialized emotions, for Korean transracial adoptees the process is further complicated due to their upbringing in families of a different race. Adoption researcher Richard M. Lee calls the phenomenon of transracial adoptees' experience of racial two-ness the "transracial adoption paradox," whereby adoptees "are racial/ethnic minorities in society but are perceived and treated by others, and sometimes themselves, as if they are members of the majority culture (i.e., racially White and ethnically European)."[37]

Most transracial adoptees are adopted into White families and as a result socialized into the White racial frame. The White racial frame "includes a broad and persisting *set of racial stereotypes, prejudices, ideologies, interlinked interpretations and narratives, and visual images*. It also includes *racialized emotions* and *racialized reactions . . .* and *embeds inclinations to discriminate*" (emphasis in original).[38] This structuring orientation to society has unique limitations for adoptees when they are racialized into their position as minoritized subjects. Unsurprisingly, scholars find transracial adoptees report feeling in between racial groups.[39] However, because race and citizenship are entangled in the US, the *transnational* transracial adoptee paradox is not only about racial-cultural expectations but also how adoptees experience national belonging. My analysis of adoptees' exceptional belonging and their conflicting racialized emotions engages Tobias Hübinette's discussion of Korean adoptee hybridity and the creation of a third space and Eleana J. Kim's investigation of adoptee identity politics and the creation of an adoptee counter-public.[40] It also builds upon Kim Park Nelson's examination of Korean adoptees' identity and feelings of belonging as shaped by and reflective of US racial ideologies.[41]

One of the first narratives of belonging adoptees learn is their adoption story. Max (b. 1984) relayed a common one: "When I was growing up, it was more of a very basic, very vague, kind of, 'Your mother couldn't take care of you, so she put you up for adoption . . . thought you'd have a better life in the United States.' That was pretty much it." Adoptees echoed this framing of familial and national inclusion. Audra's (b. 1980) parents explained her adoption saying, "Your parents loved you very much. They loved you so much that they gave you to us because they realized they couldn't take as good of care of you as maybe we could." Destiny's (b. 1995) adoption story was similar: "basically [that] my parents love me enough to give me a better life in America." While these were individual family stories of inclusion, they are situated within broader histories of immigration, kinship, and race that laid the foundation for how adoptees and non-adoptees thought about adoptees' place in their families and in the US.

The romanticized origin story of a "better life in the United States" is rooted in American exceptionalism characterizing the US as uniquely capable, virtuous, benevolent, and divinely ordained. As recipients of a "better life," adoptees are socialized into expectations of gratitude. In the popular imaginary of transnational adoption, adoptees are orphaned children in need, who are rescued from developing countries. Adoption imbues these perpetual children with hope and potential. This framing of adoption and the adoptee affect it produces enacts a form of symbolic violence. Adoption scholar Kit Myers refers to the specific harm that happens when making transnational transracial adoptive families legible through statements of love and limited notions of family as the "violence of love."[42] By situating love as the mechanism moving adoptees from an abject state in a developing country to reemerging as full of potential in a Western nation, adoption stories introduce an adoptee subjectivity forged through ideas of rescue, gratitude, and unspeakable loss.

An adoptee affect of gratitude is a consequence of racialization and assimilation expectations formed through the transnational adoption industrial complex (TAIC). Asian Americanist and adoption scholar Kimberly McKee offers the TAIC as a framework to understand the creation of transnational adoption as a global form of family-making and unmaking, one that turns adoptees into commodities.[43] Whereas adoptees are socialized into an affective position of gratitude and happiness, McKee presents the concept of the "adoptee killjoy," who enacts an adoptee "politics of refusal—refusal to engage an affective performance of gratitude."[44] In failing to perform the "correct" affect, adoptee killjoys threaten the happiness of others involved in the adoption process while also challenging the myth of adoption as solely altruistic and wholly beneficial. I build upon McKee's analysis of adoptee affect with Eleana J. Kim's discussion of adoptee affective bonds and practices of care.[45] I consider the range of adoptee racialized emotions—from adoptees' socialization into the racial group membership of their adoptive families to their racialization as Asian Americans—and how adoptees create their own social group with unique emotional group norms, confronting the competing expectations of race, family, citizenship, and belonging.

Contextualizing Korean Adoption, Institutionalizing Exceptional Belonging

Most accounts of transnational transracial adoption situate its origins in the post–World War II period. Korean adoption began in 1953 and would become the first institutionalized international adoption program; however, Mark C. Jerng locates the beginnings of transracial and transnational adoption much earlier, with Native American adoption of White captives.[46] In these instances, White captives became incorporated as kinsmen, taking on a new social identity, thereby illustrating the fluidity of racial and national boundaries. With this as a starting point, Jerng demonstrates the co-creation, contestation, and transformation of race, family, citizenship, and personhood throughout US history. Rather than adoption simply responding to existing ideas about race, in Jerng's formulation, adoption was an active part of race-making processes, or how racial categories are created and modified.

From this perspective, adoption from Korea is not so much an anomaly in adoption history but rather another inflection point in contestations over becoming and belonging as produced through ever-evolving ideas of citizenship, kinship, and race. By tracing the histories of transnational transracial adoption, adoption scholars reveal how adoption is indicative of anxieties over race relations while reflecting broader geopolitics. In the case of Korean adoption, historian Arissa H. Oh argues that post–World War II public and private spheres merged as the family became a site for Cold War domestic politics, including racial liberalism.[47] Previously, adoption practices were governed by matching policies, whereby prospective adoptive parents and children were matched by race, ethnicity, and religion.[48] Korean transnational transracial adoption transgressed ideas of race-based kinship as Asian children were incorporated into White families. But it also attempted to reproduce the monoracial family structure by ideologically and culturally whitening Korean children. SooJin Pate, too, outlines the effect of Cold War ideologies on adoption.[49] As the US expanded its global power throughout Asia, US families mirrored US-Asia relations. Thus, the US's positioning as a big brother to the fledgling Korean nation-state via humanitarian efforts in-country and through transnational adoption became ways to assert its standing on the global stage. While the bulk of work on Korean adoption focuses on White families, Kori Graves's examination of African American families in the early years of Korean adoption uncovers how child welfare organizations, press, military, and other governmental and non-governmental entities approached Black couples' transnational transracial adoption in ways that reflected Cold War civil rights.[50] Though discriminatory practices within social work prevented many interested African American families from adopting, their participation in the transnational transracial adoption project left an indelible mark on adoption practices in ways that ultimately benefited White adopters.

Broader ideological shifts joined intentional projects to make Korean orphans adoptable. Government-led public campaigns framed Korean children as especially vulnerable in a war-torn country and indefinitely separated from their biological family. Korean children's "clean break" from their biological families and birth culture mirrored the cultural expectations of absolute severance from first family (and national ties) that was codified in the first modern adoption law in 1851.[51] The portrayal of orphaned Korean children desperately in need circulated as culturally resonant images. These "iconographies of rescue" moved American couples to save helpless foreign children.[52] Scholars note that many adopted Korean children were not without family but were created into orphans through paperwork and discursive strategies, which allowed them to become legally and socially adoptable.[53] As adoptable orphans, Korean adoptees were eligible to be remade into American family members.

White American couples' desire for Korean children often resulted in individual exceptions to facilitate their immigration. To further respond to American couples' desire for Korean children and to enable adoptable orphans' immigration, some existing immigration policies were refashioned, such as the 1953 Refugee Relief Act and later the Refugee-Escapee Act of 1957, allowing others to be circumvented.[54] Although immigration from Asian countries was limited to a 100-person quota,[55] the Orphan Eligibility Clause of the Immigration and Nationality Act of 1961 recategorized Korean adoptees from "eligible orphan" to "immediate relative." As immediate relatives, Korean adoptees bypassed the quota system and instead were subsumed under national priorities of family reunification even in the face of race-based exclusionary immigration policies. Recasting adoptees as family detached them from immigrant narratives of inalienable foreignness. Eleana Kim and Kim Park Nelson argue the myriad ways Korean adoptees were distinguished from other immigrant populations because of their connections to Whiteness constitute a unique "immigration privilege."[56] Their legislative exceptionalism—particularly how adoptees' immigration was facilitated while their naturalization was not—is illustrative of adoptees' exceptional belonging.

Ultimately, exceptional belonging would facilitate the adoption of over 150,000 Korean children primarily to White American families.[57] Korean adoption peaked in the 1980s with over 66,500 adoptions but continues, albeit in decreasing numbers, even today.[58] In the late 1980s, China replaced Korea as the primary sending country of Asian adoptees. By then, international adoption was solidified as a form of family-making, and adoption from Asia as especially acceptable, desirable, and relatively problem-free in comparison to domestic adoption or adoption from other countries, even as international adoption expanded throughout the Global South.[59] Although Asian children continue to be integrated into White families—and, by extension, the national family, as I will show—their belonging has its limits.

Korean Adoptees: A Case of Exceptional Belonging

To examine how exceptional belonging shaped adoptees' belonging and becoming, I employed a range of methods, including an online survey, in-depth interviews, participant observation at Korean adoptee events in the US and Korea, and content analysis of various media. The online survey (N=107) served as my first entry point to broadly understanding how Korean adoptees were thinking of their own belonging. As with other geographically dispersed and marginalized groups, adoptees have leveraged the internet to connect with one another. In her ethnography of the Korean adoptee counter-public, Eleana Kim details how adoptees created message boards and listservs in the pre–social media internet era to begin organizing a transnational Korean adoptee network.[60] Because of the existing infrastructure, I was able to quickly distribute my survey through pre-existing Korean adoptee groups across the US. I also promoted the survey in non-adoptee, non-Korean Facebook Groups and individuals' Facebook pages.

One key finding is approximately 32 percent of survey respondents identified as a "Korean adoptee" separate from other racial, ethnic, or national identities. The "Korean adoptee" identifiers had a range of childhood experiences with Korean cultural engagement, racial socialization, and adoptee-specific or adoptive family activities. This suggests that there is a unique and specific experience created through transnational transracial adoptees' exceptional belonging.

With the survey as a guide, I began to interview adoptees (N=37) who represented some of the patterns I saw in the responses. In particular, I wanted to know more about how respondents came to a "Korean adoptee" identity and what that identity looked like in their everyday life. Adoption scholars have conceptualized the Korean adoptee identity as a personal journey of individual self-actualization, an understanding of oneself as being between racial and ethnic identities, and/or a response to experiences of marginalization.[61] Rather than approach the Korean adoptee identity as a personal identity or as a label to refer to a series of themes across individuals' experience, I was interested in understanding how adoptees themselves constructed it as a social identity, one with shared meaning, values, emotional repertoires, and culture. I wanted to know if and how the Korean adoptee group identity functioned as a response to the processes of exceptional belonging.

The Korean adoptees I spoke with and surveyed were raised in all regions of the US; grew up in large metropolitan areas, suburbs, and small rural towns; had adopted siblings, siblings biological to their adoptive parents, and no siblings at all. Most respondents were women (reflecting the gender composition of the Korean adoptee population), had at least a bachelor's degree, held liberal political views, and were adopted when they were younger than a year old. The majority were adopted by White couples. In 2016 when the interviews were conducted, most were in their late 20s to early 30s, reflective of the peak wave of adoption from Korea in the 1980s, though the overall ages ranged from 21 to 56. Some of the adoptees I spoke with were among the founders of the Korean adoptee community, some relatively new to it, and some had never spoken to another Korean adoptee outside of Facebook group messages until they chatted with me. In short, they represented a wide range of backgrounds, experiences, and perspectives. Yet one thing they shared was conflicting moments of racialization and expectations of assimilation shaping how they experienced kinship, citizenship, and race.

Race-making is an ongoing process that includes internal identification and external ascription in response to social, political, and historical conditions. Accordingly, I wanted to know how adoptees' ideas of race and belonging—their own and others—had changed, or not, over time and space. I was able to capture some of this by asking about their impressions of the racial demographics of their neighborhoods, schools, other social contexts, and close friends and corroborating with US Census data on the racial demographics of their neighborhoods and schools. Importantly, as I was starting my research, Adam Crapser's deportation case was unfolding, the Black Lives Matter movement was ongoing, and the US was in a highly divisive presidential campaign season that ended with the election of Donald Trump. This is vital context because it colored the way adoptees were talking about race, citizenship, and belonging. As you will see in the following chapters, for some, this shifting terrain was leading to new questions, for others it solidified feelings of non-belonging, and for still others it led them to double down on their identification with Whiteness.

For most of my respondents, our interview was the first time they participated in adoption research. Their motivations for participating in my study illuminate a form of "adoptee kinship" whereby adoptees feel a sense of responsibility toward one another.[62] Most stated that they felt an obligation to give back to the community, to help other adoptees—

including those who might read my study, and me specifically—or to contribute a different perspective, whether positive or more critical depending on the respondent's perception of existing research.

Even though most of my respondents were connected to the broader Korean adoptee community, even if only through Korean adoptee Facebook Groups, some did not see themselves as members of the community. Instead, they viewed belonging as limited to those who held a specific view of adoption that they themselves did not share—some viewed the adoptee community as those who had a positive adoption experience or at least viewed adoption positively, while they themselves did not share those views; others saw the adoptee community as those who were critical of adoption or advocated the end of adoption, while they were more optimistic. Even for those who would not categorize themselves as members of the Korean adoptee community, they felt it was important to share their story so that there would be a multiplicity of perspectives represented in my work. In many ways, these responses are indicative of how adoptees have often felt like outsiders to their families, to the nation, and to their racial and ethnic groups. Ironically, it is the feeling of also being outside of the adoptee community that many respondents shared.

Because race, citizenship, and family are reflected in and regulated by policy, press, and cultural production, I also analyzed a variety of media, including *Twinsters* and *aka SEOUL*, two mainstream Korean adoptee-created documentaries; *Blue Bayou*, a theatrical release directed by a Korean American portraying the deportation of an undocumented Korean adoptee; news stories about Adam Crapser's case and adoptee citizenship rights; and press releases about the Adoptee Citizenship Act. Including cultural production allowed me to situate adoptees' experiences within the collective meanings created by adoptee creatives for public audiences and those created by non-adoptees. Moreover, these media and press coverage of adoptee-related events provided shared experiences among adoptees, engendering emotional responses that act as community-building factors. By putting adoptee-created media (e.g., *Twinsters, aka SEOUL*) in conversation with other cultural constructions about adoptees (e.g., news stories, press releases, *Blue Bayou*), I demonstrate how competing narratives about race, citizenship, and kinship are created, circulated, contested, and understood.

Chapter Outline

In the chapters that follow, I examine how the multidimensional process of exceptional belonging simultaneously produced adoptable orphans and deportable immigrants. In chapter 1, I examine how Korean adoptees' exceptional belonging was enacted in their daily lives through their upbringing. Where immigration legislation, social services practices, and cultural framings positioned adoptable Korean children as assimilable to the national family, it is within the realm of the family that those beliefs were carried out. White adoptive parents reared their Korean children as if they shared racial group membership. As a result, private racialization within the family socialized adoptees into conflicting racialized emotions of belonging as White family members and non-belonging as Asians. Previous research locates transracial adoptees' racialization as non-Whites outside of the family; however, I demonstrate that adoptees first learn their racial place as Asian American outsiders *within* the family.

In chapter 2, I detail adoptees' public racialization. Through racial reinscriptions from their peers, other adults in their lives, and strangers, adoptees were disciplined into their racial place outside of Whiteness and into a shared Asian American position of presumed foreignness. Refusals of belonging variably racialized adoptees as Asian, not-White, and Black, reflecting their shifting racial in/visibility within their immediate communities and the nation. When Asian American adoptees are not knowable as people in their local and national contexts, they are that much more easily formally expelled from the nation.

Chapter 3 considers how adoptee citizenship vulnerability and the advocacy for a legislative remedy exposes the competing racialized logics within exceptional belonging. Some advocates centered their advocacy on pre-existing tropes around adoptees, family, and Whiteness as the prerequisite for citizenship, appealing to ideas of family permanency and national belonging. Others linked the fight for undocumented adoptees to other undocumented immigrants, emphasizing the joint struggles across similarly impacted groups. And some adoptee advocates connected individual impacted adoptees' citizenship vulnerability to transnational adoptees' shared experience of immigration and adoption. All of these strategies aim to activate group identity to spur people to action. The varying strategies adoptees and their allies used to garner support illuminate how racialized emotions produce material outcomes.

Chapter 4 turns to how adoptees transform the everyday experiences of their exceptional belonging into a source of shared group membership. While their in/visibility as family members and citizens were refusals of belonging that stigmatized their racial, familial, and national membership, among one another those experiences became part of the substance of a shared Korean adoptee social identity. The Korean adoptee group identity has its own cultural template and emotional group norms defying expectations of adoptee personhood constrained within normative protocols for belonging.

Where the identity meaning-making in chapter 4 is largely internal among adoptees, chapter 5 considers how Korean adoptee media offers new representation of Korean adoptees to mainstream audiences. I analyze *Twinsters* and *aka SEOUL*, two documentaries created by Korean adoptees, as cultural texts of disidentification from the dominant script for adoptee personhood. Rather than adhere to normative protocols for belonging in family, race, or nation, the documentaries present an adoptee subjectivity that re-presents who they can be and how they can feel. Additionally, I examine *Blue Bayou*, a movie written by a non-adoptee Korean American about the fictional account of an undocumented Korean, for its challenges to traditional depictions of adoptees, adoption, and Asian Americans. In addition to analyzing the alternate portrayal of adoptees within the movie, I also include how adoptees' public responses to the film demonstrate adoptees' authority over their own story. Taken together, this chapter highlights adoptees' own refusals to belong within their place as adoptable orphans or deportable immigrants.

Out of Place: The Lives of Korean Adoptee Immigrants moves beyond an isolated story of adoptee inclusion and exclusion to provide an organizing framework to examine how exceptional belonging takes shape across time and people's lives, structurally, culturally, and affectively. By uncovering the process of exceptional belonging, that makes possible dominant, interdependent constructions of citizenship, kinship, and race, we gain a better understanding of the emotional investments in in these categories of belonging. *Out of Place* charts how these informal and formal processes unfold such that Korean transnational transracial adoptees are alternately adoptable orphans and deportable immigrants, desirable yet discardable. The lives of Korean adoptee immigrants demonstrate the possibilities and challenges to reframing inclusion as adoptees themselves make sense of what it means to be out of place.

1

Feeling White, Feeling Right

"I feel completely American. I really do. No part of me feels Korean at all," Bradley (b. 1981) told me matter-of-factly. Bradley grew up on the West Coast. Most of his childhood was spent in the city, except for holidays when he visited his extended family's ranch. He continued, "When I experienced the mild racist, whatever, things that happen as you get older and you're growing up, it really made no sense to me. I'm an American, I'm a proud American and all that. It really doesn't resonate with me, it makes no sense . . . being American but looking not American, I guess. I don't know how to say it. Being in that situation is so . . . It seems ridiculous to me when people make these racist comments, because I couldn't be more American or proud of being American."

How did Bradley come to "*feel* completely American," where "no part" of him "*feels* Korean at all" (emphasis added)? How did Bradley come to *feel* race? And why could he not feel both American and Korean? Cultural constructions of Korean children as assimilable to the White American family and policy exceptions that treated adoptees as non-immigrant immigrants certainly contributed to Korean adoptees' exceptional belonging. But those weren't the only factors contributing to Bradley's feelings about who he was and his racial place. While Bradley's reflection on feeling American could be misread as a cultural-national orientation, his description of "being American but looking not American" reveals that being an American is a racialized group membership—one that is unavailable to him because of how he looks. Feeling race, then, is about individual feelings of belonging as well as socially held beliefs about racial groups and their place in society.

In the mid-1970s, Howard University Press published *Aiiieeeee!*, one of the first anthologies of Asian American literature.[1] In the preface, the editors lambasted the absurdity of the Asian American "dual personality" myth—the belief that Asian Americans could be either American or Asian as they chose or that they could be both—given Asia's and (White) America's dismissal of Asian Americans. Rejection was one part of the Asian American experience. The editors went on to describe American culture's denial of Asian Americans as racial minorities and the US's history of "legislative racism and euphemized white racist love."[2] Together these ideas placed Asian Americans outside of the boundaries of racial minorities and the racial majority, leaving Asian Americans out of place in the US racial landscape. These refusals of belonging produced an Asian American feeling of self-contempt and self-rejection. Although Asian Americans' structural, cultural, and interpersonal marginalization from US society may have led to negative self-evaluations, the editors argued that a uniquely Asian American sensibility exists—one that is not solely Asian, solely American, nor White America's stereotypes of Asians.

Several decades before *Aiiieeeee!*'s publication, W. E. B. Du Bois famously theorized "double consciousness" to characterize Black Americans' internal conflict of feeling one's "two-ness"—"two souls, two thoughts, two unreconciled strivings; two warring ideals in one dark body."[3] In theorizing Black Americans' "two-ness," double consciousness recognized the difference between African and American consciousness in a way that acknowledged the value of African distinctiveness. It also drew attention to the contradictions of belonging—of being American but excluded from the protections and privileges of citizenship because of anti-Black racism—and the sense of racial position it created.

Of course, the effect of the racial hierarchy on one's worldview and affective experience is not limited to non-Whites. In "The Souls of White Folks," Du Bois went on to describe how, in creating a racial power structure, Whites created a myth of a White identity deemed morally and intellectually superior to all other races.[4] This White identity engendered a sense of racial pride alongside a disdain for racial others. The differing positions that Asians, Blacks, Whites, and other people of color hold in the racialized social structure produce racialized emotions reflective of their racial place. Transnational transracial adoption complicates this process.

Bradley's epigraph alludes to the contradictory racialized feelings produced by transnational transracial adoption. Although Bradley "couldn't be more American," there is a disconnect between how *he* feels as a "proud American" and how *others* believe he should feel as someone who looks "not American." Further, even though Bradley reluctantly concedes to not meeting the normative protocols for being seen as American, he also doesn't feel any sense of belonging with co-ethnics. This could be read as a response to public racialization socializing Asian Americans into their position as the "foreigner within" and the concomitant Asian American racial feelings of self-rejection.[5] However, as I spoke with adoptees it became evident that it was within *their family* that they first encountered positive feelings associated with being American (i.e., White) and negative feelings associated with being Korean.

The transracial adoption paradox describes adoptees with White adoptive parents as experiencing the benefits of Whiteness within their families while locating the stigmas associated with their Asian racialized group membership as happening outside of the family.[6] However, families are not exempt from reproducing racial beliefs that marginalize adoptees, whether through assumptions of family as defined by shared biogenetics or Asians as perpetual foreigners. In this chapter, I detail what adoptees' affective sense of racial place reveals about the racial meaning-making process embedded within exceptional belonging. I draw upon adoptees' reflections on their upbringing to attend to how adoptees' *familial socialization*—not solely their experiences of public racialization in the structural, cultural, and interpersonal domains of society—shaped their understanding of their racial position as White, Asian, American, and Other.

"What I Envision Myself as Is White"

Jessa (b. 1960), who grew up in a small, rural town in the southern part of the Midwest, reflected on her sense of self, sharing:

> What I envision myself as is White, because that's what I was surrounded with. My brothers are White, my mom is White, my dad is White, my culture is White and I would say even more specifically my culture is . . . mid-western country. Small town values, small town thinking. And so when I think of myself, I have a hard time thinking of myself as Asian,. because when you think Asian, you think chopsticks, you think Geisha girl, you think Kung Fu, you think of all the stereotypes running around out there about an Asian person and I don't see myself like that. When I look in the mirror, I see an Asian face but my mind is not Asian.

Family is one of the first sites where we learn about race—our own racial group, people "like us," as well as other racial groups, people "not like us." These ideas of who we are cultivate feelings of belonging while establishing group boundaries. While most respondents reported identifying as White at some point in their lives, very few continued this identification into the present day. Among those who did, like Jessa, their explanations for why they identify as White underscore the meaning Whiteness holds for their own sense of self, their familial belonging, and national membership. Jessa learned that to be like her mom, dad, and six brothers, who were biological to their parents, was to be White.

For transnational transracial adoptees raised in White families, envisioning oneself as White is about feeling a sense of acceptance in one's family and in one's community. It includes shared values, shared culture, and shared worldview. Part of this shared perspective is the desirability of Whiteness and the undesirability of Asianness. These beliefs and the emotions they engender are part of what sociologist Joe Feagin terms the "white racial frame." The White racial frame normalizes White dominance through racialized beliefs, interpretations, emotions, and narratives that demean non-Whites and valorize Whites.[7] Although the White racial frame provides Whites with a meaning system to justify the advantages they reap through systemic racism, both Whites and non-Whites are exposed to it and can adopt it to guide their everyday interactions and to evaluate themselves and others.[8] Importantly, the White racial frame is not only about making sense of unequal social standing and inequitable distribution of resources as they already exist. It also includes embodied work to maintain White dominance. For a Korean adoptee, like Jessa, who was adopted into a White family, she was privy to the backstage performance of the White racial frame.[9] Jessa's "mind is not Asian" but rather is embedded in the racialized worldview of her familial socialization.

It is the White racial frame that portrays Asian American women as hypersexualized, submissive Geisha girls and Asian American men as desexualized, effeminate nerds.[10] Both characterizations emphasize Asian Americans' difference from normative White femininity and masculinity. Stereotypes of Asian American women offer limited ideas of who Asian American women can be. Perhaps unsurprisingly, Asian American women report feeling pressure to "comply with caricatured notions of Asian femininity" and perceive White women as having a more desirable, assertive, and egalitarian femininity.[11] These beliefs become compounded for Jessa and other Asian transracial adoptees who are adopted by White families. Whiteness is not only the marker of family inclusion, but it also offers a wider range of who you can be, a way to escape being subject to an over-sexualized subordinate racialized femininity.

Alyssa (b. 1984) also currently identifies as White. She explained:

I'm never like, "Hey, I'm Irish," or something like that, but I think I do identify as something kind of agnostic and vaguely American. If I had to say what it was, I'd probably say that it was White, or White identity, mostly because if you wanted to get down to it, my habits and my career focus and stuff like that are pretty much positions that are held by White males . . . Maybe it's just a happenstance thing. It's not happenstance because obviously I was adopted to an American family and not to a French family or something like that. I guess my parents are White and I happen to identify as White, but I don't know if it's necessarily because I identify with my parents . . . For a long time, during my whole identity-seeking phases of my life, I was independent from my parents. I wasn't looking to them for cues to tell me who I was. I was looking outside of that.

As Alyssa tries to pinpoint why she identifies as White, her response illustrates the pervasiveness of the White racial frame, which makes an "agnostic and vaguely American" identity synonymous with Whiteness. She is hesitant to credit her White identification to merely identifying with her parents, instead citing external cues for guiding her identity development; however, as she explains, her racial identity is no accident. After all, she "was adopted to an American family and not to a French family or something like that." As a member of a (White) American family she was socialized into the White racial frame. The effects of this racialized worldview are apparent in her racial identification, habits, and career focus, which she attributes to the domain of White males. The reflection also alludes to the racialized social structure that constrains opportunities—here employment, industries, and job titles—by race. Again, it is Whiteness that provides a range of possibilities for becoming. While Alyssa could be an Asian American woman *and* hold the job title she has, she instead uses it as validation of her White identity.

It is important to note that Alyssa identifies as White despite growing up in a racially and ethnically diverse area, attending high school with Asian American and Asian adoptee peers, and having support from her parents for Korean adoptee ethnic exploration. Even though some adoptees grew up in racially diverse cities, numerical diversity neither guarantees meaningful cross-racial interactions nor dismantles the overarching racially stratified organization of society. Moreover, Alyssa currently resides in a city with a sizable Asian American population. Early exposures to adoptee peers and Asian American ethnic communities are often precursors to Asian racial identification but do not guarantee it. Instead, Alyssa "happen[s] to identify as White."

Alyssa frames her White identification as a matter of chance but also as a structured choice facilitated on multiple levels—the institutionalization of Korean adoption to the US and the racially stratified organization of US society, including the racial logics embedded in family-formation via adoption.[12] Though she is hesitant to attribute her White identity to a desire to identify with her parents, for many transracial adoptees, their feelings of belonging within their family are predicated on a shared racial experience.[13] Through activities that minimize adoptees' heritage culture, adoptive parents' lack of inclusion of Asian peers within their own social networks, and parents' decision-making around family activities, holidays observed, and discussions around race, adoptees learn what is, and is not, central to the family experience.

As I spoke with Alyssa, she described a paradox of her White racial identification. She identifies as White, but she feels most comfortable around Asians. She explained: "I guess from an evolutionary perspective, people just like to see people that look like them, and I do feel comfortable when I see Asian people. It's very weird, but I do feel like a lot of times I have a lot in common with them just in terms of maybe being an introvert or how we think or feel about things. I don't know. That sounds insane." Whereas Jessa talked about feeling and thinking "White," Alyssa has the inverse explanation. She invokes a biological explanation of race connecting physical features, personality traits, and mindsets to explain her social comfort. Yet she, too, maintains commitment to a White identity.

Alyssa's mental gymnastics highlight the conflict Korean transnational transracial adoptees experience regarding the racialized emotions guiding their sense of belonging as White family members and how they experience being racialized as Asians. Her White racial identification is reflective of her socialization into the White racial frame, shaping her feelings about what it means to be a member of her family's White racial in-group and the Asian racial out-group. Being a White family member translates into White identification even as she relies on racial essentialism as an explanation for inexplicable feelings of commonality with other Asians. The similarities she assumes she has with other Asians further underscore how the White racial frame constructs Asians—as racial others with distinctly different viewpoints and dispositions. Like Jessa, Alyssa learned that Whiteness offers more flexibility in who she can become in the world.

Both Jessa's and Alyssa's explanations of their racial identification expose the logics of the White racial frame that constructs Whiteness as desirable, unrestrictive, and dominant. This poses a unique paradox in how White-identifying Korean adoptees understand themselves. For Jessa, her worldview is "not Asian," which allows her to "envision" herself as White even though she knows she has an "Asian face." For Alyssa, she too knows she shares racialized physical features with other Asians and goes as far as assuming she shares a similar disposition and feelings. Yet she sees a certain boundary between herself and "them," ultimately identifying as White. Explaining these feelings as only about a shared colorblind belonging within their family ignores how racialized family belonging is a mechanism of adoptees' racialization into a subordinate Asian position. Rather than identifying as part of the Asian racial underclass, seeing oneself as White is about feeling an alignment with White tastes, distastes, and expectations of treatment as members of the racial group atop the racialized social structure. As Du Bois and other scholars have argued, there are psychological wages of Whiteness.[14]

Returning to Bradley from the opening of this chapter, if there is a benefit to complying with the White racial frame, then there is a cost to questioning it. Bradley continued:

That's the interesting thing about these [Korean adoptee] social groups. It makes me think about identity a little bit more. I'm not some passive individual who's not thoughtful or doesn't think about this kind of stuff. I've thought about it a lot, it just doesn't . . . I think there's so many issues tied up with it that it's a lot to dive into, and I'm very comfortable with who I am. I've met my birth mother and we have a good relationship. In our relationship she doesn't want anything from me, and I don't want anything from her. We can both just exist, and then come together, and enjoy getting to know one another. There doesn't seem to be any set of expectations, which is really special because I know that sometimes these relationships can be really complicated.

I feel so lucky. Because I'm lucky, because I've had a great family, and I feel very fortunate, and I'm even in touch with my birth mother. She's happy and I'm happy. Because of all this, I don't want to question what could have been, or what is, or who am I. There's no sense . . . I feel like who I am is who I am.

Bradley has thought about his identity "a lot" and understands "there's so many issues tied up with it" that he does not want to give up the comfort his current understanding of himself as "completely American" provides. Despite engaging in activities that might signal a Korean identity—frequent travels to Korea, reuniting with his birth mother, sustained contact with his birth family—he does not find meaning in a Korean ethnic identity. Bradley shared, "The whole idea of race makes no sense, because I don't feel an affinity, or some kind of alignment in identity with that. With being Korean. It makes no sense to me, it's funny, I don't really get it." Many Whites understand their racial identity as a raceless norm, with little substantive meaning compared to non-Whites.[15] The White racial frame positions Whiteness as superior and desirable compared to non-Whiteness. Bradley's lack of affinity with his Koreanness despite his sustained engagement with his Korean family demonstrates the lengths some adoptees take to uphold the White racial frame.

Even as his Asian racialized physical features betray his White identity, identifying as White provides a sense of ease. Sara Ahmed describes the comfort of normativity as an ease with which one moves through the world. For members of the White majority who embody the norm, their belonging is effortless as the intentionality in how it is constructed goes unnoticed. For those, like Bradley, who cannot fulfill the normative protocol, he understands to preserve his happiness he must resist diving into the "many issues" of race, identity, family, and belonging. Questioning "what could have been, or what is, or who [he] is," would potentially disrupt his own comfort as well as the comfort of those around him. He would no longer be the "happy adoptee," who simply accepts his adoption without question. There is an ease in going along with what has already been laid out as the script for belonging, "to agree to where you are placed."[16]

Bradley's explanation for not incorporating his Korean heritage into his self-concept articulates what other adoptees contend with: taking on their Korean ethnic identity signals ungratefulness to and emphasizes their difference from their adoptive family and new home nation. When Whiteness is presented as the shared family experience, adoptees cannot explore their Korean heritage without also feeling as though they are rejecting their family.[17] This rigidity around what their identity can encompass means that adoptees, like Bradley, can only belong to one family and one nation, and—when both are intertwined with Whiteness—one race. How Bradley thinks about himself and the actions that he engages in present a racial identity enigma, one that can only be unraveled when understanding how entangled Whiteness, family, and citizenship are.

"We Don't See You as a Little Asian Kid"

When I asked Max (b. 1984) if he ever identified as White, he replied, "Oh yeah. The entire time I was growing up, probably until college. It's one of those things where you're like, 'What else would I be?' type of thing. You don't have to think about it." Most of the adoptees I spoke with, regardless of where they grew up, echoed the taken-for-granted nature of Whiteness, particularly as they reflected on how they felt throughout childhood and adolescence. They were not unique in this regard. One of the largest studies of Korean adoptees found that 78 percent of respondents had identified as White at some point in their lives.[18] After all, racial socialization begins at home, and most transnational transracial adoptees are adopted into White families.

Max's statement, "'What else would I be?' . . . You don't have to think about it," makes his sense of belonging via Whiteness matter of fact. Yet, as adoptees reflected on their upbringing, it was evident their Whiteness required considerable effort to construct. Adoptive parents' parenting practices were both about making adoptees one of the family through racial sameness—the normative protocol of family—and, if we understand Whiteness as an ongoing accomplishment, a way for White parents to reaffirm their own sense of racial position.

Though international adoption may have seemed progressive, the unspoken rules of race corresponded with explicit actions shaping the family in ways that reproduced the racial hierarchy. Brittney (b. 1987), who grew up in a racially diverse city in the Pacific Northwest with an older adopted Korean brother (not biologically related), shared a conversation with her mom that illustrated this point:

> I think I was in college when I asked them why they chose to adopt Korean kids versus White kids or Black kids. My parents pretty much said that at the time it was just easier, logistically, to adopt Korean kids. They had a social worker and she was Black and my mom specifically remem-

bered her asking about the whole racial issue and my mom felt like it would be much harder to raise Black children just because of how they were raised and things like that. That's why she decided to adopt Asians because she thought that it would be easier.

Brittney was adopted in the 1980s, the peak decade of Korean adoption. By then, the "Cadillac" of international adoptions was running smoothly like an assembly line.[19] So, it is likely that international adoption from Korea was logistically a smoother process. However, her mother's explanation describes how racial logics guided her adoption choice.[20] She "thought it would be easier" to raise Asian children in comparison to Black children, an assumption based in stereotypes about both Black and Asian family values. It is not uncommon for White parents to conceive of adopting from Korea as "'acceptable' boundary crossing"[21]— though this raises the question of how her social worker, a Black woman, thought about the "the racial issue" regarding White families adopting Asian children.

A decade before Brittney was adopted, the National Association of Black Social Workers (NABSW) issued a "Position Statement on Trans-Racial Adoptions."[22] In it they argued against White parents adopting Black children, speaking to the superficiality of White parents' approaches toward socialization of Black children. As the NABSW outlined, White people could not adequately prepare Black children to navigate a racist society. Furthermore, the transracial adoption of Black children into White families disrupted Black children's cultural socialization. Notably, the statement also included this condemnation:

We fully recognize the phenomenon of transracial adoption as an expedient for white folk, not as an altruistic humane concern for Black children. The supply of white children for adoption has all but vanished and adoption agencies, having always catered to middle class whites developed an answer to their desire for parenthood by motivating them to consider

Black children. This has brought about a re-definition of some Black children. Those born of Black-White alliances are no longer Black as decreed by immutable law and social custom for centuries. They are now Black-White, inter-racial, bi-racial, emphasizing the whiteness as the adoptable quality; a further subtle, but vicious design to further diminish black and accentuate white.

Here NABSW points out how children's racial status had been altered—from "Black as decreed by immutable law and social custom for centuries" to bi-racial—to make them adoptable. This change in nomenclature emphasized these children's proximity to Whiteness to establish their appeal to White adoptive parents. This same process of re-racializing non-White children was applied to Korean adoptees initially through how mixed-race Korean children were matched with prospective adoptive families and then how full-blooded Korean children were marketed.[23]

Korean children were presented as separate from ideas of a culturally distinct, foreign Yellow Peril that threatened White dominance, instead portrayed as orphans in need of rescue whose race was mutable. Further, Korean adoptees' depiction as orphans displaced them from the connotations of immigrant. Rather than emphasize adoptable Korean children's connections to their birth country, their status as immigrants, or similarity to existing Asian immigrants in the US, "orphan" stressed the severance of adoptable children's ties to the communities that made them racially inferior according to the White racial frame. Moreover, the commonly used descriptor of adoptable foreign children as "orphans in need of rescue" deracialized Korean adoptees, disconnecting them from their immigrant status, while the idea of rescue positioned adoptive parents as benevolent saviors.

In her research on adoption providers in private agencies, Elizabeth Raleigh demonstrates how racialized logics about family and culture continue to structure contemporary domestic and international adoption placement.[24] In selling transracial adoption to White prospective adoptive parents, adoption service providers sort and rank children of color according to their assimilability to Whiteness. In this consumer model of family formation, prospective parents navigate their racial preferences within the available supply of adoptable children. Their ability to parent a child of a different race, ethnicity, and/or national origin is a secondary concern.

Natalie (b. 1989) was adopted to a small city in the Northwest. The youngest of six—three boys and two girls biological to their parents—she described why she identified as White as a child: "When I was a really small child, I identified with [White identity] very strongly, because that's what I was told as a kiddo. When I was six or seven, growing up [in a] predominantly German house, would always make the German dishes, I ate the German food, and they taught me these very basic German phrases . . . part of that was because my parents would always kind of gently tease me that I was White, or that I was one of them because I was." Natalie's distinct socialization into a European ethnic group through food and language was the source of her White identification. Importantly, she did not relay a German identity or German American identity but rather a *White* identity. Although she had a specific German ethnic socialization via food and language, her family's Germanness did not detract from their Americanness in the way that her Koreanness would. American and White are frequently used synonymously, merging expectations of national belonging with racial group membership.[25] For adoptees, national, racial, and familial belonging were intertwined. Like Natalie reflected, "I was one of them [i.e., White family member] because I was."

These ideas of who we are and who we are not cultivate feelings of belonging while establishing boundaries between "us" and "them." Racial socialization within transracially adoptive families produces a unique tension. As the transracial adoptee paradox captures, adoptees are racial and/or ethnic minorities within broader society yet reared as if they are members of the White majority culture. Part of the national imagination of what it means to be White and American is that it means not being foreign. Throughout American history, this has meant enforcing boundaries around non-Whites and immigrants, specifically Asians. Historian Erika Lee argues that the 1882 Chinese Exclusion Act's significance was not only in that it was the first legislation to enforce a race-based restriction on immigration but also because of how it indelibly shaped US immigration ideology and policy.[26] The Act "established Chinese immigrants—categorized by their race, class, and gender relations as the ultimate category of undesirable immigrants—as the models by which to measure the desirability (and "whiteness") of other immigrant groups."[27] Natalie's family's teasing that she was White was as much about bringing her into a shared racial family experience as it was about her family emphasizing their own Whiteness. If Whiteness is defined in contrast to Asianness, then what does it mean for a White family's sense of racial understanding to have an Asian family member?

Heather Jacobson's work in *Culture Keeping: White Mothers, International Adoption, and the Negotiation of Family Difference* gives us some insights. She describes how international adoption of children from China and Russia brought awareness to her interviewees' Whiteness. Parenting internationally adopted children resulted in a loss of both White privilege and biological privilege regarding family formation. Through culture keeping—the intentional ethnic practices "meant to replicate partially the cultural education internationally adopted children would receive if they were being raised within a family of their own ethnic heritage"—adoptive parents navigate a delicate balance of Americanness and Chineseness (or Russianness) for their adopted children and their family. White adoptive mothers described the importance of providing the appropriate amount of cultural enrichment to their Chinese adopted children without "going overboard" and overshadowing their American cultural belonging.[28] As Jacobson shows, parents' choices were as much about facilitating a healthy sense of ethnic identity for their children as it was about ensuring adoptees were American like them (i.e., White). Culture keeping allowed White adoptive parents to preserve the normalcy of their own White identities.

Angela (b. 1983) remembered something her parents would say: "We don't see you as a little Asian kid. I see you as my daughter." This raises the question—what meaning does "a little Asian kid" hold that Angela's parents could not see her as Asian *and* as their daughter? White adoptive parents' characterization of not seeing their Korean children as Asian was meant to be complimentary in its ability to fold them into the family "as if" they were begotten. Yet where is the compliment in not being fully seen and accepted? As Kristi Brian uncovered in her interviews with White adoptive parents and Korean adoptees, White parents often reproduced the existing racial order through their colorblind approaches to race.[29] Parents' inability to see Asianness as complementary with their understanding of race, family, and citizenship is reflective of the White racial frame that positions Asians as unassimilable and inferior. Asianness and Whiteness have been constructed in White racial ideology as a difference that cannot be overcome.

Angela and her older sister, a White domestic adoptee, grew up in a small, racially diverse city in the Northwest. The city itself had a 14 percent Asian American population, 8.5 percent Black population, and 7.6 percent Latino population. However, similar to other adoptees, who grew up in larger cities with more overall racial diversity, their immediate neighborhood remained predominantly White due to structurally facilitated racial residential segregation[30] and Whites' self-segregation.[31] Angela and her older sister were raised in the same neighborhood where their parents, who were high school sweethearts, grew up. In a tight-knit community, Angela was "everybody's granddaughter." There were perks, like freshly baked cookies, but as the only Asian in a predominantly White neighborhood, it also meant she didn't quite know what meaning her Asian racial identity held. She reflected, "I always knew I was Asian but I feel sometimes that I was Asian but I really didn't identify. I feel like I was, I thought of myself as a little White kid even though I knew I wasn't. I don't know. That's so weird to say it but I don't know how to describe it."

Angela's parents felt comfortable raising her in the predominantly White community of their upbringing even as people suggested moving to a more racially diverse neighborhood. They sent Angela and her sister to a predominantly White school. They attended a predominantly White church. One way that Whiteness is reproduced in transnational transracial adoptive families is through the cultivation of White space. As Margaret Ann Hagerman argues, White racial socialization practices include parents' intentional creation of White racial contexts that then shape their child's ideas of race.[32] Though Angela knew she was not White, in the predominantly White social contexts that comprised her childhood and with her parents' colorblind approach, she did not have opportunities to explore what being Asian meant. How can one identify as something without meaning—or, as previous respondents noted, with negative meaning according to the White racial frame?

Angela did not have the tools to make sense of her racial conundrum. Instead, as she reflected, "I just wanted to be a normal kid." Part of being a normal kid was playing sports and not having to navigate her racial difference from White peers. Sports were also an activity that bonded her and her dad. Her dad was present at all her practices and games, even coaching her soccer team at one point. In the summer, they traveled to other cities, often staying overnight to compete in soccer tournaments.

When Angela was in seventh grade, her soccer team competed against a team with two Korean adoptee players. Angela vividly remembered that game. "There was only three Asians on the field, and everybody was like, 'Oh, is that your sister?' I'm like, 'Oh, no.' We found out we were adopted so then I became actually really close with them throughout high school as well." This was the first time she had met other Korean adoptees. Angela continued, "I remember my dad thought that was so cool that I found other Korean adopted girls like me and how we became best friends. Even now, I still think of them as my sisters even though they live far away." While Angela's interactions with other Korean adoptees and other peers of color were left to chance, her parents made specific decisions to cultivate predominantly White social contexts. The happenstance meeting between Angela and the two other Korean adoptees indicates how, despite the many ways that Angela felt like her parents didn't see her as an "Asian kid," her father did see her race. He just may not have had the tools, desire, or awareness to teach her about her racial group membership.[33]

Moments like these—when adoptees' racial belonging as White family members was interrupted and their ascribed racial category emphasized—challenged the legitimacy of their family structure. As a transnational transracial adoptee, Angela couldn't "just . . . be a normal kid." The comments from her and the other players' teammates reinforced the expectations of mono-raciality within families. While it is likely that both Angela's and the opposing Korean adoptee players' teammates were familiar with their respective families, the racialized assumptions defining family are so culturally ingrained that, when seeing the three Asian players, teammates' prior knowledge was replaced by expectations of shared race and kinship. Incidents like these reminded adoptees that while they may have been raised as family members and generally felt accepted within their immediate social contexts, they were seen as racial outsiders.

Angela's enduring perception of the two Korean adoptee players as her "sisters" was not merely recreating a norm around race and family. Rather, their kinship designations reflect the need to find similar others, who experience the same lived realities of race. For Korean transnational transracial adoptees adopted to White families, that racialized experience included White socialization, which often translated into feeling White, reminders that they were seen as Asian though their Asian racial group membership felt empty, and conflicting feelings on how to resolve being White family members in the face of expectations of a shared familial racial experience.

"I Don't Think of Myself as Korean"

While most adoptive parents' White racial socialization of their adopted Korean children excluded positive, proactive communication about Asian racial group membership, several respondents mentioned their parents' attempts at Korean cultural socialization. Cultural socialization practices are the parenting practices that incorporate the adopted child's heritage culture into the family, ranging from preparing or eating cultural meals, engaging in religious, social, or recreational groups and/or activities, visiting the child's birth country, celebrating ethnic holidays, attending cultural events or culture camps, and reading, watching, or listening to various forms of media from and/or about the heritage culture.[34] Contemporary research on White adoptive parents' cultural socialization practices finds adoptive parents include a variety of cultural socialization activities in contrast to earlier decades of adoption, though most of this engagement continues to be for the adopted child and not integrated into the everyday racial routine of family life.[35]

Patrick (b. 1986) grew up in a suburban city in the Midwest with a younger non-biological, Korean adoptee brother. He characterized his community, school, and friend group as predominantly White but described the following ways that his parents incorporated Korean culture into their lives:

My mom put me through taekwondo for three years [beginning around the age of 8 or 9]. We did go to Korean picnics once a year in which a group of ajummas from a church, they put together a really, really, really nice picnic with all this Korean food . . . To me and my brother, it was just this thing where we went to get Korean food, hang out with all the

Korean kids for a day. It wasn't really . . . Not a lot of excitement going on with understanding their culture or your background, but it was good. I mean there was some exposure . . . my parents did efforts to connect us to events and some types of cultural events.

This cultural socialization was not frequent enough to impart a Korean identity or to make Patrick feel pride in his ethnicity. Patrick continued, "I didn't feel like it was okay to embrace my Korean background, nor did I have a network that can help me understand it . . . Quite frankly, most of my life, in my mind, I thought I was [White] and figured, 'Why not?' because I grew up just as if they gave birth to me." Growing up as if his White adoptive parents gave birth to him meant no sustained integration of his Korean heritage culture. Instead, it meant being raised like any other White kid—enrollment in extracurricular activities and the occasional non-White ethnic meal. Patrick "grew up just as if [his White parents] gave birth to [him]," just like Natalie "was one of them [i.e., White family member]." Part of this White socialization was an absence of sustained interracial contact. Without ongoing, engaged interactions with a Korean ethnic community, adoptees like Patrick felt disconnected from their heritage culture and an ethnic identity as Korean.

Although Patrick and a minority of respondents mentioned the occasional Korean cultural activities or sporadic interactions with Korean American communities, when I asked adoptees about their connections with other Koreans or Asian Americans when they were growing up, they overwhelmingly described if and how their parents provided opportunities for connecting with Korean *adoptees* and Korean *adoptee* activities. Adoptee activities, particularly adoptive family activities, normalized White adoptive parents' transnational transracial adoption. James (b. 1988), whose family was very active in an international adoptive family organization, described his participation: "There was a lot of just generally fun stuff for kids. So, it was almost like going to a birthday party once a month. It was pretty cool." While adoptive family activities provided social connections for adoptees, they prioritized White adoptive parents' comfort rather than adoptees' racial and/or ethnic socialization.

Several respondents from the 1980s cohort mentioned participation in Korean culture camps as how their parents exposed them to other Koreans and/or Asian Americans, reflecting the simultaneous increase in adoption from Korea and shift in social work practices that recommended parents incorporate heritage culture. Even for adoptees who grew up in areas where there was a significant Korean American community, Korean culture camps remained the primary way that adoptees were introduced to their heritage culture.

Korean culture camps are weekend or weeklong cultural immersion programs historically spearheaded by adoption agencies, such as Holt and Bethany Christian Services. In rare instances, in areas with a critical mass of adoptive families, adoptive mothers also organized culture camps. Through the camps, adoptees learn about their heritage culture's history, art, music, language, and food. While Korean culture camp may seem like a proactive step toward teaching an adopted Korean child about her culture, and in many respects, it is, this form of connection to Korean culture is also limited. As the respondents explained, most participants were other adoptees and not adoptive families, and in some cases these camps were led by other adoptees.

Culture camps give adoptees a space to make connections to other adoptees, but they are divorced from Korean communities and the concomitant racial socialization. In many ways, culture camps operate as a safe and symbolic way for adoptive parents to engage with their child's birth culture.[36] As Heather Jacobson uncovered, this form of "culture keeping" allowed White adoptive parents of Chinese transnationally adopted children to meet contemporary mandates around heritage culture exposure while leaving their own understanding of race unchallenged.[37] Similarly, Carla Goar and I find that although some White adoptive parents who attend culture camps reported *feeling* "browner" or as if they are honorary members of their adopted child's heritage culture, these changes did not generate a critical understanding of their Whiteness.[38] Instead, White adoptive parents were able to symbolically take on non-White racial and/or ethnic identities because of their belief in Whiteness as the unmarked racial norm. Ironically, while participation in culture camps led some White adoptive parents to feel more ethnic, a few saw their adopted children as incapable of being authentically ethnic because of their overall unfamiliarity with their heritage culture and lack of connections to a heritage culture community. White adoptive parents allowed themselves to embody their adopted child's ethnicity while barring them from doing the same.

Additionally, the infrequency of these interactions bolsters its symbolic nature. Culture camps are not integrated into the everyday routine of adoptive families. Because of the lack of sustained engagement, it was much harder for respondents to continue what they learned or to develop an identity around their heritage culture. For my respondents, even maintaining the friendships they made at Korean culture camp was relegated to the summers as they were growing up. The other most common avenues through which parents connected the adoptees I spoke with to their heritage culture—homeland tours and Korean food—were likewise intermittent activities that reinforced the symbolic nature of their Korean culture. These activities allowed families to introduce cultural elements while maintaining their and their adopted child's White racial frame.

Kendra (b. 1984) grew up in a small city in the Midwest with her younger, non-biologically related Korean sister, in an area with several Korean adoptees. Her parents provided a range of opportunities for the two sisters to connect with adoptees and explore their heritage culture. Both sisters participated in a Korean adoptee group with about a dozen other Korean adoptive families. The two sisters went to Korean culture camps in the summer, and as a family, they all went on a homeland tour with a group of Korean adoptee families when Kendra and her sister were adolescents. However, like other respondents, when I asked Kendra how she thought about herself, she said, "Instantly, I don't think anything about race or ethnicity . . . I think about my personality and my goals and my drive more than anything besides race and ethnicity." Despite her parents' proactive approach to Korean *adoptee* socialization, these activities did little to inscribe a *Korean* identification. Kendra attributed her identity to her parents: "I think I attribute that so much to being adopted and being adopted into the family that I was, and how lucky and fortunate I was to have parents who pushed me to do whatever I wanted to do and be whoever I wanted to be, but also instill in me a fundamental relationship with Korea and that culture and that part of me *to whatever degree I wanted it to be, however I saw that fitting into my life*" (emphasis added).

In *Ethnic Options: Choosing Identities in America*, Mary C. Waters found that middle-class Whites claimed European ethnicity devoid of specific meaning or participation in ethnic organizations and/or communities. Through temporary displays of ethnic symbols such as attire, food, and historical cultural icons,[39] White Americans draw upon ethnic ancestry to capture the essence of community without the commitment of community ties. Though these symbols foster a connection to ethnic identity, one that is often strongly felt, it is rarely permanent. This symbolic ethnicity is largely voluntary, and while it has a "lack of demonstrable content" it "combines individuality with feelings both of community and conformity through an exercise of personal choice."[40] Here Kendra describes a similar level of personal choice as she refers to incorporating Korean culture "to whatever degree I wanted." Through symbolic ethnicity, adherents feel unique but also part of a community to the extent that they choose.

When White Americans publicly express their ethnic option, it can be invoked when and how they want insofar as the portrayed ethnic identity is believable to those whom it is presented.[41] It also does not detract from their American identity. However, Korean adoptees do not possess this public ethnic flexibility. Instead, racialized expectations dictate that they be accountable to their presumed ethnic background.[42] When interacting with people outside of their immediate family, they are expected to be authentically ethnic, enacting their Korean culture, language, and values. Ironically, within the family, transracial adoptees are often perceived as incapable of being "authentically" ethnic due to their lack of same-race relationships and integration into ethnic communities,[43] ties that their adoptive families hindered. Regardless of their familial racial socialization, Korean adoptees incur social costs when they do not live up to the racialized expectations of ethnic authenticity. These social costs range from the seemingly innocuous (e.g., questions about ethnic background) to more harmful (e.g., racial teasing, racial slurs, hate crimes). Simply put, Asian Americans do not have ethnic options.[44] Moreover, their American identity has always already been contested by virtue of the history of Asian exclusion from the national polity. Korean culture and Korean identification, while presented as an individual choice in their "personal lives" within their adoptive families, were not optional in their "public lives."[45]

Though Alyssa attended a Korean culture camp, it was too infrequent to be an important part of her childhood or how she thought about herself: "I don't think I would think of myself as Korean even except that every once in a while, I'll be reminded by someone saying something like, 'You're Asian,' or whatever. I've completely forgotten at that point because I just think of myself as a person. I would not say that being adopted or being Korean even factors into my daily life . . . I feel like there's quite a few of us out there that don't feel a connection." Given adoptees' familial socialization into the White racial frame and the external cues that reinforced this worldview, it is unsurprising that respondents' Korean identity wasn't a factor in their daily life. Instead, several respondents defaulted to *feeling* as if their race shouldn't be a factor as they moved through the world. This feeling of their racial place is the White racialized emotion reflective of being atop the racial hierarchy.

"Your Own Kind"

White adoptive parents encountered a unique challenge to parenting their adopted Korean children "as if" they were White when their children reached dating age. Returning to Angela, she recalled a family conversation: "I remember my dad sitting down and talking with us, with my mom, about, 'We don't care what color you are.' . . . I think it was when my sister started dating, they were like, 'We don't care who you bring home. If you bring home somebody that's not White or whatever, it doesn't matter. We don't care if you're green with orange stripes, we love you.'"

Although Angela's parents said that race "doesn't matter," their seemingly colorblind approach emphasized that race did, in fact, matter. Of course, people are not "green with orange stripes." The idea that either sister would find, let alone, date someone with such a variegated complexion is absurd. But so is the likelihood that they would bring home someone that blatantly challenged the racial preferences communicated through their parents' countless other family decisions.[46] Up until this point, conversations directly addressing adoptees' race or racism were rare. When it came to dating, however, adoptive parents were vocal about what made an appropriate love interest. As Asian adoptees grew up, they were no longer cute little kids whose race was a non-factor.

Jessa remembered one of the lessons her mother taught her about who was acceptable for her to date:

> I think it was in the eighth grade and I went to the school dance by myself. All through school though there was this young . . . This boy who I realized liked me, but in my head was weird because what White person wants to like an Asian person? I'm different, you know, you should be going with the White girls . . . I can remember him writing notes to me and carrying my books for me and, you know, just, he liked me! So, he

went to the dance by himself as well and we wound up having our picture taken together, pictures that I had to hide from my mother. Then we . . . When it was time for my folks to come and pick me up, he kissed me! It was dark and my mom couldn't see him, but I hid the pictures from my mother, and she found the pictures of us together and she looked at me and said, "You should be dating your own kind."

As a teenager, Jessa couldn't pick up on the cues signaling her White male classmate's romantic interest. The belief that she was "different" and that her difference was undesirable—at least according to the White racial frame—prohibited her from accepting that a White boy could like her. Her interpretation of her classmate's interest as "weird" was her internalization of Asian inferiority. Through the White racial frame, she knew that the acceptable romantic interest for a White boy would be a White girl. She understood that by liking her—an Asian girl—her classmate was putting his Whiteness at stake.

Jessa attended the dance by herself, which is revealing. No one else asked her to the dance, not even the classmate who liked her. In her ethnography of Korean adoptees, Kim Park Nelson relays how adoptees, whether those adopted in the assimilationist era of the late 1950s or those who grew up in the multiculturalism of the early 1980s, quickly learned that, for the most part, their White peers were not interested in them.[47] Even for Whites who expressed interest in them or adoptees or expressed interest in White peers, other White classmates policed racial boundaries by explicitly discouraging their romantic interests.

Jessa and the boy both went to the dance by themselves, signaling that there were constraints around him asking her to be his date and obstacles to navigating interracial dating with their parents. Jessa's hiding of the evidence of her interracial intimacy was not simply about the secrets teenage girls keep from their parents. It was a logical response to what her family had communicated about the norms of White same-race relationships. Those racial preferences became concrete in her mother's reprimand that she should be dating her "own kind."

But who was Jessa's "kind"? Her upbringing communicated she had left her Koreanness in her birth country. Her parents were explicit in their assimilation approach to raising her, even going as far as assuring her that "You're an American and that's all the matters." However, her mother's racial disciplining for having a White romantic interest showed that there was a limit to the Whiteness that they would extend.

Destiny (b. 1995) reflected, "I feel like they didn't care one way or the other [about acknowledging her race] . . . until I hit that dating age. Sometimes my mom would try to set me up with random Asian guys she would meet. And I would not be interested in them at all. I'm like, 'I don't even know these people so just stop trying.'" Whereas Destiny described her parents as actively avoiding conversations about adoption and race, to the point where she eventually felt uncomfortable asking questions, her mother was comfortable in taking a proactive approach to her dating prospects. Implicit and explicit dating guidance that communicated who were appropriate romantic interests reinforced the differing racial positions adoptees and their White family members held. Given how White parents structured predominantly White social contexts for their family, they themselves had limited interracial relationships, including few Asian American acquaintances. The "random Asian guys" Destiny's mom encountered were those working in the personal care industry, notably nail salons.

Several of the women adoptees I spoke with mentioned how their dating experiences brought to light issues of race, racism, and racial objectification, particularly White males' Asian fetish. Some were able to identify these racializing experiences in the moment as they began to realize the disconnect between the White shared family racial experience and their position as Asians. For others, it would be much later as they retroactively reflected on dating in their adolescence and young adulthood. Regardless of when they came to these realizations, these were not topics of conversation they raised with their parents.

Women were more likely to mention explicit dating guidance from their parents, reflecting gendered cultural norms.[48] This is not to say that men didn't experience racism within the realm of dating.[49] Thomas (b. 1970) also described how he "had no dates in high school." As he explained, "It's kind of odd, but in a way I almost feel like I knew that I wasn't that attractive to White people." While Thomas may not have been able to pinpoint exactly why he knew White people didn't find him, as an Asian man, attractive, his familial racial socialization impressed upon him a general feeling of racial undesirability.

Greg (b. 1983) mentioned how he felt his dating options were constrained because of his race. In a small, predominantly White town, he believed Asian stereotypes prevented Whites from seeing him as a viable romantic partner. His belief is well founded. Historically Asian men were constructed as undesirable and desexualized, and early anti-miscegenation laws locked Asian men out of the marriage market.[50] Though interracial marriages are no longer legally outlawed, long-standing tropes about Asian male undesirability are circulated in popular media. Asian male characters in movies and television series are rarely presented as leading male characters or as romantic love interests. Research on dating finds that these racialized views show up in dating preferences, with Asian men being perceived as less datable than men of any other race.[51] Although adoptees were reared as White family members, the possibilities of cross-racial dating exposed the racialized assumptions governing romantic partnerships that positioned adoptees outside of what was acceptable to Whiteness.

* * *

Adoptees commonly described how their White adoptive parents "just saw beyond the ethnicity. They didn't see us as really different to them." While this has often been read as a colorblind acceptance that shaped adoptive parents' approaches to Asian racial socialization and Korean ethnic socialization, not seeing Korean children as racially or ethnically different from themselves was also a way for adoptive parents to navigate the challenges transnational transracial adoption posed for their own racial identity. After all, family is an active site of the race-making process not just for children but for all family members.

Early framings of adoptable Korean orphans and then later the model minority stereotype popularized general ideas about Asian Americans' assimilability; however, it is within the family domain where we see the limitations of these racialized beliefs. Adoptees were raised within the White racial frame learning that to belong—within their families, community, and nation—meant enacting a White way of knowing, seeing, and being. Yet they were simultaneously raised into their racialized positions as outsiders to Whiteness. When and how parents addressed race and ethnicity—both their own and their adopted children's—whether through what they said or didn't say and other choices they made regarding where they lived, school enrollment, extracurricular activities, friendships, romantic relationships, and other interpersonal interactions, illustrate how adoptees' exceptional status functioned as a mechanism of racialization into an Asian American feeling of rejection in their daily lives.

2

Refusals of Belonging

"I'm sure you've heard all the questions," Greg (b. 1983) began. "But, whenever you're talking to someone and they ask, the first thing that I always get is the fun, 'What are you?' Fun things like that." He continued, "Then, start asking you about your parents. That's where it leads into, 'I was adopted,' which leads into the fun questions like, 'Have you thought about trying to figure out who your birth mother was?'" As Greg relayed this frequent exchange, his tone of resignation betrayed the casualness of his words. There is nothing "fun" about your existence being questioned.

The question "What are you?" is a variation of the more common phrasing, "Where are you from?" Both versions are rooted in the historic belief of Whiteness—here White racialized physical features—as a requirement for US national belonging.[1] For Asian Americans, this line of questioning is also reminiscent of the historic belief of Asians' ineligibility for citizenship.[2] Asian Americans share this experience of their presence in the US being questioned and interlocuters' desire and even excitement in attempting to get the truth of their origins.[3] "What are you?" revives ideas of Asian exoticism and objectification stripping the addressee of their humanity. Greg grew up in a predominantly White, blue-collar, rural town in the Midwest. Of the 20,000 or so residents, the overall Asian American population was about 1 percent, which he recalls was primarily Hmong. Greg was an anomaly among anomalies, not even legible as the Asian racial other.

Greg's visibility as non-American is rooted in deep-seated beliefs linking family, race, and citizenship. Greg's initial response, "I'm American," not explicitly stated here in his retelling but implied, and its unacceptability to the questioner is what leads to the inquiry about his parents. Where the speaker may have conceded to Greg being born here and therefore having birthright citizenship, the assumption was that his parents were not from here and therefore he too was not really American. This was the logic US Solicitor General Holmes Conrad used in 1898 when appealing Chinese American Wong Kim Ark's citizenship status in what would become a landmark case for birthright citizenship. At question was not merely *if* Wong Kim Ark was a citizen but if he, a Chinese person, *could* be a citizen. Even if he was born in San Francisco, as he claimed and as White witnesses attested, could he be a citizen if his parents were Chinese subjects?

According to Conrad, being Chinese by blood meant he could not. One of the claims against Wong Kim Ark's eligibility for US citizenship despite being born in the US was his indisputable, interminable Asianness. As stated by the opposition, he could not be a citizen "because the said Wong Kim Ark has been at all times, by reason of his race, language, color, and dress, a Chinese person."[4] In the end, the Supreme Court ruled in Wong Kim Ark's favor (6–2), solidifying the 14th Amendment's provision for birthright citizenship. This decision was not a solely magnanimous interpretation of the law. Justice Horace Gray, writing for the majority opinion, argued, "To hold that the Fourteenth Amendment of the Constitution excludes from citizenship the children born in the United States of citizens or subjects of other countries, would be to deny citizenship to thousands of persons of English, Scotch, Irish, German, or other European parentage, who have always been considered and treated as citizens of the United States."[5] Therefore, to deny Wong Kim Ark's citizenship would be to put White citizenship in jeopardy.

Greg's present-day interaction illuminates the durability of the right type of blood ties in authenticating national belonging. Although transnational transracial adoptees may be naturalized citizens and have White (adoptive) parents, they lack biological connections to their

White American family. The interlocuter's questions about Greg's birth parents and expectations that he would want to find them demonstrate the expectations of bionormativity and monoraciality within families, delegitimizing adoptees' claims to citizenship, family, and personhood. Although adoptees are immigrants, most did not think of themselves as immigrants. These types of questions acted as racial reinscriptions disciplining adoptees into an Asian American status as presumed foreigners.

Adoptees commonly experienced refusals of belonging through xenophobic exchanges, like the one Greg detailed. These interpersonal encounters were frequent enough for Greg to be certain that I, as well as the other adoptees I had spoken with, had experienced them, too—in fact, a well-founded assumption. How did adoptees make sense of public racialization challenging their familial and national belonging considering their private racialization that imparted the belief that they had a right to an American identity and American acceptance? What do these patterned experiences reveal about the false promises inherent in exceptional belonging? And how do they socialize adoptees into a particular *feeling* as Asian Americans? In this chapter, I examine adoptees' common experiences of public racialization, including particularly salient childhood memories involving community members, peers, and strangers, for what they reveal about the contradictions of exceptional belonging. Korean adoptees' transnational transracial adoption status made them hypervisible within their families, yet their upbringing was predicated upon maintaining a certain level of invisibility around their racial difference.[6] Public racialization, however, made their racial status as non-White hypervisible, rendering their family relationships and familial socialization invisible. Exceptional belonging attempted to recreate adoptees into citizens but the process by which it did reified existing racialized logics of citizenship. Public racialization reinforced boundaries around family, race, and national belonging, disciplinary reminders that adoptees were out of place.

"Go Back to Where You Came From"

As Greg and I continued to talk, he shared another common refusal of belonging: "The typical insults growing up of like, 'Go back to where you came from,' I didn't understand. When people told me that, I was like, 'You want me to drive back home to [rural Midwest town]?' That stuff didn't click for me until I got older." There is a reason for Greg's not understanding. Transnational transracial adoptees confuse the "us" and "them" of in-group/out-group boundaries. Korean adoptees raised in White families are one of "us"—White family members—and one of "them"—Asian foreigners—conflicting racialized positions.

As political scientist Claire Jean Kim argues in her model of racial triangulation, Whites, Blacks, and Asians are racialized in comparison with one another in multiple ways.[7] In this field of racialized positions, racial groups are evaluated on axes of cultural superiority and inferiority and assumed foreign or insider status. In this model, as Asian Americans, Korean adoptees would be assessed as culturally inferior to Whites but culturally valorized compared to Blacks. However, adoptees raised in White families are insiders to White culture and often adopt the White racial frame leading adoptees to feel as if they are also insiders to the nation. At the same time, as Asian Americans, Korean adoptees are assessed as foreigners despite how they were raised as if their national membership was a given. This is the transracial adoptee paradox[8]—adoptees break the rules of the racial order.

Nadia Y. Kim draws attention to visibility and invisibility as a contributing process to racial triangulation. She details how Asian Americans are visible as model minorities for their presumed socioeconomic achievement and invisible within the national conversation about race and racism. Asian transnational transracial adoptees are visible as emblems of racial progress and traditionally invisible within conversations of racialized minority immigrants. However, in their lived experiences

Korean transnational transracial adoptees experience hypervisibility, particularly in their White racial contexts. The failure of "Go back to where you came from" to hail Greg as a non-citizen, however, is a result of his being socialized into White racialized emotions.[9] Greg not only doesn't understand why he, as an in-group member, would be treated as a foreigner but he also doesn't know where it is he should go back to.

The feeling of being caught between two impossible places is a common racialized emotion shared among immigrants of color. David L. Eng and Shinhee Han refer to how Asian Americans, and other immigrants of color, feel because of their immigration histories and suspended assimilation as racial melancholia.[10] Broader social processes that legally, socially, and culturally exclude immigrants of color lead to a socially determined group feeling of unresolved grief for being unable to attain full citizenship. Racial melancholia is not an individual pathological state but rather a normative psychic state due to structural conditions, such as discrimination, assimilation, and ideologies intertwining Whiteness and citizenship. An Asian American structure of feeling is shaped by the ongoing conflict between Asian Americans' foreigner status—though they are citizens—and inability to attain the markers of social citizenship—because their racialized physical features make Whiteness unattainable.[11]

Among Asian transracial adoptees in White families this feeling of racial melancholia is compounded—broader ideologies like the model minority myth characterize Asians as assimilable to Whiteness, and family socialization rears them into White familial bonds and the White racial frame. Asian adoptees learn firsthand the rules of the racial game, but as much as they are insiders to Whiteness, they too know that "the ideals of whiteness are perpetually strained—continually estranged."[12] Furthermore, although racial melancholia is a component of Asian Americans' racialized emotions, unlike Asian Americans raised in Asian American families, transracial adoptees and their parents cannot share in these racial feelings. Adoptees are left on their own to make sense of their racial positions as Asian Americans, including why they were often assumed foreigners. For many, like Greg, it didn't "click" until they got older.

Exceptional belonging created the conditions for adoptees' misunderstanding of their place as Asian Americans and immigrants in the racial order. On a policy level, Korean transnational transracial adoptees are the beneficiaries of their adoptive parents' citizenship privileges. Transnational adoptees were classified as "immediate family members," a designation prioritizing their migration over that of other immigrants and distinguishing them from other immigrant groups.[13] Where their legal reclassification as immediate family members severed their ties to their birth family, their socialization minimized their connections to birth country. Most adoptees relayed adoption stories that erased biological family ties, whether through beginning their stories with orphanages or relaying adoption records that certified unknown family origins. As a result, they did not cultivate an immigrant identity, and their emotional connection to national belonging was to the US. Demands to "Go back to where you came from," therefore, did not affectively resonate.

Although adoptees' physical entry into the US was expedited, there were no corresponding naturalization privileges (at least not within the first five decades of transnational adoption).[14] Since joining Korean adoptees with their US families neither required it nor affected their adoptive parents' citizenship status, there would be no reason to. As scholars demonstrate, at its inception adoption from Korea was seen as a way for US couples to join the fight against communism, enact their Christian values, and attain the happiness that the traditional, nuclear family was supposed to bestow.[15] These motivations were all expressions of adoptive parents' American citizenship, none of which required ensuring adoptees' legal citizenship. As a result, adoptees were recognized as family members via legal adoption but not as citizens via legal or social citizenship.

Kyra (b. 1988) shared similar public racialization emphasizing her racial visibility: "I definitely got 'Go back to China' or 'Squinty-eyes' or those types of comments," she said. "When you're a kid, 'cause kids are kids and don't know what they're talking about, then even as an adult, I think just ignorance." The invective to "Go back to China" or "Go back to where you came from" is a shared experience across Asian ethnicities. It harkens back to responses to the "Chinese Question" of the late 1800s. Back then the rallying cry on handbills, posters, newspapers, and at town halls was "The Chinese Must Go!" Whites perceived Chinese as a threat to their economic standing, culture, and families that had to be eliminated. "The Chinese Must Go!" was codified in the Chinese Exclusion Act of 1882 barring Chinese immigration, the first legislation to prohibit immigration of all members of an ethnicity and nationality.[16] It also banned Chinese individuals from naturalizing.[17] Anti-Asian sentiments expanded to include the Asiatic Barred Zone in 1917 before the Immigration Act of 1924 effectively barred all Asian immigration. It would not be until the Immigration and Nationality Act of 1965 that the ban on Asian immigration was lifted.

That Kyra was not ethnically Chinese was not the point. As an Asian person, she was Chinese, a synecdoche for the Asian racial other. Unlike adoptees who failed to grasp why they were being racialized as Asian foreigners, Kyra made sense of these racializations through another aspect of the White racial frame—the denial of racism. Her dismissal of the accusations of her difference from the norms of Whiteness—as kids' not knowing and adults' ignorance—makes racism unknowable. As sociologist Jennifer Mueller argues in her theory of racial ignorance, Whites' ignorance is a "cognitive accomplishment grounded in explicit and tacit practices of knowing and non-knowing."[18] Ignorance and non-knowing, then, are intentional maneuvers to retain the privileges of Whiteness while upholding White supremacy and resisting accountability for one's contributions to the racial stratification system. The adoptees I interviewed all relayed similar experiences of interpersonal racism despite ranging in age from 21 to 56 and growing up across all regions of the US. The theory of racial ignorance sheds light on how across time and space kids and adults alike have not come to know what they are saying even as they know how, when, and toward whom to deploy racism.

To what extent does Kyra and other adoptees' upbringing socialize them into explaining away these racist encounters? In Kyra's retelling of this common public racialization from childhood to adulthood, it is not the speakers who pled ignorance. Rather it is Kyra who relieves the speakers of responsibility for their words. The White racial frame explains why Whites would be invested in upholding an unequal social system.[19] The theory of racial ignorance complements this by explaining the efficacy of Whites' denial of racism to that end.[20] As detailed in chapter 1, adoptees are intimately familiar with the White racial frame and in some cases take on the worldview that normalized anti-Asian sentiments. Acknowledging racism goes against the White racial frame and the White racial experience defining the family. Giving people the benefit of the doubt then operates as a protective mechanism to maintain the family. What happens when anti-Asian racism perpetuated by your family, or people who look like your family, cannot be explained away?

Asian transracial adoptees were confronted with this dilemma in March 2021 when Robert Aaron Long, a 21-year-old White male, opened fire at Atlanta area spas, ultimately killing eight people, six of whom were Asian women. Long described having a "sexual addiction" and that his actions were attempts to eliminate his "temptation."[21] This mass shooting occurred amid ongoing anti-Asian racism instigated by racist scapegoating of COVID-19. Stop AAPI Hate, a national coalition addressing anti-Asian racism, tracked nearly 4,000 incidents of anti-Asian racism and violence over the previous year.[22] Although on-the-ground protests to "Stop Asian Hate" had been ongoing, particularly in cities with large populations of Asian Americans, more broadly Americans were unaware of these coordinated efforts. However, the nature of Long's crime and the national media coverage that followed made it impossible to ignore anti-Asian violence. As Asian Americans grappled with this event and grieved with one another, many Asian adoptees did not have an Asian—or Asian adoptee—community to communally mourn with, leaving them to process on their own. Grieving with their White adoptive family was limited because of the difference in how this event was affectively experienced given their racialized positions.[23] "It is hard to process violence against people who look like us when the perpetrator of that violence looks like our family," Kaylyn Brown, Korean transracial adoptee and poet, reflected in a viral Instagram post shortly after the shootings.

Asian Americans made connections between Long's mass shooting and the rising anti-Asian violence during the pandemic as well as historic anti-Asian violence against Asian women for their presumed sexual deviance. Media, however, did not immediately characterize Long's actions as a racially motivated hate crime.[24] In one of the initial statements by Captain Jay Baker, spokesperson for Cherokee County, where Long was apprehended, Baker characterized Long's rampage as the result of "a really bad day," as if killing people was a justified response. However, if Asians are dehumanized and viewed as culpable for Whites' woes and if Whites are perceived as a sympathetic in-group, then Baker's empathy for the shooter and not the victims is an obvious outcome of those racialized logics. Baker's anti-Asian racist response was not an isolated racial feeling. Shortly after his statement, Baker's social media post promoting a "humorous" T-shirt blaming China for the COVID-19 virus surfaced.[25] Captain Baker was relieved of his role.

Sociologist Raúl Pérez's analysis of racist humor demonstrates that racism is not just hatred, like what may have motivated Long.[26] Racism is "also a practice deeply rooted in a pleasurable solidarity grounded in an amused contempt for racialized others."[27] The T-shirt's racist humor reinforced ideas of Asians as disease-carrying threats to Americans in

a manner that demeaned, ridiculed, and ostracized Asians while providing solidarity among Whites. Pérez's examination of racist humor
within law enforcement illuminates the link between racist joking as
an in-group mechanism and structural and direct violence. In this case,
though Baker's anti-Asian COVID-19 humor was conducted off the
job—though we might assume many of his Facebook friends were other
officers—it still influenced racial dynamics on the job. In Baker's case,
he produced harm by minimizing Long's actions. Complicating Baker's
anti-Asian racist beliefs is his own family relations. Baker has a Vietnamese adoptee brother, Tony. Although Tony did not join the Baker
family until he was around eight years old and Jay was six, because of
their closeness in age they grew up together. As Jay recalled, "Tony was
always family."[28]

Being family does not guarantee shared interpretations of events,
nor does it necessarily extend feelings of shared group belonging. Well
before Long's mass shooting or the rising anti-Asian violence during
COVID-19, adoptees had learned that their parents could not affectively
relate to their experiences of racism. It was rare for adoptees to recall
their parents proactively preparing them for racism that they may experience. Even when adoptees told their parents about racist encounters,
the most common response was for parents to minimize the encounter, typically explaining it as not racism but rather general childhood
bullying. For example, Mi Na (b. 1994) described how her mom would
respond when she shared racist encounters with her when she was growing up: "My mom would say something like, 'I get made fun of all the
time because I'm ugly and I have a big nose. People said this and that
about me.'" Even when hearing their children tell them about racism
they experienced, some parents delegitimized adoptees' knowing, attempting to convince adoptees that they did not understand their own
experiences. The theory of racial ignorance explains why even when
confronted with evidence, such as firsthand testimony, parents engage in
"refusals to know" in order to uphold White domination.[29] If one does

"not know," then one can "not do." In not knowing and not doing, racism is allowed to continue unchecked. Anti-Asian racism was rendered unknowable in national consciousness and in adoptees' personal lives.

Public racialization was not only about adoptees' racial place. It also maintained racial group boundaries by affirming the speakers' sense of racial position. Jessa (b. 1960) recalled a particularly hurtful childhood memory:

> I was in the sixth grade. So, there's certain things that stick with me, right? So, in the sixth grade, there was a group of about three other girls, and I hung around with them and went to their houses and, you know, just we were friends. One day I got a note that says, "You can't be our friend anymore." I was like, "What?! What? What did I do? What did I do?" It turned out that their grandfather saw me, and he was a POW during World War II and basically said, "You can't have that Jap in the house." So, I was like, "But I'm not Japanese! I'm Korean! And I speak with a perfect American accent, so I've been told!" You know, and that was actually kind of a hard blow, you know, I was discriminated against because of the way I looked. With no question, with no seeking knowledge, no nothing. Then, I wasn't allowed to be these girls' friend, you know, it was a very hurtful thing.

Despite her "perfect American accent" that challenged previous speakers' assumptions of Asian unassimilability, Jessa was still seen as outside of the bounds of American citizenry. She did not *do* anything except evoke a particular racialized threat—her existence was a yellow peril. To her friends' grandfather, her "Japanese" features were reminiscent of the dangerous enemy aliens of World War II. President Franklin Roosevelt's Presidential Proclamation and Executive Order[30] reinscribed Japanese Americans' inalienable difference from real Americans, irrespective of their educational achievement, socioeconomic standing, community ties, language proficiency and unaccented enunciation, or even nationality. While over 120,000 Japanese and Japanese Americans were incarcerated in internment camps, hundreds of Japanese Americans were deported under the guise of repatriation, cementing beliefs that Asians could never be American citizens regardless of birthright citizenship.[31] Similarly, the grandfather's aversion to Jessa reinscribed her position outside of what it means to be American. Regardless of her adoption, upbringing, or White cultural familiarity, Jessa was subsumed under a racial system that drew a sharp line between Whites and Asians of any ethnicity. Jessa and similar racial others might be permitted in the nation, but they were not welcomed inside this grandfather's home or permissible as friends to his granddaughters.

Jessa wasn't the only one disciplined into the racial order. Her friends, too, received a racial lesson about with whom they could interact. Their reprimand was so resolute that they dared not remain friends, even at school. Boundary enforcement excludes out-group members and bolsters inclusion among in-group members through defining the behaviors, values, and attitudes that are appropriate for group members. While this can be accomplished through familial socialization, everyday practices, and racist humor, it is also enforced through direct disciplining. Previous geopolitics, policy decisions, and cultural constructions of Asians in America influenced the grandfather's xenophobic, nativist view of Jessa, which the girls then reproduced, without hesitation, as they terminated their friendship. The girls' dismissal of Jessa enforced their shared White racial position. Jessa understood the racial significance of their actions and knew she could not share what happened with her family without disrupting their assumed White racial family experience.

Adoptees learned from friends and strangers that they were out of their racial place. Despite how they were raised or what they believed about their own national belonging, they were not seen as members of the nation. Adoptees may have felt this difference in minor ways (detailed in chapter 1), but explicit refusals of belonging, such as invectives, slurs, and discrimination, made it clear. Through public racialization, adoptees were disciplined into Asian American racialized emotions of exclusion due to their presumed foreignness. For adoptees this is complicated since they are, in fact, not from "here" yet have little affective connection to where they were born. Korea was hardly a place in their personal lives, and they learned it was not a place in the public imaginary of Asianness, as they were commonly racialized as Chinese or Japanese. Korean adoptees are visible as racial outsiders to the nation, but Korea is invisible. Adoptees were out of place with nowhere to go.

Asian Racial Ambiguity

Alex (b. 1986) described a particularly troublesome conversation between herself and a teacher: "For the longest time I thought I was White. It was really in middle school, I had a teacher who was a person of color who sat me down and was like, 'You are not White.' . . . I thought it was highly inappropriate [for her to say that]. I was sitting there going, 'This is not your place. If I think I'm White, I think I'm White.'" Alex grew up in a large racially diverse city on the West Coast with a younger brother, also a Korean adoptee (not biologically related). Like most adoptees raised by White adoptive parents, she learned that Whiteness was the shared family experience. According to the logics of the White racial frame, Whiteness was superior, desirable, and the identity that offered the full expression of personhood; Asianness was inferior, undesirable, and devoid of positive meaning. Despite living in a racially diverse neighborhood and attending schools with Asian peers and Asian teachers, Alex identified as White throughout childhood.

As much as adoptees may have aligned themselves with Whiteness, others repeatedly shepherded them into their place within the racial order. Here it was a teacher of color who attempted to educate Alex on the incorrectness of identifying as White. While we do not know the motivation for this teacher's extracurricular lesson, research shows that racial and ethnic identity promote positive psychological development and act as a protective measure against adversity among Black, Latino, and Asian children and adolescents.[32] Perhaps Alex's teacher was trying to awaken Alex to her racial group membership to protect her from future psychological harm, something that her parents were unwilling or incapable of doing.

Although it should have been adoptive parents' place to help adoptees understand race and prepare them for experiences of racism, most adoptive parents' racial socialization practices left adoptees vulnerable to experiences of Asian racialization. While Alex's teacher takes on the responsibility of racial identity education, attempting to push Alex out of a White racial identity, she does not tell her why Whiteness is unavailable to her or what her racial identity should be. Asian is not White, but what *is* Asian? Alex's teacher's racial lesson leaves her on her own to figure out the meaning of a group identity. Unsurprisingly, Alex is resistant to thinking of herself as anything other than White; locating herself somewhere is better than resigning herself to a racial nowhere.

The racial nowhere that Asian adoptees experience is similar to that of Asian parachute children, youth whose parents send them to live and study in the US by themselves. Eng and Han describe parachute children's racial experiences as racial dissociation, whereby individuals have racialized experiences but lack the language or support to identify them as such, resulting in a psychic, emotional, and racial "nowhere."[33] Parachute children have a lack of cultural, emotional, and social rootedness because of their solo migration that leaves them to navigate the politics of immigration alone. Adoptees also navigate immigration, assimilation, and racialization alone because of their upbringing within non-Asian American families. I find that their racial dissociation takes unique forms. Adoptees experience a multivalent racial dissociation via three avenues: (1) when the ideologies of colorblind racism that permeate society and their parents' approaches to race and racism conflict with their racialized experiences both inside and outside of the home;

(2) as an outcome of their immigration histories and dislocation from a homeland and heritage culture while also feeling not quite a part of the American experience; and (3) as a result of their socialization into and experience of conflicting racialized emotions associated with their transracial adoption. In short, Asian transnational transracial adoptees' racial dissociation is an outcome of adoptees' exceptional belonging. Racial dissociation joined racial melancholia as part of the shared substance of adoption that contributed to adoptees' racialized emotions.

Sarah (b. 1982) grew up in a small predominantly White city in the mountains of the Pacific Northwest. At a young age, she learned from her peers what her racial identity should be. She recalled:

> I think I was so out of touch with my ethnicity, and I know my friends never told me this or anything, I just somehow gathered that if you weren't White, you were Black. I went through this time period that I thought I was Black. Oh! It was because of this kid. I was in a daycare and this kid, actually he was one of the older brothers of my friend, and he looked at me and said to one of the other kids, "Hey, have you ever seen a Black person before?" And then pointed to me. That's why I got the idea I was Black.

Sarah's understanding that "if you weren't White, you were Black" reflects the US's enduring Black-White racial binary.[34] In Sarah's case, where the total population of non-white residents in her hometown city of 52,000 was 6 percent, or around 3,000 people, "Black" became a catchall category lumping together everyone on the non-White side of the racial divide. The racial boundaries around Whiteness were rigid, whereas ideas of Blackness afforded a certain flexibility in incorporating other non-Whites.

Sarah's peers' categorization of her as Black was not only because Asians weren't a substantial numerical presence in her hometown. It is also a reflection of how American culture renders Asian Americans invisible. For example, in a nationally representative survey of Americans, nearly 60 percent of respondents could not name a prominent Asian American figure.[35] Of those who did, the most frequently cited were Jackie Chan, who is not Asian American, and Bruce Lee, who died in 1973, speaking to their status as cultural icons as well as the dearth of Asian American leading actors.[36] In fact, analysis of the top 100 grossing films from 2007 to 2019 found only 44 of the 1,300 films, or less than 4 percent, featured an Asian American or Pacific Islander lead or co-lead.[37] Moreover, Asian American characters are overwhelmingly depicted through racist stereotypes.[38]

Asian American invisibility also characterizes K–12 public education. The limited coverage of Asian American history focuses on Chinese and Japanese Americans to the exclusion of other Asian ethnic groups and portrays Asian American as victims of nativist racism, ignoring their active resistance.[39] These depictions perpetuate stereotypes of Asian Americans as foreigners, passive, and a monolith. By excluding Asian American histories of activism and coalition building, anti-Asian racism is unknowable in the present. As Nadia Y. Kim argues, "Asian Americans' racialized status as foreigners goes beyond being *visibly* different from the norm. . . . Rather, it also involved being nonexistent on the national radar, in other words, invisible or almost so" (emphasis in original).[40] White America's lack of familiarity is a central component of Asian American racialization. While Asians have been in the US since 1750, it was not until July 2021 that Illinois became the first state to mandate Asian American history in public school curriculum. Almost a year later, Connecticut became the first to allocate state funding to these efforts.[41]

The relative absence of Asian Americans throughout the cultural domain of society, coupled with adoptees' upbringing, meant that adoptees were uncertain about the meaning of their Asianness, leaving them vulnerable to others' interpretations of who they were and where they belonged. Sarah never shared this unforgettable race lesson with her family, but it influenced how she thought about herself. She described how this racial lesson impacted her: "I remember being super nice to them [the Black customers at her family's business] because I thought I was going to be nice to the Black people because they were like me." Like other transracial adoptees, Sarah knew she was not White like her adoptive family even though she was raised as if she were a member of the White racial group; and, as with other Korean adoptees, being Asian did not have any substantive meaning, particularly absent of a visible Asian American community. Sarah was left to make sense of her racial identity through her peer's external categorization of her. While an individual's reflected race may or may not influence their racial identity, in this case it very much did, resulting in Sarah self-identifying as Black. Though thinking of her racial identity as Black only lasted a couple years, this line of thinking is the outcome of the Black-White binary that categorizes Asian Americans as "near Black" or "near White" in ways that are historically and locally contingent but always work to reinforce White domination.[42]

Sarah wasn't the only adoptee who mentioned that their childhood peers categorized them as Black. Hannah (b. 1986) grew up in a small, predominantly White, rural town in the Midwest. She recalled, "When I was a student [K–12], students would immediately think I was related to another Asian student in a class because there aren't really many Asians around the area and so I had to be related to them, or they thought I was African American, which really threw me off. Those were pretty young but still I think you should know the difference between African American and Asian." There is an interchangeability and depersonalization of non-Whites. To her peers, Asians were indistinguishable from one another and lumped together with other non-Whites even though to Hannah the racial differences between Black Americans and Asian Americans should have been apparent. Jennifer Ann Ho argues the ways Asian Americans "have been variously and multiply interpreted"[43] informs an Asian American racial ambiguity. Throughout history, Asian

Americans have been conceptualized as a threatening Yellow Peril and an assimilable model minority. Depending on space, place, and economic interests, Asian Americans have been aligned with Black Americans and seen as "colored" or aligned with White Americans and seen as honorary Whites and used as a racial wedge against other people of color. Ellen Wu charts White America's changing interpretation of Asian Americans in relation to national and global racial politics. She details how Japanese and Chinese Americans went from being definitively not-White prior to the 1950s to definitively not-Black by the mid-1960s, based on the US's foreign relations agenda and ideology of racial liberalism.[44] These shifting racialized perceptions are not about extending rights to Asian Americans. Rather, as Leslie Bow argues, Asian Americans' "racial intermediacy represents a flexibility of convenience" usually for economic or legal reasons benefiting White elites.[45]

Korean adoptable orphans' framing as permissible for inclusion into White American families is an extension of Asian "differential inclusion" into the realm of intimate relationships. Yen Espiritu defines differential inclusion as "the process by where a group of people is deemed integral to the nation's economy, culture, identity, and power—but integral only or precisely because of their designated subordinate standing."[46] As scholars have detailed, Korean adoption was a result of White interests—a way for the US government and its military to save face considering their failure during the Korean War.[47] It also was evidence of US racial liberalism, a necessity given the government's foreign relations. Of course, transnational transracial adoption does not confer White racial status even as Korean transracial adoptees learn the racial rules of the cultural system from the vantage point of their White parents. The mismatch between adoptees' private familial socialization and public racialization explains why some adoptees do not understand where they racially belong. However, regardless of their perception, Korean adoptees' racial group membership is held accountable to society's categorizations of race and where people who look like them should fit within that framework. As the racial reinscriptions by peers and adults demonstrates, adoptees possess a racial flexibility depending upon their local contexts. However, whether adoptees are categorized as Black, Asian, or broadly not-White, what is definitive is that Asian is not American.

"I Will Never Be Thought of as Just American"

Grace (b. 1984) succinctly stated, "I don't feel quite American, which in no uncertain terms nowadays means Caucasian." As much as their families socialized them into Whiteness, Whiteness was untenable considering refusals of belonging disciplining them into their expected racial place as Asians in America. While Grace describes the linkage between Americanness and Whiteness as a contemporary racial feeling, it is the continuation of historic precedent of citizenship defined by Whiteness.[48]

Brianne (b. 1985) explained, "Because I look like this, I could never be a part of White people, I guess . . . I don't think I was ever given the opportunity to ever identify as White, I guess, even though my family is White . . . I will never be thought of in America by Americans first and foremost as just American. I'll always be seen as Asian first, racially." To be seen as Asian first—and therefore non-American—is the common Asian American experience.[49] While we can assume—and, in fact, Brianne later detailed in our conversation—that the Americans who don't see her as American are White Americans, Asian Americans' assumed foreign status is a broadly shared component of Asian racialization across racial and ethnic groups.

Brianne relayed a range of common experiences among adoptees that impressed upon them that they were different from the White norm and therefore could never identify as White, regardless of how they were raised. She remembered a childhood incident where her mom caught her in the mirror squishing her eyelids in an attempt to make them look rounder and achieve White racial beauty standards. She talked about a particularly hurtful time in high school when she was bullied because she stood out as one of the few non-White students in a predominantly White high school. But, ultimately, it was the everyday experiences of intrusive questioning that socialized her into her position as non-White:

> I was something that was really different and didn't really fit in physically. Also, I think my presence raised a lot of questions that, at the time when I was real shy, I was very uncomfortable answering because I knew that every question that was raised towards me meant that I was seen as something that was "other" and not part of the collective. I think when you're younger, you're more concerned with fitting in. Now, I don't. I don't give a shit now, but I think that back then, you just wanted to be part of this whole so you can just exist without being questioned. That was very difficult to do when you're the only not-White face in a sea of White faces including your own family.

To exist without being questioned was a luxury that transnational transracial adoptees could not possess. Their exceptional belonging ensured that they would be conspicuous in the nation. To exist without being questioned is the (White) American experience—the feeling of belonging that enjoying legal, cultural, and social citizenship provides. Despite Brianne's parents raising her as if she were part of the White collective—cultivating White racial contexts and explaining away interpersonal racism she experienced—she learned that her claim to Whiteness was conditional, at best.

As Brianne reflected on how she thought about herself now, she shared, "I think that I'm very aware of, in general, a lot of minority experiences in America, from any non-White background. I think I identify more with just the general minority experience than I do with my adopted experience." Although Brianne knew that she was an adoptee and not White, she did not find a community of other adoptees with which she could understand her transnational transracial adoptee experience.

Instead, once she moved away from home, she found a community of people of color. Whereas it was her adoptee experience that was an early source of her feelings as a racial outsider, it was the overall similarities to other racially marginalized groups and the network of relationships she created that fostered a salient identity as a person of color. After all, you cannot cultivate a group identity individually. Without a critical mass of adoptees in Brianne's immediate social contexts, her adoptee identity did not have an opportunity to form.

Although Brianne came to identify as a person of color, most adoptees that I spoke with and surveyed did not identify in this way. Angela reflected on her own racial awareness: "I knew I was Asian, but I wasn't a person of color. That was . . . I guess I always thought a person of color is an African American, Black person, not Asian because Asians are Asian." Angela's discomfort with claiming the designation of person of color as an Asian American woman can be attributed to a confluence of factors—her upbringing in a White family and community, dominant culture's unfamiliarity with Asian Americans as a historically disadvantaged racial group, and the origins of the term "person of color." Traditionally, "person of color" was used to refer to people of African heritage. More recently it has expanded to include any non-White group, in some cases to the point of obscuring anti-Black racism. Given the socioeconomic advancement of some Asian American ethnic groups, East Asians in particular, there is debate about whether Asian Americans fall under the umbrella of "people of color" as a term referring to the systematic exclusion of racially minoritized groups. The boundaries around the "person of color" category highlight how Asian Americans are seen as a monolith, who are honorary Whites. It also demonstrates an unfamiliarity with historic and contemporary anti-Asian racism as well as Asian American histories of interracial solidarity. However, the few adoptees I spoke with who identified as a person of color recognized their racial experience as one of shared marginalization with other non-White communities and a commitment to cross-racial solidarity.

Adoptees' alignment with "person of color" as an identity of political solidarity also reflects how the racial classification "Asian American" has been divorced from the political consciousness that initially led to the creation of the pan-ethnic identifier. The term "Asian American" is so commonplace today that it is no more than shorthand to refer to the over 20 million Asian Americans in the US with disparate ethnic origins. Yet at its inception it was a self-defined label of pan-ethnic political organizing. Coined in 1968 by two student activists, Japanese American Yuji Ichioka and Chinese American Emma Gee, the name signified a pan-ethnic Asian unification of traditionally separate groups of Asian students while challenging the derogatory term "Oriental." "Oriental" was a pejorative label applied to people from Asia emphasizing their inferiority to and difference from people from Western nations. "Asian American" was a signal of Yellow Power, a power for self-determination, anti-racism, anti-imperialism, and social justice.

Since then, "Asian American" has been largely divorced from its political roots. Most adoptees who identified as Asian American used it simply as a term of expected racial categorization. However, for some, its political origins shaped their identification with the pan-ethnic label. These adoptees were actively involved in Asian American communities, political organizing, and grappling with issues of social justice.

As the many refusals of belonging reinscribing Korean adoptees' racial status accumulated over their lives, it produced a specific racial feeling related to their position as Asian Americans. Mi Na reflected on how she thought about herself: "No, I never forget it [that she is Asian and how others view her]. I never got that chance. I was never comfortable enough ever . . . I never really forgot. I was always worrying about how I looked on the outside." The awareness of how you are perceived as an Asian in America—foreigner, non-American—permeates accounts of Asian Americans' racial feelings across ethnicities, generations, immigration status, and time periods.[50] While some Asian Americans may be temporarily lauded as racial success stories or welcomed into the nation because of their economic contributions, Asian Americans' inclusion is subject to the whims of Whiteness.[51] Throughout history Asian Americans have been reminded that they can never be fully part of the national family.

Mi Na described how she felt as though she always had to be prepared for someone to remind her of her racial place, to ask her "No, where do you really come from?" She continued, "If you're not prepared. You go out, somebody says something . . . You forget that you're Asian for a second. Somebody says something, then you're totally caught off guard and then your whole day is ruined because you didn't prepare for it ahead of time because if you're colored, that's your responsibility to not let it get you down."[52] As Mi Na describes, there is a psychological toll to not being White in America. There is a disposition of cautiousness and a state of alertness. This includes a mental fortitude, an emotional resilience, and a repertoire of responses that allow you to maintain your dignity. As Mi Na understands the racialized social system, people of color are responsible for how they react to racism rather than perpetrators being held accountable. Racism is an inevitability, one that non-Whites must learn to skillfully navigate. To "forget that you're Asian" and simply move about the world is to be caught off guard when someone reminds of your racial place. Asian Americans learn that forgetting has a cost.

* * *

Is the adoptee one of *them*, a non-White foreigner? And if so, what happens when the adoptee becomes one of *us*, a White American? As much as exceptional belonging conceptually and culturally constructed adoptable orphans as distinct from other Asian immigrants, enduring racialized beliefs about who can be from "here" disciplined adoptees into their racial place as presumed foreigners. Refusals of belonging, including racial slurs, invectives, discriminatory behavior, innocent questions, and jokes, reinforced racial boundaries positioning adoptees outside of Whiteness and Americanness.

Adoptees learned that they were not White but what exactly was "not White?" Adoptees' amorphous position as "not White" was subject to the racialized logics of those around them. Adoptees were not-White, Black, and Asian. Their undefined position racialized them into a broader Asian American structure of feeling. These racial feelings include racial melancholia, racial dissociation, and an inability to feel comfortable at home in the US. Many adoptees characterized the effect of racial rein-scriptions as an inescapable feeling that they could never be accepted in the US without question. For others, it was a feeling of confusion over why they would be perceived as non-Americans. And, for some, it was a feeling of identification with other people of color.

Despite being adopted to White families, socialized into the White racial frame, and growing up in White spaces, Asian adoptees cannot be received as White; they are "racially subjectivized as non-White."[53] Transnational transracial adoptees should be evidence of the possibilities of assimilation. Korean adoptees were culturally constructed as assimilable and have an intimate familiarity with Whiteness to the point that many adoptees self-identify as White at some point in their lives. Yet the concept of assimilation itself ensures that non-Whites can never reach social status with Whites; assimilation already assumes difference from the standard. The more attempts are made to prove Asian Americans' assimilation by offering up select Asian American ethnic groups' socioeconomic attainment or intermarriage rates, particularly without situating these outcomes in past or present immigration policies, or heralding transnational transracial adoption as racial progress, the more their racially subordinate position is inscribed.[54] As the public racialization detailed in this chapter demonstrates, Asian Americans may reside within the national borders but they embody a difference that marks them as perpetually out of place.

3

Adoptable Orphan, Deportable Immigrant

During the 2015 holiday season, a couple dozen Korean adoptees and their significant others gathered for a family-style dinner at a local restaurant. The mood was festive as people dressed in ugly Christmas sweaters chatted about upcoming travels and family get-togethers. Among the revelers were regulars, newcomers, and special Korean adoptee guests from out of town: Mary Hiatt, Me & Korea, Inc., Board Member,[1] and Zeke Anders, who was embarking on a multi-city tour documenting adoptees' views on their identity. Zeke's project would become *The KAD Diaries*, a photo and video series exploring the questions "Who am I?" and "Where do I belong?" For the photo op, Korean adoptees encountered a backdrop of a US and Korean flag hanging side-by-side—a visual representation of a question adoptees face throughout their lives. Where they stood was up to the adoptees themselves.

As Zeke flipped the question of belonging to center adoptee choice, Mary took the holiday gathering as an opportunity to connect common adoptee experiences questioning their belonging with formal removal from the nation. In front of a captive audience, Mary shared information about Adam Crapser's deportation case and the concurrent push for the Adoptee Citizenship Act of 2015. Making an impassioned plea, she rallied her audience: "It is our duty to support it [Adoptee Citizenship Act of 2015, S. 2275] and call our senator, congressmen to get this bill pushed through. *This could be any of us.*"

Mary's assertion of "any of us" was in stark contrast to the individual way adoptees experienced their belonging for most of their lives. Adoption had primarily been a fact of personal history, one that did not engender a sense of emotional connectedness or denote membership in a group identity. Rather than adoptees' individual understanding of who they are or where they belong, Mary's words called upon the shared history among Korean adoptees, who have the longest record of sustained adoption to the US and are the largest population of adult transnational adoptees in the nation. More than that, however, it also emphasized the responsibility Korean adoptees have to advocate for themselves and one another. "This could be any of us" was a redirection to the idea that adoptees were united by their exceptional belonging, the multidimensional process that fashioned Korean children into desirable adoptees and just as conveniently constructed Korean adults as discardable immigrants. For Korean adoptees, national belonging was not a personal choice.

Social movements—like, at the time, the burgeoning adoptee-led adoptee citizenship rights movement—rely on collective identity to propel people to action.[2] That evening Mary emphasized her audience's shared transnational adoptive status to engage them to identify with and act on behalf of vulnerable transnational adoptees. Mary's declaration that the potential deportation of one adoptee could happen to *any* adoptee recast adoptive status from a biographical footnote to an ongoing, active, and shared part of who adopted persons are. Although most adoptees are not vulnerable to legal expulsion from the US, the informal exclusions they experienced throughout their lives and shared racialized emotions as Asians in America served as a basis for adoptees to identify with Adam and other undocumented adoptees.

Mary's words and other similar calls to an adoptee collective identity were not the only ones being used to garner support for adoptee citizenship rights. Adoptee deportations were a collective refusal of belonging, racializing adoptees as non-White foreigners. However, some strategies adoptees and other advocates used in advocating for citizenship rights attempted to leverage pre-existing tropes around adoptees, family, and Whiteness as the prerequisite for citizenship—a tactic that required adoptees to be seen through the lens of their White family ties.

This chapter charts how responses to adoptee citizenship vulnerability exposed the competing logics of exceptional belonging—at times relying on the racialized logics of conditional inclusion and at others using previous exclusions from full citizenship to reframe adoptee belonging. Each tactic attempted to activate a shared group identity through appealing to group emotions. By uncovering the racialized logics used for adoptee citizenship advocacy, this chapter demonstrates the material consequences of racialized emotions, from advancing deportations to organizing for adoptee citizenship rights legislation.

Forever Foreigners: "I Am Capable of More"

As I began formally interviewing adoptees, Adam Crapser's deportation case entered mainstream news. Kevin Vollmers of Land of Gazillion Adoptees, an adoptee-centered multimedia company, and Gazillion Strong, an advocacy group, began advocating around adoptee citizenship in February 2015, shortly after ICE served Adam his deportation paperwork. With Adam's April 2, 2015, ICE deportation hearing looming, 18 Million Rising, an online Asian American advocacy hub, launched a social media campaign to #KeepAdamHome. This was one of the first and largest social media campaigns to raise awareness for Adam's case and the loopholes of existing adoptee citizenship legislation. Long-standing Asian American blogs, such as Angry Asian Man and Reappropriate, signal boosted the petition.[3] Readers were encouraged to tweet using the #KeepAdamHome hashtag, sign 18 Million Rising's petition asking Raphael Sanchez of the Office of the Chief Counsel for an administrative closure of Adam's case, and support an amendment that would address the citizenship loophole left by the previous Child Citizenship Act.

By bringing attention to Adam's case, 18 Million Rising's campaign positioned Adam, and by extension Asian adoptees, as part of Asian America, and adoptee citizenship rights as a cause that affected the

Asian American community. This inclusion within Asian America was significantly different from how adoptees were often excluded from Asian American networks throughout childhood and how Asian transnational adoption has typically been omitted from Asian American history. Adam's undocumented status, while a result of adoption and immigration policy failures specific to international adoption, was reframed as another instance of Asian Americans' conditional inclusion. Advocating for Adam and adoptee citizenship rights more broadly, then, was one way that Asian American supporters could proclaim their own belonging.

18 Million Rising's campaign identified Asian Americans' informal and formal exclusion from the nation as unjust; however, the imagery that they used to garner support for Adam's case invoked racialized tropes about adoptees as rescuable children. 18 Million Rising's campaign presented a black-and-white image of a smiling child-age Adam with the quote "I am capable of more. There is good in me." Using young Adam as the poster child for the call to action for adult Adam's vulnerability invoked visual tropes of need linked to practices of international adoption.[4] By representing Adam in this way, it reinforced the infantilization of adoptees. Although undocumented adoptees need community and ally support as they advocate for themselves, they do not need to be saved, nor do they lack agency. Positioning adoptees as children continued their objectification, putting supporters in the role of benevolent rescuers.

18 Million Rising's choice of visual imagery and quote paralleled the culturally resonant redemption narrative. The plea of an innocent child could spur people to action, whereas that of a middle-aged Asian man asking for yet another chance after breaking the law would not. An adult Adam conjured more sinister imagery, that of a Yellow Peril—sneaky, criminal, and conniving. If it was the former that helped mobilize ideologies of rescue resulting in international adoption of foreign orphans

to the West,[5] then it is the latter that all but ensured Adam's formal expulsion from American citizenry.

The subsequent media coverage zeroed in on another common adoption trope—adoption's promise of forever family. Adam's life history was a heart-wrenching challenge to the feel-good stories of adoption. Rather than a story of abandonment and rescue, Adam's "life in this country quickly became a nightmare"[6] as he faced abuse at the hands of his first adoptive family, who relinquished him to state custody. His second adoptive family was no better. Dolly and Thomas Crapser physically and sexually abused Adam and their other children.[7] In 1991, the Crapsers were arrested on charges of physical child abuse, sexual abuse, and rape. They were convicted on multiple counts of criminal mistreatment and assault. Despite the unimaginable violence of his childhood, Adam managed to create a better life for himself, eventually finding stable employment, marrying, and starting his own family. He was able to find his American dream.

Yet, in 2015, he, like other vulnerable transnational adoptees before him, found himself faced with a stark reality. Though adopted to the US by an American family, he was not an American citizen. Due to legal loopholes in adoption and immigration policy, a child could be legally adopted from abroad but not have US citizenship. Similarly, an international adoptee could be naturalized without their adoption being finalized.[8] Adoptees' immigration privilege,[9] particularly pre–Child Citizenship Act, ensured that some adoptees would be forever foreigners. Thus, the policy decisions and cultural constructions that created adoptable orphans ensured they would be deportable immigrants.

For Adam, his citizenship vulnerability felt like a betrayal of America's promise. Quoted in *Gazillion Voices*, Adam said, "America signed a bill to bring us over from Korea in a military action. . . . They promised us a better life over here. All I'm asking is to keep their promise and do what they said they'd do. And if not for me, then for my children."[10] Whether it was through the US military's creation of Korean orphanages during the Korean War, US couples rescuing orphans from a war-torn country, or the adoption stories that centered on birth mothers' desires for a better life for their children, the belief was that the US was better suited to address the needs of these Korean children.[11] The fact that the US was responsible for contributing to the conditions that led to the economic, political, and social instability of Korea or other foreign countries in need was irrelevant when the US could now rescue the children left in its aftermath. The assumption was that adoptees would fare better in a society where they could be accepted, integrated, and free from the stigma of single parenthood or mixed-race lineage. The irony was that for undocumented adoptees this better life was similar to the life they may have had in their home country. They existed on the fringes of society, unable to partake in the benefits as citizens. In Adam's case, not only did the US fail to provide his forever family during his childhood and thereby his better life, with his current deportation proceedings the US was also destroying his children's forever family. However, by signing petitions for Adam's release, readers were able to collectively fulfill the promise of permanency.

Deportable Immigrant: "It Was Their Parents' Responsibility"

Prior to the Child Citizenship Act of 2000 (CCA), it was incumbent upon adoptive parents to know that their adopted children were not automatically citizens and how to apply for citizenship for their child. There was no formal federal-level process informing adoptive parents about the citizenship process, and as a result, many parents did not secure citizenship for their child. Some failed to do so out of ignorance, others out of laziness, and still others out of willful neglect. The CCA was a result of the efforts of adoptive parents who believed their transnationally adopted children should automatically receive US citizenship upon adoption and that the naturalization process for adoptees should be eliminated. As Eleana Kim and Kim Park Nelson argue, adoptees had already been framed as non-immigrant immigrants "whose legal and cultural citizenship are considered to be, like transracial adoptive kinship itself, (as-if-) natural-born and (almost-) white."[12] The CCA was the formalization of this belief.

Though the CCA addressed the citizenship issue for the thousands of international adoptees who were under 18 years old upon the legislation's passing and the tens of thousands of international adoptees since, it left those over 18 without a clear pathway to citizenship. Seeking to address the thousands of adoptees who were not covered by the CCA, in 2009, the House and the Senate introduced the Foreign Adopted Children Equality (FACE) Act.[13] The bill sought retroactive citizenship for all adoptees regardless of age, as long as they had been adopted before they were 18 years old. It also sought to clarify another loophole of the CCA; it would confer citizenship at the time the adoption was finalized in the country of the child's birth rather than once the child entered the US to reside permanently. Doing so would remove adopted children from the immigration process entirely and curtail situations where adopted children entered the US under visas not covered by the CCA. Another key component of this bill was citizenship from birth. Whereas the CCA simply sought to rectify adoptees' citizenship status, the FACE Act wanted to remove the final legal distinction between internationally adopted children and biological children by classifying adopted children as "citizens from birth." This change would afford internationally adopted children all the rights and privileges of "natural born citizens." Though both House and Senate bills were referred to Committee, neither saw any other legislative action.

In 2013 an amendment to the CCA,[14] which would have closed the loophole and granted retroactive citizenship to adoptees not covered by previous legislation, was introduced and later included in a broader immigration bill, which did not pass.[15] As was the case then and continues to be the case now as adoptees and allies fight for adoptee citizenship rights, adoptees with criminal records are stumbling blocks to Congress and House support.[16] Elected officials do not want to be perceived as providing citizenship to criminal immigrants. As adults, adoptees are no longer vulnerable foreign children. They are seen as immigrant adults who are taking advantage of the system.

The shift in framing from vulnerable children to criminal immigrants was apparent in responses to Adam's and other similarly situated adoptees' cases. As I was speaking with Natasha (b. 1975), she shared a shocking response she'd encountered when talking about Adam's case: "This whole thing with Adam Crapser, like I didn't even know that was an issue, and it's important to me, but I was really surprised at how many people, it wasn't important to them." I asked if it was adoptees that did not see its importance. She clarified, "No. Regular people. They're like, 'No. They need to go through the legal ways to get citizenship, too.' And I'm like, 'You're talking about a baby. A six-month-old baby. Should've gone through the legal way?' 'Well, then it was their parents' responsibility.' Yeah, but we're talking about adults now whose parents didn't do what they were supposed to do. How are they penalized? I couldn't believe some of the statements that I got from people."

For many Americans, like the ones Natasha encountered, there was a disconnect between conceding to adoptive parents' responsibility to secure adoptees' citizenship when they were children and placing the blame for adoptees' undocumented status on adult adoptees. Acknowledging parents' failure in the past does little to help resolve adoptees' citizenship issues in the present. Yet parents were absolved of their responsibility and instead the fault was put solely on the adoptees once adoptees reached adulthood. No longer minors, no longer under the protection of their parents, and no longer children in need of rescue, adoptees became subsumed under tropes that accuse immigrants of being lazy and siphoning off resources from deserving Americans. Without a clear script for making sense of undocumented adults whose status is the fault of their parents' inaction or, more accurately, the government's failure to ensure adopted children's citizenship, people default to the easily accessible framing they know—criminal immigrants.

Beginning in the 1960s, policies and public attitudes laid a foundation for the intertwining of criminal law and immigration law that currently characterizes the US's approach to immigrants. Changes to immigration policy, such as the end of the Bracero program in 1964 and the introduction of the Immigration and Nationality Act of 1965, abruptly halted the legal flow of immigration from Mexico while dismantling the quotas on immigration from other countries. These policy changes were later joined by the War on Crime,[17] which created a fear that crime was omnipresent, and the War on Drugs,[18] which introduced the idea that non-citizens were smuggling drugs across the southern border. In response, policing increased, laws expanded the scope of confinement, and incarceration grew exponentially—all of which disproportionately affected Black and Brown communities.

The fear of rising crime by people "not like us" drew upon historic fears of "others," cementing racialized beliefs around who was constructed as citizens and moral judgments about who should receive the benefits of citizenship. Immigrants, particularly those from non-European countries, were no longer perceived as "Americans in waiting," who could contribute to society, but rather as "criminal aliens" to be feared, controlled, and deported.[19] As historian Erika Lee traces in *America for Americans: A History of Xenophobia in the United States*, "fear of the stranger" is part of the United States' national identity, guiding politics, shaping economics, and defining culture.[20] Research shows immigrants are less likely to commit crime, yet public opinions about immigrants operating outside of the law are strongly held.[21] These misbeliefs bolster ideas of citizenship as a conferred right given only to those deemed worthy—historically this has meant Whites, people with certain morals and values, and those who are either professional class members, highly educated, or with specialized skills.

One outcome of the overlap of criminal law and immigration law enforcement was the change in criminal activity classifications. The 1988 Anti-Drug Abuse Act introduced the immigration law classification "aggravated felony." During the mid-1980s through the 1990s, Congress expanded the range of crimes that were deportable offenses, notably broadening the category of aggravated felonies. Many actions by immigrants that were once classified as civil violations became criminal offenses and/or carried harsher penalties. With the passage of the 1996 Illegal Immigration Reform and Immigrant Responsibility Act (IIRIRA), nonviolent offenses such as bribery, forgery, and some types of theft, burglary, and fraud were included. The IIRIRA was also retroactive. Non-citizens with a prior conviction for an offense now defined as an aggravated felony were subject to deportation. At the same time that the scope of deportable offenses was broadened, judges' discretionary power was limited and the eligibility criteria for cancellation of removal were narrowed. In political scientist Lina Newton's analysis of Congressional debate about the IIRIRA, she reveals how policy makers' discussion of immigrants and immigration policy shifted from a more complex framing acknowledging the humanity of immigrants to one that framed immigrants as unlawful and undeserving, a perspective that continues to shape immigration policy and attitudes today.[22]

The response to the September 11, 2001, attacks further intertwined criminality with immigration. Terrorism was linked to immigration, resulting in the creation of the Department of Homeland Security (DHS). One of DHS's objectives was to enforce immigration law. The safety of the nation was at the forefront, and the War on Terror promised to protect it from "terrorist aliens" through immigration control and criminal law enforcement. Whereas immigration law and criminal law had been separately enforced, these two systems of law were merged into what is now referred to as "crimmigration."

Beginning in 2001, the now defunct Immigration and Naturalization Services began entering civil immigration information into the

FBI's database. Police officers use this database when they run a person's identification. Although immigration law enforcement is a federal responsibility, in 2007 Congress granted states the authority to enforce both criminal and civil immigration violations.[23] As state officers effectively became deputized to enforce immigration law, the merging of immigration policy and policing blurred the lines of these two regimes of law enforcement. The effect can be seen in due process procedures. Whereas a person who violates criminal law faces arrest and incarceration with due process protections, a person who violates the Immigration and Nationality Act faces arrest, detention, and deportation *without* due process protections. For immigration law violations that are pursued in conjunction with criminal offenses, courts routinely default to the laxer interpretations of civil immigration procedures. This includes a more lenient application of the Fourth, Fifth, and Sixth Amendments.[24]

Once an immigrant is entangled in this convoluted system of law there is little chance that they will not be deported,[25] especially given Fourth Amendment violations characterizing "speed deportations."[26] The absence of due process protections, the increased scope of crimes included as deportable offenses, and the limitations on judges' discretionary power all but ensure this outcome. Under the Trump administration, the application of immigration laws became more punitive as the role of prosecutorial discretion was increasingly used to detain and deport immigrants with devastating effects.[27]

Jessa (b. 1960) and I were discussing Adam's case when she divulged, "I more than feel for them, I'm part of that, myself. I'm 56 years old, I've been in this country since I was two, I am not an American citizen. I am not faced with the plight of many of those who do not have citizenship, mostly because I am . . . wouldn't say I am 100 percent law abiding citizen because there's no such thing, but I truly don't do really anything that causes attention to me. I know the reasons why I'm not a citizen, some of them are my mistakes, some of them is stupid government and I'm going to call them stupid." Though Jessa is not an American citizen, she does maintain lawful permanent residence. She sees herself as part of a class of adoptees who should, but do not, have citizenship, even as she distances herself from targeted adoptees by offering up her own good behavior. Her framing of her status as a function of her own "mistakes" belies a commitment to personal responsibility narratives while absolving responsible parties, such as parents or the government, from their role in adoptees' lack of citizenship.

Approaching citizenship as an earned entitlement became evident in another common response to Adam's deportation status, which was that if Adam had not broken the law, he would not be facing deportation. This "personal responsibility" framing paints Adam's plight as a moral failure. If only he had the correct values and morals to be an upstanding citizen, this would not have happened. However, it is not Adam's moral failure that created his deportability but rather the US's long history of imperialism and xenophobia. US imperialism led to the conditions facilitating international adoption of Korean children; US xenophobia guaranteed that when those children became adults they aged out of the "orphans in need of rescue" framing and into that of a foreign threat. Though the US government took pains to ensure international adoptees would be able to immigrate, even making special legislation to do so, and media and social services framed international adoptees as family members like any others, there were no federal policies put in place to certify adoptees' inclusion in the national family.

Undergirding the personal responsibility explanation is the idea that citizenship should be earned—an idea that citizens by birth are immune from. The situations for which these moral arguments are mobilized illuminate who is considered worthy of being citizens and who is considered foreigners. Even if one's behavior could justify or revoke one's citizenship, in a previous time, Adam's burglary conviction from when he retrieved his personal childhood items that the Crapsers would not return to him would not have classified him as a felon. Just as who is eligible for citizenship changes over time following the caprices of the law, so too do ideas of criminality. However, the arguments in support of Adam's deportation show that what endures is Asians' exclusion from American belonging.

Jessa went on to explain,

> I was denied my application because I took five dollars too much money one time. Five dollars and they refused my application, they rejected it, and all I could think of is, "Are you fucking idiots?!" I was furious! I plan on applying for my citizenship again, probably towards the end of this year if this bill [Adoptee Citizenship Act] does not get passed. I will become potentially part of the lawsuit against the United States.[28] I do not know if that's a good thing, or if this is going to be a detrimental thing to me. But I figured, what better way to bring attention to what I feel is a . . . America needs to make those of us who are international adoptees, they need to make us whole, and they need to make us citizens. I look at it like I will pay the money, I will prove that I am here legitimately, I will prove that I'm an American citizen, but why insult me to take the test? . . . Those of us who've been in this country for years, our entire life, you're going to make us jump through these hoops.

As Jessa points out, the naturalization process can be tedious. Forms must be filled out exactly as specified; fees must be correctly paid. The process can often take years. Jessa had attempted to go through the process four or five times but to no avail. For adoptees who have known no other country, applying for citizenship is an affront. Jessa's frustration underlines the belief that she is already a citizen, one who is in the US "legitimately," and separate from other immigrants who should take the naturalization test, undergo the naturalization interview, and be tested on their English and civics knowledge.[29] When Jessa says, "I will prove that I'm an American citizen," she emphasizes the shared misbeliefs that undocumented migrants, who entered the US as children, often have. They grew up in the US, attended US schools, participated in life as

American citizens, expecting to enjoy the full rights and responsibilities as US citizens only to find out that they are not citizens at all.[30] Though Jessa believes she can "prove that I'm an American citizen," the irony is that if she could prove it, she would not need to go through the naturalization process. Though she entered the US legally and has maintained her legal status with a green card, it does not make her an American citizen, only a lawful permanent resident. The paperwork needed to prove her pre-existing American status does not exist.

Though Jessa is an adoptee without citizenship, there is, in her mind, a sharp distinction between herself and those she "feels" for or identifies with who, like her, are here "legitimately," and those who have done it the wrong way. She continued:

> I get a little bit indignant about illegal aliens. You know, those individuals who have hopped their way into this country, swam their way into this country, smuggled their way into this country, and yet at the same time, they can get all the same privileges as those of us who did it the right way. Then when I see folks, you know, like Adam Crapser, who's going to get deported, but yet they can't deport the Mexicans when they catch them and they know that they're not legally here in this country, but yet they can't deport them. So, I get a little . . . My fire gets up of the, what I consider, the injustice of it all.

Using the racialized logics of good immigrants versus bad immigrants, Jessa identifies those who deserve the privileges of US citizenship, like herself, and those who should be deported, those who are unlike her. The conjuring up of "Mexicans" as the "bad immigrant" is connected to a long history of race-making that racializes Mexican as not fully American and inherently illegal. Historian Natalia Molina details how the immigration regime of the 1940s and 1950s racialized Mexicans as undocumented, criminal, and disease-carrying—logics that continue to shape debates about deportation and citizenship (in)eligibility today.[31] She argues that race-making happens relationally between racialized groups and across time so that the "attitudes, practices, customs, policies, and laws" that defined African Americans' and Chinese Americans' race and belonging in the 19th century were used to categorize Mexicans as non-White and therefore similarly ineligible for citizenship.

Even though Asians are the fastest growing population of undocumented migrants,[32] the discourse on illegal immigration continues its focus on "Mexicans" and public attitudes follow suit. While Jessa wants justice for undocumented adoptees, going as far as wanting to sue the US government, the "injustice" of capricious citizenship laws is applicable to certain populations only. The pervasiveness of anti-immigrant sentiment and the conjoining of criminality with immigration make it difficult for some people to consider the plight of undocumented immigrants. For adoptees, like Jessa, who learned that "immigrant" means "criminal alien" or whose socialization into the White racial frame led to seeing themselves aligned with Whites, there is a cognitive dissonance precluding them from thinking of themselves as immigrants. The distancing from seeing oneself as an immigrant along with viewing citizenship as an earned entitlement and deportation as the just outcome of individual moral failure are the internalization of exceptional belonging. Jessa has aligned herself with legal citizens who deserve privileges and against "illegal aliens" who unjustly "can get all the same privileges as those of us who did it the right way."[33] The cruel irony in Jessa's identification as one of "those who did it the right way" is that the legal process of adoption does not guarantee citizenship. One can do everything "right" and still never become American.

Adoptable Orphan: "A Family Issue Not an Immigration Issue"

Cognizant of the challenges of stand-alone legislation for retroactive adoptee citizenship, a coalition of Asian American advocacy groups, including the National Korean American Service and Education Consortium (NAKASEC), the Adoptee Rights Campaign, 18 Million Rising, and Gazillion Strong, began meeting with lawmakers to support the Adoptee Citizenship Act (ACA).[34] Throughout 2016, they continued to bring public awareness to the issue of adoptees without citizenship and attempted to secure co-sponsors for the legislation. In addition to online support and fundraising for Adam's case specifically and the Adoptee Rights Campaign more broadly, NAKASEC organized days of action on Capitol Hill. At least once during each 2016 quarter, Korean adoptees, other international adoptees, and their allies met with elected officials on the Hill to urge their support of the ACA.

Advocacy for the ACA was distinct from previous adoptee citizenship legislation, as it was primarily spearheaded by adoptees for adoptees rather than by adoptive parents or adoption agencies. The Adoptee Rights Campaign was intentional about who could be in leadership positions within the organization—first having both adoptees with citizenship and undocumented adoptees and later deciding that undocumented adoptees should lead the charge.

By 2016's end, the ACA had bipartisan support in the House and Senate.[35] Senator Amy Klobuchar (D-MN) along with six co-sponsors led the Senate bill, and Representative Adam Smith (D-WA) along with seven co-sponsors introduced the House bill. The bill "amends the Immigration and Nationality Act to grant automatic citizenship to all qualifying children adopted by a U.S. citizen parent, regardless of the date on which the adoption was finalized." The delicacy of a bill advocating for citizenship of what were now undocumented adult immigrants and in a charged anti-immigrant political context was a conscious concern. At a strategy meeting during one of the Days of Action on Capitol Hill, Hill staffers reviewed the talking points of the bill in preparation of Adoptee Rights Campaign meetings with potential Congressional and House co-sponsors. In that meeting, one of the staffers reminded volunteers to "frame this as a family issue not an immigration issue," a strategy to try to gain the support of more conservative representatives by separating the ACA from broader discourse about immigration.

Pitching the ACA as legislation to protect family unity also shifted the focus from adoptee citizenship rights to ensuring the interests of White parents. This approach recast ACA activists as children in need, something that adoptee-led advocacy attempted to push against. Yet the reality was that legislators could be moved by thinking about White interests more than immigrant interests just as they were at Korean adoption's inception. Framing the ACA as a family issue activated potential legislative co-sponsors' shared identity as (White) Americans. The emotional plea inherent in family separation and the outrage for deportation of White Americans' children could elicit group-based emotions. Though legislators may not be adoptive parents themselves or have a direct connection to adoption, events that affect groups with which people identify can produce a shared emotional response, influencing people to action.

Emphasizing the family angle rather than the immigration issue of the ACA was a strategy to create common ground and a shared goal between advocates and potential co-sponsors. Given Adam's high-profile deportation case and his criminal background, the ACA could be easily linked to broader controversies around undocumented immigrants. This too could elicit group-based emotions—fear of foreigners, concerns for safety—leading legislators not to support the ACA. Without a framework to think about adoptees as adults, the strategies to mobilize people to action were limited to existing frames around immigration, family, and race. These frames had mixed possibilities for mobilizing not only legislators but also the public and adoptees.

In fact, early organizing by the Adoptee Rights Campaign distinguished between adoptees without citizenship and other undocumented immigrants. Narratives of adoptees' "deservingness" through terminology such as "adoptees without citizenship" are attempts to leverage their exceptional belonging into formal citizenship benefits. Adoption scholar Kimberly McKee outlines how language choice reinforces harmful stereotypes about immigrants: "the term *adoptees without citizenship* privileges noncitizen adoptees as 'good' undocumented immigrants, while others who lack citizenship are rendered 'bad' immigrants" (italics in original).[36] As Eleana Kim and Kim Park Nelson point out, this dichotomy between "good" and "bad" or "deserving" and "undeserving" immigrants hinges on adoptees' non-immigrant immigrant status created from their proximity to Whiteness.[37] The use of "adoptee without citizenship" attempts to recall adoptees' past immigration privilege to shore up present priority in securing citizenship rights.[38]

Despite Korean adoptee and broader Asian American organizing, on October 24, 2016, immigration judge John C. O'Dell ruled that Adam Crapser be deported to Korea.[39] The different strategies to appeal to racialized emotions provide futile. 18 Million Rising's campaign attempted to #KeepAdamHome by appealing to adoptee rescue narratives, and ACA advocacy tried to distance the legislation from broader debates about immigration, instead emphasizing the family unity angle. In Adam's case, however, he was merely another deportable immigrant. Whether administrative relief was not granted because of his non-Whiteness, criminal background, or estrangement from his White adoptive families cannot be known for certain. However, his deportation confirms that adoptable orphans are deportable immigrants because of—not in spite of—their exceptional belonging.

Although the face of advocacy was deported, efforts continued, and in the spring of 2018,[40] the Adoptee Citizenship Act was reintroduced in the House and the Senate.[41] Since then, the bill has been reintroduced to the House and Senate in 2019–2020 and 2021–2022.[42] However, the 2018 bill was unique because of a key change in the bill's language. Adoptees and their allies had been fighting for "citizenship for all adoptees," but this new bill had an important caveat—adoptees who "have been found guilty of a violent crime and have been deported" would be excluded. In other words, adoptees like Adam, who was the face of the movement and the impetus for renewed advocacy and the introduction of the ACA, would not be included. This shift in strategy relied on the good/bad and deserving/undeserving immigrant dichotomy in attempting to secure citizenship rights for some at the expense of validating exclusionary immigration policy.

Shortly after the bill was introduced, Adam vehemently opposed the new bill and the adoptees who had been working behind the scenes to get it introduced. Other Korean adoptees, namely those who had been involved in advocacy for the initial iterations of the ACA, made statements voicing their lack of support for this new bill as well and called for the Adoptee Rights Campaign to make a statement clarifying how the current bill diverged from their motto of "citizenship for all adoptees."

The Adoptee Rights Campaign (ARC) responded to the critiques of the new legislation, and in a Facebook post entitled, "How ARC Came to Support the 2018 Adoptee Citizenship Act," stated,[43]

> Since 2000, many of you have helped support campaigns for adoptee citizenship. Unfortunately, since 2016, the legislation had remained stalled in Judiciary Committees. The bill faced opposition in Congress because it included adoptees who had been deported—even if they had completed their sentences long ago. The political climate has harshened. . . . Last year, under a new administration, ARC was forced back to the drawing board with a new bill and needed to recruit new Congressional sponsors. . . . After a year of discussions, extensive research and advocacy on our part, along with close analysis from our legal experts, the government's legal experts, and USCIS, ARC's legal counsel advised in favor of the revision.

The response to the 2018 ACA brought to light what had been happening behind the scenes—the shift from "citizenship for all" to "citizenship for most," the fracturing of ARC volunteers, and the continued distancing of ARC from other immigrant groups. By the end of 2018, the splinter among adoptees leading the fight for adoptee citizenship legislation became formalized as a new adoptee advocacy group emerged, Adoptees for Justice (A4J). Formed with support from NAKASEC, HANA Center, Korean Resource Center, and Asian Americans Advancing Justice—Atlanta, A4J is, at the time of this writing, at the forefront in strategizing the best way to move forward on the ACA[44] Many of the adoptees who were initially involved in ARC, both those directly affected and their allies, are now at the helm of A4J. Whether or not "citizenship for all" was a feasible goal or if "citizenship for most" would be better than citizenship for none seemed to characterize the break between adoptee groups.[45]

In May 2019, another Adoptee Citizenship Act was introduced in the House and Senate.[46] Most significantly, neither of the bills had the deportable offense clause. In press releases announcing the new bill, the change was not mentioned. However, the racialized logics undergirding international adoption that constructed Korean adoptees as exceptional were invoked to justify legislation rectifying adult adoptees' citizenship needs. Central to this framing was adoptees' deservedness as good immigrants and their White familial ties. Senator Susan Collins (R-ME) was quoted in the ACA 2019 press release, saying, "Individuals who were legally adopted by loving U.S. parents, raised with American values, and are now contributing members of our society should not be denied citizenship due to a technicality in current law. . . . Our bipartisan bill would address this loophole, and I encourage our colleagues to support it."[47] Senator Collins's statement reinforces assumptions of immigrant worthiness, positioning undocumented adoptees as "good" immigrants who are in the US legally, like "us" (re: White Americans), and "contributing members of society." In short, undocumented adoptees are not illegal crimmigrants who must be deported but rather model minorities. Her inclusion of the role of "loving U.S. parents" sets the tone for who these affected individuals are—not the children of people who illegally entered the US but real

US citizens who themselves did nothing wrong. Instead, a "technicality" is at the heart of this issue absolving anyone of responsibility.

Throughout the press release for the Senate's bill, Senate co-sponsors emphasized that vulnerable adoptees were "raised in the U.S., by American parents" (Roy Blunt, R-MO) and "raised as Americans in American families" (Mazie K. Hirono, D-HI). As Senator Amy Klobuchar summarizes, "These adoptees grew up in American families. They went to American schools. They lead American lives. This bill would ensure that international adoptees are recognized as the Americans that they truly are." The proof of adoptees' Americanness—their cultural upbringing, education, and assimilation—recalls historic constructions of Americanness predicated on Whiteness. Nearly one hundred years earlier, Takao Ozawa made a similar argument for his naturalization, citing his acculturation—educated in the US, Christian, and using English at home with his wife and children. In short, Ozawa had forsaken Japanese culture and was leading an American life. As he compellingly stated in his legal brief, "At heart, I am a true American." The Supreme Court, however, was unmoved and ultimately upheld the racialized naturalization law of the time that restricted citizenship to "free white persons."

The co-sponsors' statements draw on the implicit link between Whiteness, citizenship, and family. By aligning adoptees within their (White) American families, adoptive parents' citizenship privileges are invoked. Whereas other undocumented immigrants may have grown up in the US, attended American schools, and now lead American lives, what sets undocumented adoptees apart is that they have American parents. Assimilation does not ensure citizenship—social, cultural, or legal. Instead, it is the familial connection to (White) Americans that is most compelling. Without this distinction, the argument for citizenship for other children brought to the US by loving parents would be one and the same. Adoptees are made exceptional by how they came to be undocumented Americans, under the care of true Americans. By framing the ACA in this way, support of this bill is for the benefit not only of adoptees but also of their families. Thus, the ACA serves the interests of White family members, those whose citizenship should confer certain benefits.

The language in the Senate and House bills' press releases, of course, did not refer to vulnerable adoptees as immigrants. Rather, they were referenced as "foreign-born adoptive children," "internationally adopted children," "children adopted from abroad," or "children adopted to the U.S." The sound bites emphasized adoptees as children with little to no mention of who the affected adoptees are now as adults. By infantilizing adoptees, it positioned potential co-signers and the public at large in roles as generous benefactors. In framing adoptees as children, these official statements conjure the image of foreign orphans in need, a culturally resonant script positioning adoptees as worthy of rescue. It also clarifies who is eligible for citizenship: children. Korean adoptees remain divorced from racialized framing of Asian adults as unassimilable, untrustworthy foreigners. Yet it is this continued emphasis on adoptees as children that precludes them from full personhood and the ability to be recognized as complete citizens.

Congressman Adam Smith focused on another aspect of this framing:[48]

> I am proud to introduce the bipartisan Adoptee Citizenship Act of 2019 to help achieve the vision of the original Child Citizenship Act of 2000, which sought to ensure that adopted children and biological children are treated equally under U.S. law. By closing an existing loophole in the Child Citizenship Act, this bill will extend citizenship to thousands of foreign-born adoptive children who have joined their families here in the United States. . . . Unfortunately, not all adoptees were able to benefit from the Child Citizenship Act when it originally passed, as it was limited to apply only to minors age 18 and under. Adopted individuals should not

be treated as second class citizens just because they happened to be the wrong age when the Child Citizenship Act became law.

By highlighting that adopted children and biological children deserve the same rights, the idea of "as if begotten" is retrofitted to include equal treatment under the law. By referring to undocumented adoptees as "foreign-born adoptive children who have joined their families here in the United States," the shift is from adopted children to children who simply had to sojourn to join their families. The distinction may be slight, but it is a rhetorical move further emphasizing adoptees' clean break from their birth country and any other family. Adoptees were always already part of their American family; they just needed to physically join them. Congressman Smith's excerpt ends with the familiar absolution of responsibility for undocumented adoptees' status—"they happened to be the wrong age when the Child Citizenship Act became law." Yet in 2000 the CCA could have included all internationally adopted individuals regardless of age. As Kim and Park Nelson point out, legislators' anxiety over appearing "tough on crime" ultimately led to the exclusion of adult adoptees from the CCA.[49]

In one of the only statements that references adoptees as adults, Congressman Rob Woodall (R-GA) is quoted saying, "It is estimated that between 25,000 and 49,000 children adopted to the U.S. between 1945 and 1998 lack U.S. citizenship. Most of them did not become aware of their lack of citizenship until well into their adulthood. . . . The Korean American community is home to tens of thousands of adoptees that lack eligibility for U.S. citizenship despite their legal entry and lifelong residency here. Our legislation will provide a solution to close this loophole and grant the adoptees the right to citizenship they deserve."[50] Why adoptees do not have citizenship is left unanswered, but what readers do know from the Congressman's statement is that despite a lack of citizenship, Korean American adoptees entered the US legally and have lived here their entire lives. As such, they deserve a "right to citizenship." This right hinges on their legality. While legal entry can change capriciously, it is the legal aspect that makes them deserving.

Woodall's statement also activates racialized assimilation expectations when he references adoptees' inclusion within the Korean American community. Even as Korean adoptees often do not see themselves as integrated within their Asian American ethnic community, Woodall's positioning of them as contributing members connects adoptees to tropes about the successful assimilation of Asian Americans. Affected adoptees are worthy of citizenship by virtue of their model minority status.

The various press releases announcing the latest version of the ACA emphasized discourses of family, citizenship, and race. For the most part, adoptees were constructed simply as children within (White) American families, who happen to not have citizenship. Who is at fault for their lack of citizenship is of little consequence. These press releases impress that what is important is that adoptees are citizens due to upbringing, legal entry, and their moral character. When adoptees are referenced as adults, they are connected to broader cultural messaging around Asian assimilation. It is imperative that statements by the bill co-signers divorce undocumented adoptees from other undocumented migrants not only due to public perception linking immigrants to criminality but also due to the moral obligation that they would then have to address the plight of other undocumented migrants.

"This Could Be Any of Us"

In light of adoptee deportations, some adoptees, like Jessa, relied on the White racial frame to distinguish themselves from undocumented adoptees and immigrants, while others were spurred to rethink their understanding of who they were and where they belonged. This was evident when I asked Alex (b. 1986) how important being an adoptee was to how she thinks about herself. She answered by talking about her involvement in ACA:

It feels like I'm not so alone, because at one of the latest Days of Actions [for the Adoptee Citizenship Act] one of the women was like, "I always felt like I was unique in this circumstance," and she never really knew how to feel. And listening to her talk, I was like this feels sort of similar because I've never really known how to feel about this. And I've always . . . Because of the way that my parents kind of holed us in this isolationist silo, feeling like . . . not really knowing how to accept the adoption and everything . . . Doing the advocacy for the Adoptee Citizenship Act, because knowing how some of the people that I've met, and have either done the Days of Action with or just have gotten to know online, I'm trying to learn their stories, doing presentations for other areas . . . Knowing that how some of them were abused mentally and emotionally, in similar ways that my little brother and I were, and probably thinking how close me and my little brother possibly were to maybe being in the same boat if my parents had realized that, "Oh hey, we could have actually had just one more thing to hold over their heads" [by not getting them naturalized][51] . . . Now I'm feeling like it's part of my duty to help these other adoptees that, through no fault of their own, don't have citizenship. So, that's one thing that I'm trying to do to actively accept [who I am as an adoptee].

Undocumented adoptees very publicly demonstrate the complexities of adoption, offering a more nuanced depiction of this form of family-making beyond feel-good stories of rescue. By bringing the failures of adoption to the forefront, adoptee citizenship advocacy provided an opportunity for adoptees to reconsider their position as transnational transracial adoptees beyond expectations of gratitude and framings of adoptees as exceptional immigrants. Where being an adoptee may have previously been synonymous with being happy or grateful, this category of vulnerable adoptees provided a new way for adoptees to think of themselves, resolving the uncertainty of how to feel about their adoption or about themselves as adoptees.

For adoptees like Alex, who often are unsure of where they fit in, understanding themselves as part of a coalition fighting for undocumented adoptees provided a sense of belonging that may have previously been missing. The identification with undocumented adoptees is similar to Mary's assertion at the beginning of the chapter that "This could be any of us." Through these declarations and testimony of undocumented adoptees, a shared sense of we-ness is forged among adoptees, regardless of their citizenship status. In drawing on ideas of a linked fate[52]—both a linked history that led to their adoption and a linked future, whereby adoptee deportations could happen to "any of us"—there is a shared responsibility. We see the alignment toward a collective identity happening in Alex. Through ACA advocacy, Alex came to understand and accept herself as an adoptee while connecting that personal identity to the broader adoptee community. This shared identity leads to a sense of "duty to help these other adoptees."

One reason identifying with and acting on behalf of undocumented adoptees is compelling even for adoptees who have legal protections or who had more positive upbringings is all the other ways that adoptees experienced limitations to their citizenship—refusals of belonging through invectives to "Go back to where you came from!" and invisibility within mainstream media and school curriculum. Adoptee deportations become a tangible representation of adoptees' countless revocations of their social and cultural citizenship throughout their lives. Participation in adoptee rights advocacy provides a space for adoptees to combat their own feelings of alienation, whether past or present. By creating a sense of community as they do so, adoptees are able to transform feelings of marginalization into empowerment.

Given the global network of Korean adoptee organizations,[53] information about Adam's case was frequently circulated. Roughly half of the adoptees I interviewed were involved in some type of advocacy around the ACA, including signing online petitions, contacting their elected officials through letter drives or phone calls, spreading awareness to non-adoptee friends and family, participating in Days of Action on Capitol Hill, or serving as spokespersons for the ACA at other events.

In addition to these activities, James (b. 1988), who was an active member in a local Korean adoptee group in the Mid-Atlantic, described his participation:

> So I do a lot of helping [my local Korean adoptee organization], in doing a letter drive to our Congress people, and getting the awareness out in the greater adoption community. And we also keep an open channel of community with AAAW, which is the Asian Adult Adoptees of Washington Organization, Seattle. I had actually visited Seattle this past weekend and I stayed with their president, so I asked, "What's the status of Adam," "How is he doing?" She actually visited him recently at the detention center and I told her we got a lot of stuff going on out here and we actually have a rally on the Hill coming up pretty soon, next week. Even though I'm not taking a lead on any of these projects, I am helping out where I can. And I really hope that we can get it resolved as soon as possible.

Given the pre-existing infrastructure of Korean adoptee organizations, they were able to quickly disseminate information and calls to action across groups. This became important as adoptee groups, like AAAW, which was geographically closest to Adam, or Adoption Links DC, which is based at the nation's capital, had insider information that could not be gleaned from mainstream news. Importantly, Korean adoptee organizations view their programming and outreach for all Korean adoptees regardless of their involvement in the Korean adoptee community. Even though Adam was not involved in the local Seattle Korean adoptee group, or any adoptee group, AAAW proactively reached out to him to assist in any way they could. Later when Adam was deported to

Korea, adoptee groups in Korea, such as Korean Adoption Services,[54] which provided pre- and post-adoption services, reached out to him to assist in his transition.

The expectations of kinship and care were also seen through adoptee conference programming. Annual adoptee conferences, such as the Korean American Adoptee Adoptive Family Network's annual conference and the International Korean Adoptee Association Network's annual Gatherings and its associated International Research Symposium on Korean Adoption Studies, included sessions on adoptees without citizenship. From 2016 until the present, each of these conferences included programming focusing on "Adopted, Without Citizenship,"[55] which featured transnational adoptees without citizenship as well as members of the Adoptee Rights Campaign; "Adoption, Immigration, and Citizenship,"[56] which was led by members of Adoptees for Justice; or other similar topics. Because conferences often capture newcomers to the adoptee community, through these sessions they were socialized into a collective identity—one that was intricately linked to their lived experiences and that required action. Newcomers regularly remark on how through their entrance to the community they find similar others, often for the first time. This may make getting behind a cause, like adoptee citizenship rights, particularly compelling.

Like Alex, Julia (b. 1987) viewed her advocacy as intricately linked to her identity as a Korean adoptee:

> I feel like when I talk to people about my experiences in a way I'm sort of advocating about adoption and trying to educate them as well as about the experience. Because some people want to say, "Oh, you're so lucky you were saved" and stuff. And that's one perspective but I also want to show them the other side of the coin that not everything is so black or white, even just the Adoptee Citizenship Act, and people not knowing that people had to make their kids citizens and they could be deported. I

think my role in letting people know that I'm adopted is also advocating about the adoptee experience, at least the Korean adoptee experience and educating people about it.

Because of international adoption's long history of being linked to ideas of benevolent rescue, it is hard for people to consider the negative ramifications of adoption. When adoption has been framed as rescue and adoptive parents as saviors, critiques of adoption or parenting practices challenge the beliefs undergirding these institutions, namely that US intervention and adoptive parents are the best choice for these children in need. Thus, acknowledging abuse, failed placements, or, in this case, undocumented adoptees, may seem like an indictment of the US. Among those whose American identity is central to how they think about themselves, such a critique can feel like a personal attack, leading to resistance to adoptee citizenship rights advocacy.

Furthermore, the idea of adoptees being saved by adoptive parents presents a stumbling block to understanding adoptees' citizenship challenges. Being saved requires a posture of gratitude. Although some adoptees may not have citizenship, the idea of rescue implies that even without citizenship, adoptees are in a better position than they would have been if they had not been adopted. For some, their rescue from foreign countries and welcome into American families were benevolent, selfless acts that required unyielding gratitude, leaving families and the US above critique.

Though early stages of ACA advocacy separated undocumented adoptees from immigration, the reality that undocumented adoptees were undocumented migrants could not be ignored. In the public imaginary, adoptees are children, not adults with their own families. Adoptee adults are not seen through the prism of adoption, Whiteness, and rescue; rather, Asian adoptee adults are assumed immigrants, foreigners who are unassimilable.

When I spoke with Kendra (b. 1984), she described how the harshening political landscape was changing how she thought about herself as an adoptee:

> It's more important now than I think before, especially I think in the political environment that we're currently going down. I think it gives me a different perspective on a lot of people's stories. I think it has made me more of a sympathetic and empathetic person when I can be in trying to . . . Advocating for people, the whole anti-immigrant fever that's going on in a lot of the political environments. It's advocating for those people who are trying to go through the system and have lost or can't. There's not this just easy process. It's not like you just go in and apply, and they stamp and whatever. I think using personal experience to help people have a different perspective on other people's lives and stories I think is really, really important and how I use being an adoptee.

Acknowledging adoptees as on the receiving end of broader anti-immigration attitudes, Kendra sees adoptees as being joined to other immigrant communities. Although she had not previously thought about ethnicity or race as primary components of her identity, the current political environment expanded her understanding of how she, as an immigrant herself, might be perceived. She began to connect her own immigrant background to the challenges facing undocumented migrants to advocate for more nuanced understandings of immigration.

Many adoptees cite the immediate changes in social context—from their predominantly White hometowns to more racially diverse college settings—that facilitate their exploration into their racial and ethnic identities.[57] As the political context changed—from more covert racism to overt policy changes targeted at various immigrant groups and increasing anti-immigrant attitudes—the adoptees I interviewed wrestled with their own identity as immigrants, many for the first time. Adoptees' exceptional belonging constructed them as separate from immigration histories and immigrant communities, yet collective racial reinscriptions via adoptee deportations and anti-immigration policies accentuated their position as immigrants. Adoptees previously experienced xenophobia through direct threats or more benign assumptions of foreignness, and adoptee deportations highlighted how their acceptance in the US could be formally revoked. This led many adoptees to consider their own citizenship status. Among those who were naturalized citizens, the increasing restrictions to immigrant groups and the immigration process itself made them question if their legal status could be nullified. The Trump administration's creation of a "denaturalization task force" in June of 2018 highlighted adoptees' citizenship precarity. While denaturalization does not guarantee deportation—rather, it reverts a naturalized citizen to a permanent lawful resident—the restrictive immigration policy, expansive deportable offenses, and overall anti-immigrant climate justifiably caused panic. Adam's case and the immigration policy reversals awakened some adoptees to a shared political consciousness as immigrants.

In repositioning themselves as immigrants, adoptees reclaim parts of their personal immigration history that special adoption legislation, adoption discourse, and their familial upbringing distanced them from. Even though, in an anti-immigrant political environment, undocumented immigrants are viewed unfavorably, ACA advocacy provided the adoptee immigrant identity with positive evaluations. Adoptees were able to see themselves as part of a collective. The collective identity forged through ACA advocacy also created emotional group norms of care that then facilitated advocacy. This advocacy was not limited to adoptee citizenship rights legislation.

Many adoptees involved in ACA advocacy, understanding the joint struggles across immigrant communities, wanted to build coalitions with other immigrants' rights groups. As ACA advocacy continued and threats to other immigration policies surfaced, such as those against the DREAM Act and Temporary Protected Status, adoptee rights organizations joined movements for immigration rights more broadly. In the midst of continued advocacy for adoptees, NAKASEC also began a 22-day, 24-hour vigil in front of the White House to draw attention to other immigrant rights. From August 15 to September 5, 2017, NAKASEC led "DREAM Action" or #DreamAction17 to protest the end of the Deferred Action for Childhood Arrivals (DACA) and the Temporary Protective Status (TPS) programs. DREAM Action drew together wide-ranging members of the immigrant community. Korean adoptees joined this around-the-clock action. In the current political climate, heightened immigration scrutiny and adoptees' precarious citizenship rights appear to have facilitated an awareness of a linked fate, whereby the conditions and outcomes for one are connected to the many, among and between immigrant groups.

* * *

Adoptee deportations are the legal outcome of questions adoptees experienced throughout their lives, such as "Where are you *really* from?" and "What about your *real* parents?" Where these questions highlighted assumptions that Korean adoptees could neither be from "here" nor belong here, adoptee deportations brought home their precarity. The racialized assumptions undergirding these refusals of belonging resurfaced within adoptee citizenship rights advocacy. This is apparent when considering the multiple racialized logics used in crafting a bill granting citizenship to undocumented adoptees. Prioritizing the family component rather than the immigration aspect was one element, which served to separate adoptees from politically charged discourse about immigration. Reminding legislators of adoptees' proximity to Whiteness was another, which emphasized beliefs equating Whiteness with citizenship. Referring to vulnerable adoptees as "adoptees without citizenship" rather than "undocumented adoptees" conjured imagery of Whiteness, family, and belonging rather than illegality or criminality.

How racialized logics mobilized various stakeholders to support adoptee citizenship rights advocacy—or not—demonstrates the material consequences of racialized emotions. For Whites and for adoptees reared into and identifying with Whiteness, there is an expectation for their outrage, fears, and desires to produce an anticipated outcome. When the ACA was paired with ideas of White family permanency, elected officials identified with the affected White parents and supported the ACA. When the ACA was joined to ideas of immigration, their identity as citizens, who are distinct from non-citizens, non-Whites, and foreigners, was activated and they opposed the ACA. For most adoptees who experienced racial reinscriptions reminding them of their place as Asians in a racialized social structure, the framing of adoptees as having a shared experience of exclusion mobilized their advocacy for the ACA and a sense of linked fate with other immigrant populations. Adoptee citizenship vulnerability illuminated the false promises of exceptional belonging, providing tangible confirmation of the multiple exclusions adoptees often felt throughout their lives. Through these exclusions, adoptees began creating a collective identity, reimagining their inclusion outside of the confines of their exceptional belonging.

4

Korean Plus Something Else

One of the first interviews I conducted was with Harry (b. 1986). We met for lunch at a local Korean restaurant, and as we were talking, he said something that, at the time, I didn't expect: "It wasn't only until probably the past two years where I really felt like I could identify as that [a Korean adoptee]." He clarified, "not in the sense that I didn't identify myself as that but in the sense that I never really thought of it as a category that people could fit into, if that makes sense. Growing up it's pretty easy to know that there's White people, there are Black people, there are Asians, there are Native Americans, the list goes on and on. Never had I really thought critically that there's a group of people out there called Korean adoptees, who sort of fit in the same cultural understanding of each other as White people, Black people, Native American." Harry grew up in a predominantly White town in the Midwest, and outside of his two adopted Korean siblings, he had virtually no engagement with other adoptees, Koreans, or Asian Americans throughout childhood. How, then, did Harry come to understand being a Korean adoptee as a social identity and not merely a fact of personal biography? What meaning did adoptees, like Harry, come to impart to "Korean adoptee"?

Part of my surprise at Harry's conceptualization of "Korean adoptee" as a shared identity was because, as another adoptee remarked to me, being adopted was not the "whole of [their] identity or even the most salient part." As a social psychological concept, the salience of an identity can be measured by how you would describe yourself to someone you'd just met.[1] In other words, how you'd answer the question, "Tell me about yourself." The initial responses of who you are and how you spend your time typically reflect your most salient identities. As Harry alludes to, there is a difference between identifying as a Korean adoptee to acknowledge how you came to be a part of your family and identifying as a Korean adoptee to denote shared cultural understanding, affective bonds, and ongoing relationships with similar others.

Although being transnationally and transracially adopted very much shaped adoptees' experiences, it did so in a way that stigmatized their belonging. Adoption rendered their family formation as less real than bionormative families, their Asian racial group membership as less authentic, and their national belonging as less legitimate.[2] The policy exceptions and cultural constructions that crafted adoptable orphans facilitated their stigmatization. Exceptional belonging marked adoptees as apart from some of the primary ways we identify who we are and our place in the world.

For most adoptees, even though others frequently drew attention to their adoptive status,[3] being an adoptee was not an identity that they felt connected to in any meaningful way. The social groups we are a part of contribute to how we see ourselves,[4] and for adoptees they perceived that others saw their group membership as conditional. Most adoptees understood their adoption as an individual experience, one prohibiting them from complete acceptance in various social groups, rather than an identity joining them to similar others. Yet as I would come to learn, for Korean adoptee identifiers, theirs was not a "forced connection over adoption history" as one of the adoptees I spoke with assumed. Adoptees weren't just making sense of adoption as an isolated act in their individual lives. They were finding shared meaning in their patterned experiences and using that foundation as a basis for creating a group identity.

These patterned experiences were like what previous research identified among adoptees from earlier adoption cohorts. Research conducted in the early aughts with adoptees born or adopted from the 1950s through the mid-1980s consistently found adoptees were overwhelmingly raised by White families in racial isolation and were not prepared to navigate racism.[5] Adoptees felt racially in between the White racial group membership they were raised in and the Asian racial group they were racialized into.[6] Eleana Kim's ethnography on the beginnings of the global Korean adoptee network identified adoptees' "self-consciousness about not fitting into dominant categories of race, family, and nation" as one contributing factor in making a Korean adoptee counter-public.[7] Similarly, in detailing how Korean adoptees have been rendered racially invisible, Kim Park Nelson's oral histories of Korean adoptees described the Korean adoptee identity as a response to "experiences of marginalization that were difficult to reconcile in White or nonadopted circles, or out of meeting other adoptees with whom they felt a meaningful connection."[8]

Even though adoption best practices have changed dramatically since the beginning of Korean adoption, from assimilation to cultural engagement, research finds that adoptive parents often overestimate the amount of cultural engagement they offer their children.[9] Moreover, although the US's prevailing racial ideology has shifted from assimilation to multiculturalism to colorblindness, Asian Americans' racial status as perpetual foreigners persists.[10] This contributes to why the adoptees I spoke with, who were born from the 1960s through the mid-1990s, with the majority in the 1980s and 1990s, reported similar experiences and feelings to adoptees in earlier research. The continuity across Korean adoptee experiences speaks to how the conditions and processes of their exceptional belonging have remained relatively unchanged.

I continue in the line of Korean adoptee identity research, giving particular attention to how adoptees transform their conflicting racialized emotions into the basis for a shared social identity with its own emotional group norms. In this chapter, I detail adoptees' refusals to conform to the normative rules of belonging. I find that adoptees communally rework exceptional belonging's inclusions and exclusions, ultimately creating a Korean adoptee social identity with its own emotional repertoire, culture, and group norms. Approaching the Korean adoptee group identity through this lens demonstrates how it is not a passive reaction to others' expectations for who they should be but an active rethinking of what it means to be Korean, American, and adopted. Of course, not all adoptees consider themselves members of a shared Korean adoptee group identity even as they experience refusals of belonging for their failure to adhere to the normative protocols for racial, familial, and/or national membership. Therefore, the chapter concludes with an examination of adoptees who reject the Korean adoptee identity and what their perception of it and themselves tell us about adoptee personhood and affective belonging.

"It's Just a Different Group"

Thomas (b. 1970), who had lived in Korea on two different occasions, made an important distinction characterizing the Korean adoptee identity: "Even as much as I want to be a part of that [Korea] again, you know, I could certainly live there, and I have lived there, but you know, *I'm Korean plus something else*" (emphasis added). Thomas *is* Korean, a declaration starkly contrasting how most adoptees felt at earlier ages. Because of their interrupted Korean socialization, disconnection from Korean communities, and upbringing as White family members, many adoptees in White families saw Whites as their reference group. Reference groups teach us norms, attitudes, and values and provide the standard to evaluate our personal characteristics and belonging.[11] Although adoptees were racialized as Korean (or, more generally, as Asian), the absence of co-ethnic relationships and ethnic exposure meant that their Korean identity did not have significant meaning.[12] Now, even though Thomas has the language skills and cultural knowledge to navigate Korean society, internally he feels distinct. Being Korean does not completely capture who he is.

To identify as a Korean adoptee is not the same as identifying singularly as Korean, as Thomas's qualifier of "plus something else" indicates. It is also not the same as the bicultural identification Korean American. Korean adoptee is not dual Korean and American cultural fluency—though Korean adoptee identifiers certainly do engage in Korean cultural exploration—instead the "plus something else" becomes a defining element of the Korean adoptee identity.

"Something else" includes adoptees' experiences of exceptional belonging by way of their adoption, which shaped adoptees' inclusion and exclusion within and across racial, ethnic, and immigrant groups. "Something else" includes how adoptees felt the conflicting racialized emotions produced by their transracial adoption. And, for those who had traveled to Korea or lived there for an extended time, "something else" captured their distinction from Koreans, who had grown up in Korea. Notably, the acknowledgment of being "Korean plus something else" reframes adoptee identity from one defined by the *absence of* to one that is created by the *presence of*. Rather than accept external messaging for who they should be, where they belonged, and how they should feel, many of the adoptees I interviewed were active in recreating what being "Korean plus something else" meant.

Hannah (b. 1986) described the reframing of her adoptee identity:

> I am not Korean and I'm not American but it's like this category that I share more attributes with Korean adoptees than I would with Koreans or would with Americans. Maybe it's the adopted part but the Korean adoptee community in terms of the individuals that I've met that share that identity, I feel like I have more things in common with them in terms of trying to figure out my own identity or questions that I have . . . I feel like it's almost like that place in between or maybe it's not even a continuum, maybe it's just a different group. It's something that I've just more recently thought about. I felt like it was either Asian or American or Asian American, there wasn't anything else.

Prior to participating in a month-long homeland tour with other Korean adoptees, Hannah felt constrained by the identification options of Korean or American. On homeland tours, adoptees participate in cultural education, language classes, tourist activities, and birth search. Tours range from a week to a month long and are often financed by the Korean government and organized through adoption agencies. Because of the highly coordinated nature of these programs attempting to reintegrate adoptees into Korean society and a Korean subjectivity, homeland tours have been likened to "rites of passage."[13] However, rather than revive adoptees' inherent Koreanness, the tours often bring awareness to adoptees' lack of cultural belonging, spurring adoptees' "'disidentification' with hegemonic versions of being 'Korean.'"[14]

For Hannah, the homeland tour sparked her understanding of being Korean with a difference. As she explained, her adoptedness modifies her sense of Koreanness and Americanness. She no longer viewed her identity through the mutually exclusive options of Korean or American. These constrained identity options reflect a traditional view of acculturation, with one's heritage culture on one end (Korean) and complete assimilation into the receiving dominant culture on the other (American). This view of acculturation assumed that two cultures could not be maintained. Instead, to be high on the heritage culture meant being low on the new mainstream culture and vice versa. Accordingly, acculturation was thought of as a linear process and used synonymously with assimilation.[15] Newer models of acculturation, however, identify various outcomes, including biculturalism, demonstrating that acculturation is not simply about assimilation but rather can have various outcomes depending on one's desire and ability to maintain one's heritage culture and have contact with members of the mainstream culture. Social contexts, including national (e.g., immigration policies, national approaches to multiculturalism), regional (e.g., ethnic enclaves), and interpersonal (e.g., parental socialization), are identified as key components of this process.[16]

Transnational transracial adoptees complicate traditional assimilation theories. For example, adoptees benefited from unique immigration policy that sets them apart from other immigrants.[17] Adoptees typically immigrate alone and do not grow up in immigrant communities. Furthermore, most transnational transracial adoptees are adopted at such a young age that they have no conscious recollection of their heritage culture. Rather than assimilate into mainstream American culture according to the trajectories that immigrant incorporation theories outline, adoptees are raised within the majority culture as if it were their birth culture, unlike other first-generation immigrants.

Because of the way they immigrate to the US, the possibility for adoptees to attain a bicultural identity is also not as straightforward as immigrant incorporation theories assume. As Hannah reflects, the bicultural designation of Asian American does not accurately capture her and similar others' identity as Korean adoptees. "Biculturalism" refers to a cultural dualism whereby individuals understand and express cultural norms, beliefs, and/or languages of the two cultures and/or identify with both cultures (e.g., I am Korean American).[18] Although "bicultural individuals are in the unique position of potentially holding two such cultural social identities and navigating two potentially different cultural frameworks,"[19] this may lead to difficulties in identity development or negative behavioral and psychological outcomes when the two cultural identities are valued differently in a given context or when the individual holds simultaneous membership in two different in-groups.[20]

Thirty-seven percent of my online survey respondents stated that they sometimes identify as White and sometimes as Korean, depending on the context. This may hint at bicultural alternation, whereby they can identify and respond to the cultural cues in both White and Korean social settings with the appropriate cultural capital. However, the racial and cultural code-switching that adoptees engage in is not always reflective of the cultural alternation identified in biculturalism literature. Patrick (b. 1986) described his engagement with White and Korean

American peers: "Growing up in a White community in high school and social groups, there is no doubt that I feel part of these groups. There is this one percent of me that feels different . . . I never felt 100 percent comfortable in my skin or with the people who were my friends and family. I mean, 99 percent. I felt 100 percent loved and loved everyone. But, there is that 1 percent where it's like I'm just a little bit different." He went on to describe that same feeling regarding Korean Americans, providing examples of his lack of cultural knowledge that made him feel that difference. It wasn't only that Patrick perceived that he was seen as not fully a part of the group by others. He also experienced it. He disclosed, "In the same way I'd be teased with White kids, I would get teased by Koreans and they'd say, 'Well, Patrick is White.'"

Adoptees reared in White culture understand White cultural nuances, given that they were privy to the private sphere of Whiteness in ways that other non-Whites typically are not. As many of the adoptees I interviewed reported, they are comfortable and feel accepted in White spaces. However, most adoptees do not possess the Korean language fluency or understanding of Korean cultural nuances to alternate in the ways outlined in biculturalism theories. Adoptees may feel Korean based on the racial and ethnic composition of the specific social context. In certain instances, adoptees may identify as Korean when among Korean peers or in other instances when among White peers, when their racial difference is accentuated. As Patrick's quote highlights, because of how he was perceived by Whites and Korean Americans he had lower regard for himself as a member of either group.

To identify as a Korean adoptee, then, is not simply to have bicultural competency in White culture and Korean culture but to have merged those two cultures—or more specifically elements of the heritage culture based on adoptees' cultural exploration—and their racialized emotions as experienced through the adoptive status into a third, distinct culture. The Korean social identity is not a form of biculturalism, which centers identification through dominant ideologies of assimilation. Instead, the

Korean adoptee identity and its emotional group norms transform the stigma created through exceptional belonging. Instead of feeling different, ashamed, or not confident in themselves because of how others perceived them, the Korean adoptee group becomes a reference group with positive regard. Patrick described the effects of the Korean adoptee community: "I don't have to fake it to make it. I just fit in, so that's always a good feeling . . . it gives me confidence . . . I feel 100 percent confident in myself, whereas I used to not." Through sustained relationships with similar others who identify with and create meaning into the Korean adoptee identity, adoptees gain a new conceptualization of their own belonging, one that defies traditional assumptions for immigrant incorporation and the White racial frame of their upbringing.

"Everyone Can Relate"

Although he was initially hesitant to meet with other adoptees in person, Harry shared what happened the first time he attended an adoptee get-together: "But, you know, I went, introduced myself, and there were like a good four or five people who were extremely welcoming, and just open to hearing my story, where I was from, where I grew up. They shared stuff about themselves too, which was like, 'I can relate to that. I can relate to that.'" Storytelling is a key component of identity formation.[21] Through storytelling we integrate our experiences into a cohesive story of who we are and how we fit into our social world. Importantly, how those stories are received by our audience can confirm or challenge our understanding of ourselves. Although the stories we tell about ourselves are central components to identity formation for everyone, storytelling takes on heightened importance in Korean adoptee community building.[22]

In Korean adoptee circles, whether online groups or in-person meet-ups, the process of sharing and listening to each other's story is paramount. These are not just individual stories that bolster personal

identity. This type of storytelling takes on the characteristics of testimony and witnessing, whereby the act of giving testimony—a subjective
account of an event—to an audience who can bear witness and identify
with it creates a community.[23] Harry's reflection on the mutual storytelling that happened at his first in-person adoptee meet-up illustrates
the role of the telling and hearing of one another's stories in positioning
Korean adoptees as a reference group whose evaluations matter.

I asked Harry what some of the relatable experiences in the other
adoptees' stories were. He shared:

> How growing up whenever you were introduced to people, always being
> asked like "Are you gonna find your birth parents?" That's definitely a
> big one. You know, simple jokes honestly, like, "Oh, you're good at math"
> or whatever. I'm sure you can understand. Being on the other side of
> that and how that makes you feel, everyone can relate. It's different when
> someone who isn't Asian makes that joke versus someone who is. It's, in
> its nature, the exact same joke but the meaning is inherently different,
> and it's really hard to explain to someone who isn't the subject of that
> joke. So, yeah, to me those are the things that sort of created a feeling of
> connection.

Whereas several of the adoptees I spoke with remarked how validating
it was to learn that other adoptees grew up in racial isolation, too, what
stood out most to Harry was the shared experience of microaggressions.
Harry's example of a common adoption microaggression—here asking
about birth parent search—hinges on beliefs of adoptive parent inade-
quacy and the permanency of blood ties.[24] Through a range of adoption
microaggressions, adoptees feel the stigma of adoption, reminding them
that they are outside of the normative protocols for family belonging.[25]
The recurrence of intrusive questions throughout adoptees' lives imparts
that adoptees' stories are not theirs to tell but rather required disclosures
for anyone who asks. Adoptee storytelling in community with similar

others who can affectively relate allows adoptees to share as much or as little detail as they desire. These stories do not differentiate them from the group. Instead, the act of sharing one's adoption story becomes a cultural norm defining group membership, and the content of the stories point to a shared cultural experience within the Korean adoptee social group.

Harry also offers racial microaggressions as a relatable experience that surfaced through adoptee storytelling. It was not only the experience of being subject to racial jokes, stereotypes, or slurs that was shared. It was also that when they were growing up adoptees did not have anyone who could validate those experiences as racist or who could prepare them for racism they would face. Most adoptees who were adopted into White families were raised as if they were White themselves, which meant no acknowledgment of anti-Asian racism. Racism was not a part of the shared family experience. Adoptees learned that they could not admit these experiences to their parents.[26] Due to the differences in their racial positions in society, adoptive parents could not affectively relate, and most adoptive parents dismissed interpersonal racism. In the community of other adoptees, however, Harry found similar others who could affectively relate to both experiencing racism and having to navigate those experiences with little family guidance.

As Harry relays the stereotype of Asians being good at math that "everyone can relate" to, Korean adoptees become the "everyone" who matters, even me. Harry draws me into the cultural understanding among Korean adoptees, intimating, "I'm sure you can understand." Previously, adoptees oriented toward their White family members or White peers as the reference group whose opinions, values, and behavior shaped their own understanding of themselves. After participating in the Korean adoptee community, adoptees saw Korean adoptees as a potential reference group whose evaluations mattered. Whereas adoptees identified with and were included within Whiteness and Asianness to varying degrees, the Korean adoptee reference group provided a sense of belonging in ways that other groups could not. The shared experiences as Korean transracial adoptees, including intrusive questions and racialized teasing, coupled with the genuine desire to hear one another's story facilitate what Harry described as "that instant identification and comfort level with someone who understands you without really knowing you."

Christine (b. 1978) reflected on a shared emotional repertoire among adoptees:

> There's the [local Korean adoptee] meetings where we're all adoptees. What I like about being there is there's an unspoken, we all have a similar story so no one needs to break it down or explain. You can be like, "So, did you find your parents yet?" It's all just very cut and dry. Instead of, my other friends get very emotionally invested in everything that I have to say. "Oh my gosh, I'm so sad for you." I'm like, "No, it's not sad. It just is." Sure, I'm sad. Sure, I cried when I found out the truth about things, but it comes with a gravitas when I'm talking with, especially, my White friends. It's harder on them than it is on me. I'm like, "You okay? Do you need a tissue?" I'm fine.

Sharing testimony assumes an audience that can affectively relate, and when relaying one's adoption story to non-adoptees there is a limit to their understanding, given their own family formation. This example of birth search and the way it affectively resonates among adoptees contrasts with Harry's example. Here Christine relays the same question inquiring about searching for birth parents, but when asked among fellow adoptees it is not an invalidation of adoptees' family experience. Among adoptees, there is a collective affective response that is activated through sharing various "cut and dry" aspects of their birth search and relinquishment. What creates community among adoptees, however, leads to distance among non-adoptee friends. Christine's attempt to connect with her non-adoptee friends by disclosing important details of her life resulted in her taking on emotional labor to respond to their feelings.

The act of witnessing facilitates communal mourning of the different losses associated with transnational transracial adoption. Grieving birth country, culture, and family is paramount for adoptees, as these separations have traditionally been discounted as losses at all. Sara Ahmed argues, "One has to recognize oneself as having something before one can recognize oneself as losing something. . . . Loss implies the acknowledgement of the desirability of what was once had."[27] Adoption discourse erased adoptees' pre-adoption histories to produce their subjectivity as American citizens and (White) American family members. These erasures were not meant to be grievable losses. In acknowledging their pre-adoption histories as valuable and desirable, adoptees act outside of the expectations of adoptee personhood. The grief felt from these losses is not solved or eliminated; rather, the Korean adoptee identity provides a space for that grief to be held and transformed from private feelings to group emotions. Importantly, this is not an expression of loss as a form of dissent or rebelling against adoption discourse that demands an adoptee affect of gratitude.[28]

Illustrating this, Stacey (b. 1978) reflected: "I can think about these things and figure out how I really feel about it aside from what I've been taught and aside from having to worry about people's feelings." Similar to how Christine noted that non-adoptees' emotional response to her adoption story moved the focus from her experiences, interpretations, and needs, Stacey acknowledges how her regard for other people's feelings left her without the space to have her own emotional response. Adoptees often cite consideration of their parents' feelings as reasons why they have not explored their heritage culture, traveled back to Korea, or undertaken a birth search.[29] More broadly, adoptees have been expected to perform gratitude for their adoption.[30] With Korean adoptees as a reference group instead of non-adoptees, adoptees receive validation for their desire to interpret their experiences separate from others' perspectives. This reorientation also expands the possibilities for how adoptees can feel beyond binary constructions of adoptees as happy/angry and of adoption as good/bad. The Korean adoptee affective community provides a new lens to evaluate the role of adoption in their lives, one that acknowledges the complexity of the adoptee experience.

Julia (b. 1987) described the adoptee community as a space where you are "able to say things to people with them being able to understand, that you can't say to maybe even your regular family or your friends because they have no idea how to comprehend or relate." She shared a recent example:

> Last Saturday I had like a mini breakdown, and I was feeling all these like intangible hard-to-describe things related to adoption and I want to talk to my husband about it. I couldn't really verbalize it. And then I got on Facebook messenger and KaKao talk and talked to some of my adoptee friends and was able to work it out and get it out of my system. But, it was something to my husband I had no idea how to verbalize it, and he is so supportive. He's gone to KAAN [referring here to the annual Korean American Adoptee Adoptive Family Network conference] with me, and he goes to the [monthly Korean adoptee] events and he's very interested. But it was still something. And he's read blogs about dating adoptees and stuff like that. He's invested, but it was still something I just couldn't communicate to him.

Julia locates the disconnect between herself and her husband in an inability to communicate exactly what she was feeling in a way that he could understand the affective significance of the event. However, the "intangible hard-to-describe things related to adoption" would be unrelatable to non-adoptees, whose racial and familial positions created a different disposition than that shared among adoptees. Julia's adoptee friends had a shared emotional repertoire allowing them to be affected in a way that aligned with her experience of the event in question. Their shared disposition acted as a shortcut in understanding, whereas despite her best attempts and her husband's commitment to understanding the adoptee experience, Julia could not convey what she was feeling in a way that her husband could respond to supportively.

As adoptees created relationships with one another through Korean adoptee online groups and in-person meet-ups, they came to identify Korean adoptee as a reference group, whose appraisals mattered. Through shared storytelling, adoptees normalized their experiences of exclusion from the other reference groups that had previously been a primary way they thought about themselves. Rather than continue to understand these exclusions as individual experiences, through shared witnessing, private feelings were given shared substance. It is the shared substance that gives meaning to being around other adoptees. Private failings to adhere to normative protocols for race and family were revealed as natural outcomes of adoptees' circumstances of exceptional belonging. Instead of internalizing these private failings as personal shortcomings, adoptees reconstructed the exclusions they experienced because of their exceptional belonging as a mundane part of their belonging as Korean adoptees. Similar to the racialized emotions adoptees learned as White family members and Asian Americans, adoptee emotional group norms foster shared feelings among one another and a disposition to past, present, and future events.

"A New Way of Thinking"

Natasha (b. 1975) described surprise at how her participation in Korean adoptee groups was causing her to reappraise some of her previous viewpoints: "I literally am not sure how I should feel because this is such a new way of thinking for me. Like I know the things, the triggers that I have, you know, and like certain racial topics can really get me going, but the adoptee community is *very* sensitive. And so, I'm like, 'Wow. I didn't know I should be upset about that.' But now, I find myself getting upset like, 'What the hell. Don't say that shit. That's rude.' You know, whereas normally I'da just laughed about it. You know. Now, I'm just like wow" (emphasis in original).

I asked her if there was anything specific that came to mind. She shared: "Like when we were growing up, right, we used to always make jokes like I'm speaking Korean [makes "Asian" language sounds]. You know whatever, like making the angry sounds and stuff. And now I know that that's like totally offensive and it's rude. But like I would totally do that [laughs] with my brothers. And my parents would be like, 'What the hell are you guys doing?' [laughs] I'd be like, 'I'm speaking Korean to my brothers.' So now I just know that that's like wrong." Although Natasha describes the adoptee community as "*very* sensitive," it is more accurately a *different* sensitivity to behaviors, experiences, and events. Whereas adoptees' other social groups evaluate actions like mocking Asian language and intonations as harmless, the Korean adoptee community Natasha is a part of views it as racially insensitive. This particular example is reminiscent of one of the ways Korean adoptees—and other Asian Americans—were taunted as they were growing up.[31] Some adoptees were able to stand up to interpersonal racism, while others may have internalized it, particularly when their friends or family were the perpetrators. Now in the company of others who have experienced similar forms of racism, adoptees could name it as offensive.

She continued, "But you know like, somebody from the outside looking in would hear him say that to me, and he'd be like, 'That asshole. I can't believe he . . .' but that's like totally something *we* used to do with each other. So, and just, now I'm like, 'Yeah, no. We can't do that.' Even my husband . . . now I'm like, 'Well, you can't do that anymore because that's offensive to me.' And he's like, 'What?!' thirteen, fourteen years of marriage we've been doing this and now it's a problem" (emphasis in original).

Natasha's reflection speaks to the process of emotional change precipitated by identification with the adoptee reference group. Her appraisal of her communication with her brothers and husband was seen no longer as innocent joking but as racially insensitive. These changes in appraisals, even for events that an individual proactively and frequently participated in throughout their life, are not unusual.[32] Respondents shared reappraisals of current events, social issues, and adoption-specific phenomena. Respondents also reevaluated their own adoption histories, situating them within the context of adoption from Korea and international adoption, more broadly.

Harry shared how he started to rethink his own perception of adoption: "I started to learn more about the other side, like why Korean families or mothers gave up their children for adoption, which I really hadn't thought about before. It was always about me, and why was I given up for adoption, and how did that make me feel, and how did I adapt, and blah blah blah." Most adoptees had very little background information in their adoption files. Adoptees were left to make sense of their relinquishment through orphan narratives and stereotypes of birth mothers as promiscuous and irresponsible. Many adoptees felt like they had simply been "thrown away" and had negative perceptions of their birth mothers. These stories not only shaped their sense of self but also discouraged them from conducting birth family searches.

Some adoptees learned more about the sociopolitical context in Korea through their own research, and others learned more about Korea and the international adoption industry through their connection with other adoptees. Learning contextual information that was largely absent from how adoption was discussed as they were growing up helped adoptees to reframe their perspective toward Korea from feelings of shame, anger, and judgment to empathy. Whereas previously Harry had only considered how adoption made him feel and the utility of a birth search for satisfying his personal curiosity, this reappraisal of Korean adoption spurred him to reconsider. With his birth mother's potential feelings and desires now a consideration, Harry decided to start a birth search.

By seeing Korean adoptees as a community that they could belong to—rather than a descriptive for their entry into their adoptive families—Korean adoptees became a reference group that shaped their interpretation of events, actions, and their own adoption history. Adoptees were able to express beliefs that ran counter to those of their other reference groups—instances of racial teasing that their adoptive family or non-adoptee peer group dismissed were reinterpreted as offensive; perspectives of adoption that erased birth families or maligned them were replaced with consideration for birth family's desire. Rather than take on the stigma associated with adoption, adoptees gained a new perspective from which to think about their communal experiences.

It's Okay to Embrace My Korean Background

Patrick described another way that the Korean adoptee community changed his perspective: "Back when I was in [home state], I didn't feel like it was okay to embrace my Korean background, nor did I have a network that can help me understand it. So, I got the validation that hey, these are people that are really obsessed with Korea, understanding Korean culture, too. It's okay to be that way and to learn more." Although adoptees like Patrick were curious about their Korean ethnicity, their unique immigration pathway separated them from their ethnic community. For adoptees raised in White families, there was limited, if any, interaction with other Asian Americans or Korean Americans. Instead, adoptees were raised as if they were White, including being socialized into the White racial frame that negatively constructs non-White culture.[33] Whereas Patrick could have explored his Korean heritage by himself, it is not only cultural knowledge that Patrick was looking for. It was also relationships with similar others. In fact, is the extensiveness and intensity of relationships in everyday life that bolster commitment to an identity. Once he moved to a larger, more racially and ethnically diverse city, Patrick connected with a network of people with similar interests, validating his desire to learn more about Korea and bringing him into a shared Korean adoptee identity.

Patricia (b. 1962) also identified how being in community with other Korean adoptees reframed adoption microaggressions challenging the authenticity of her ethnic group membership. She reflected:

> I just remember the first real experience I had [with other Korean adoptees] was going to a Korean restaurant with 20 adult adoptees. I think this was maybe 2009. We went to a Korean restaurant together; we all met up there. We had this backroom to ourselves, and all sitting there chatting. Then the Korean waitress comes to order our food, and we're all speaking English. She starts off in Korean, because all she saw was a room full of Koreans. We're all looking at each other like, "What did she just say?"
>
> That was the first time I felt like, "I belong here. I feel like I'm part of this group. I'm in the same place as they are." Whereas before I was like, "Uh, I don't know what to order. I don't know what to say. I feel like I have to explain, but I don't want to." Anyway, when the waitress came and she started babbling off in Korean, we all looked at each other like, "What is she saying?" Then, we looked at the waitress and the blank look on her face and we all started cracking up. It was so funny. That was like another, "Ah-ha!" moment. That was a pretty neat experience. That's when I knew I wanted to be around adult adoptees more often.

Adoptees frequently reported judgment from other Asians and Korean Americans about their limited Asian ethnic cultural knowledge. This came in the form of accusations of being "basically White" or "not really Asian."[34] Adoptees mentioned being referred to as "Twinkies" or "bananas."[35] "Twinkie" and "banana" are to adoptees' racial group membership as "real" parents is to their family belonging. Both delegitimize their inclusion while essentializing race and culture. Through the pejoratives "Twinkie" and "banana," adoptees are simultaneously racialized and invalidated as Asian. Both terms convey that there is an expectation of what it means to be Asian, with Asian transracial adoptees falling outside of what is deemed authentic.

However, in the communal space of fellow adoptees, instead of shame for not already knowing what to say or feeling pressured to explain why she did not know how to respond, Patricia's limited cultural knowledge because of her adoption fostered a sense of belonging among other Korean adoptees. The adoptee space allowed adoptees to be Korean as they had always been, even if their cultural experience differed from other Koreans. As another adoptee I spoke with asserted, "I see myself as Asian and Korean. I don't see myself as White or part-White or anything like that. I get that culturally I grew up with White parents." The idea that adoptees are White or inauthentic Asians ignored that while they may have been raised culturally by White parents, they still experienced the world as Asians.

During adoptee-initiated heritage culture exploration, adoptees seek out *Korean* culture, including learning Korean history, contemporary Korean culture (e.g., music, television, movies, fashion), Korean language, and Korean food.[36] Amanda Baden and colleagues define this process of "reclaiming one's birth culture" as reculturation.[37] There are several possible reculturative activities that transnational transracial adoptees engage in to regain cultural knowledge and skills, become comfortable in their racial and/or ethnic identities, and/or identify with their adoptee community. These range from the aforementioned activities to building relationships with same-race and/or same-ethnicity peers to actively seeking out more racially and ethnically diverse social contexts, exploring the Korean American community, traveling to one's birth country, and connecting with other adoptees. All the adoptees I spoke with had engaged in reculturative activities to various degrees. The Korean adoptee identifiers I spoke with actively participated in multiple reculturative activities and had sustained relationships with other adoptees in the Korean adoptee community. The extensiveness and importance of adoptee relationships fostered a sense of belonging as Korean adoptees in contrast to how they may have simply used "Korean" or "adoptee" as a descriptive.

It is important to note that for the most part adoptees I spoke with did not seek out *Korean American* culture or *Korean American* communities. Rather, they sought out *Korean* culture and *Korean* connections. Respondents regularly shared that they traveled to Korea as part of their heritage culture exploration, in contrast to traveling to cities in the US with large Korean American communities. Even for adoptees with Korean American communities nearby, the focus was on learning about Korean history, culture, and customs (even though adoptees also attended Korean American festivals or other cultural events hosted by Korean American organizations). This is important because adoptees are not necessarily seeking out connections or shared experiences with other Korean Americans, at least not initially.[38] It is not Korean American culture that is integrated into the Korean adoptee identity. Rather, the adoptees that I spoke with conceptualized the Korean part of their Korean adoptee identity as a signifier of their roots in their ancestral homeland.

This exploration is partly a response to expectations for their Asian ethnic enculturation. Identity is not only about personal meaning or self-identification but related to a larger system of social interaction, one with expectations for interpersonal behavior and relationships. Similar to other Asian Americans, who report assumptions of ethnic "authenticity," adoptees, too, reported demands from others that they have fluency in their heritage culture.[39] Although adoptees may self-identify and experience being racialized as Asian, they also contend with accusations of being "not really" Asian because of their White cultural upbringing.[40] Moreover, they themselves may feel unable to be "completely Korean" because they do not meet the expectations of group membership. Koreans are expected to be knowledgeable about and participate in a rich

Korean ethnic culture, have a dense network of Korean co-ethnics, and have Korean pride.[41] Throughout their lives, adoptees had to contend with these expectations and their own internal understandings of themselves racially and ethnically. Some interviewees remarked that adoptees could never be fully Korean, internalizing the belief that there is a specific way to be Korean, which was inaccessible to them because of adoption. Through their reculturative activities, adoptees reclaim their heritage culture and, in the process, redefine how they think about themselves outside of the racial and ethnic socialization of their upbringing.

The Korean adoptee community offered support for reculturation that some adoptees were already undertaking, and for others, the reculturative activities were a distinct departure from their existing cultural template. Christine reflected on her participation in a local Korean adoptee group: "there are moments when I'm like, 'Oh god, is this the world?' We went to dinner [to a Korean restaurant] and then went over and did karaoke. Which it's like, 'Huh. Okay. Is this what I should be enjoying?' I don't know." Christine's excerpt highlights some of the activities Korean adoptee groups prioritize for their in-person meet-ups. She identifies the explicit incorporation of Korean food, Korean culture, and participation in common Korean activities, in this case noraebang.[42] Her reflection of "Is this what I should be enjoying? I don't know" is a direct response to the socialization process within adoptee groups. Through their participation in Korean adoptee networks, both in-person and virtual, adoptees are socialized into the expectations that they should be interested in Korean culture and the cultural elements they should enjoy. Through the purposeful selection of activities, including topics of conversation, choice of restaurants, or participating in leisure activities, members create and transmit shared norms, tastes, and feelings of belonging.

The desire for rootedness in their birth country could be read as a symbolic connection like that of later generation White ethnics.[43] However, when examined through the lens of stigma management, adoptees' ethnic reclamation recovers the imagined and real losses of Korean culture and biological connections created through their immigration histories and transnational adoption. Although adoptees' origin stories often communicated that adoptees were unwanted by their birth countries or portrayed their heritage culture as undesirable, adoptees' reculturation defies expectations that adoptees would assimilate into American culture. Importantly, reculturation centers adoptee desire. Rather than adoptive parent–mediated heritage culture exposure, reculturation is an outcome of adoptees' own curiosity and initiative. Adoptees integrate their Koreanness into how they think about themselves in a way whereby they evaluate their Korean group membership with positive regard. This agency over cultural decision-making is something that they previously had little control over.

"The Only Thing They Have in Common"

On an episode of The Janchi Show, KJ Roelke, one of the three co-hosts of the podcast about the Korean adoptee experience, reflected on how he thought about himself: "I am adoptee. That's never going to change. So, it makes sense for me to call myself an adoptee. Right. That's not like a singular, I'm, I wasn't adopted and that's it. That's all that I had to do with being adopted. But *I am* an adoptee. That is a reality and identity that I will have to continue to live in and reckon with in the same way that I *am* Korean and that is a thing that I'll have to reckon with" (emphasis in original).[44] There is the "singular" fact of being adopted as an act that happened in the past and is complete. Then, there is the continual "reckon[ing] with" that KJ refers to as integral to what it means to *be* an adoptee. The inhabiting of adoptee as an ongoing, shared social identity and taking account of its everyday meaning is a reworking of how adoptees were supposed to identify as family members, immigrants, and adoptees. Exceptional belonging may have created a class of adoptable orphans, but having a shared group identity as adoptees was not supposed to happen.

While many adoptees feel some level of not fully inhabiting the normative categories of belonging, not all identify as a Korean adoptee. Brian (b. 1978) thought of the Korean adoptee identity as nothing more than "being from Korea and being adopted." As he considered it, "As far as identity, I feel like it's almost an overrated issue." Even among adoptees who had participated in the adoptee community, there was no guarantee of identification with Korean adoptees as a reference group.

Like most adoptees, David (b. 1987) had salient childhood memories of adoption microaggressions. He remembered how he internalized adoption stigma as a young child to the point where he was afraid that his adoptive parents might send him back. He also experienced racial microaggressions, and as with most adoptees, his parents did not proactively discuss anti-Asian racism. However, they were proactive about Korean cultural engagement. He attended Korean culture camp and Korean language classes throughout childhood, and as a result felt that he was able to "internalize and be a hybrid between both American and Korean culture, without feeling ostracized by either side."

When it came to how he thought about the Korean adoptee identity, he had this to say: "When people identify as Korean adoptees, I feel it has a negative connotation to it . . . there have been a lot [of] sort of negative opinions about us as a sub-group, as like, socially awkward and weird and not really being able to fit in. That's where my ability to socially chameleon into situations has allowed me to be like 'Oh okay, like normal dude, pretty cool.'" David distinguishes between himself as a "normal dude," who is "pretty cool," and those who identify as Korean adoptees, who are seen as "socially awkward and weird, and not really being able to fit in." In offering up stigmatizing beliefs about adoptees, he engages in othering to minimize his own categorization as an adoptee. His use of distancing as a strategy to maintain his own positive self-evaluation is common among members of stigmatized groups.[45]

It may be surprising, then, to know that David was active in his local Korean adoptee group. He described his involvement saying, "I feel like I dealt with my adoptee issues, like identifying who I am, like what I'm about, and just like finding myself, and that sense early on, where a lot of other adoptees have not. That causes them to have a lot of friction in life, and a lot of issues, and so by going to these events, I'm able to demonstrate to them like 'Hey, I dealt with it, here's how I got around it, feel free to use me as a contact or touch point if like anything comes up.'" Understanding of interpersonal discrimination and connection with others who share the same stigma can lead to a shared social identity. David, however, does not share an identification as a Korean adoptee despite his sustained social interactions. Involvement in the Korean adoptee group is voluntary, so it may seem peculiar that David would continue to participate in a group that has "negative connotations to it." However, David's view of his role in the group illustrates why he remains engaged. By being a resource as someone who has "got around" his adoptee issues, he can maintain distance between himself and other adoptees who he views as less adjusted.

Sasha (b. 1978) reflected on her interactions with adoptees. Although she did not have any exposure to Korean adoptee groups or activities growing up, as an adult Sasha had been involved in Korean adoptee groups in the various places she'd lived. She divulged, "When I meet another Korean adoptee honestly, I try really early to figure out like where are you on the bitterness scale? Can I say that? When I meet an adoptee, I'm always trying to figure out where they lie on the bitterness scale. And it is such a relief to me when I meet someone that is adopted, and I like them for other reasons." Sasha distances herself from other adoptees, even as she voluntarily participates in Korean adoptee get-togethers. She offered up adoptee bitterness as a defining adoptee emotion—one that she assessed negatively and that she herself did not hold. By making bitterness the commonality she saw among those in the Korean adoptee community, she others adoptees who have made—in her eyes, at least—their adoption central to who they are. Sasha went on to describe naming "Korean adoptee" as a primary identifier as a phase in younger people's lives, implying that to continue to identify as a Korean adoptee signaled that adoptees were stuck in a juvenile developmental phase. Like David, Sasha distinguishes herself from other adoptees, who cannot integrate their adoption history in what she deems a healthy way, and as a result are socially awkward, are bitter, or have issues.

Sasha continued her contemplation on Korean adoptee group members:

> The reason I brought up that group [of adoptees] is because you could not put, like the six women that tend to be the core of it, you could not put six more different people in a room. The only thing they have in common literally is that they are all Korean adoptees. I think it's 20-year age span, maybe more. Gay, straight, poor, rich, married, single . . . But, they do, they spend almost all of their time together, like their free social time together, which is fascinating . . . I find that most of the groups have been like that though. It's like the only thing they have in common.

As Sasha described the group of adoptees, she expressed incredulity at their commitment to one another based on this one aspect of their lives. For Sasha, adoption was a fact of biographical history but not relevant to who she was or how she saw herself, instead finding other components of her identity more salient, such as hobbies, career, or personality traits. Even though one of her best friends "happens to be adopted Korean as well," they met through their careers, later finding out they were both adoptees. While Sasha assessed adoption as being "literally" the only thing the members of the Korean adoptee group she mentioned shared, that was not how Korean adoptee identifiers viewed adoption or their connections to one another. Adoption was not simply a part of their family formation, and adoptee was not only a personal identity. Instead, the process of transnational transracial adoption via exceptional belonging created a distinct set of experiences and racialized emotions, enabling the basis for a Korean adoptee community. By giving testimony, bearing witness, and reworking the meanings of their other social group identities, the Korean adoptee identity took precedence over group memberships that are often dividing lines—"gay, straight, poor, rich, married, single."

* * *

Diane (b. 1965) reflected on the importance of identifying as a Korean adoptee: "It's more honest about who I am than anything else." She contrasted her current pride in being a Korean adoptee to how she felt growing up and throughout her early adulthood. She continued:

> My young adult life and my young adolescent life, wanting to be White, wanting to be just like, to look like my family, and now I do regret getting the eyelid surgery and the nose thing but it's, now it's, because I accept who I really am more and I am proud of it and it's just, part of, it's just more me. I'll never be Caucasian. I'll never be a lot of things that I tried so hard to be in my life. It's more part of me and I'm very proud of it. There are so many of us . . . [for] so long I think I was ashamed of it but now I am very proud to be Korean adoptee.

Through identifying with other adoptees and understanding their individual lived experiences as part of a patterned response to the structural conditions facilitating their transnational transracial adoption, adoptees transformed how they thought about themselves as adoptees. Adoptees' lived experiences were previously interpreted through conflicting racialized emotions. Adoptees raised in White families tried enacting Whiteness while simultaneously being excluded from it because of how Asianness is negatively constructed in the White racial frame. Adoptees were racialized as Asian but also seen as inauthentic because of their upbringing by non-Asian families. Through a range of refusals of belonging, adoptees were acutely aware of the many ways they did not adhere to the normative protocols for familial, racial, and national membership.

The Korean adoptee identity transforms experiences of exclusion into inclusion, and it is these experiences that comprise the shared substance among adoptees. The Korean adoptee identity is a refusal of adhering to the expectations of adoptee personhood. It challenges adoptees' upbringing that excluded Korean heritage culture, cultural constructions of Asians as honorary Whites, and beliefs that Asian adoptees are raceless. It also defies assimilation assumptions that immigrants want to and will assimilate and instead draws attention to how this group of immigrants affectively experience their racialized positions. Through the Korean adoptee identity new emotional group norms are created alongside a new space for belonging outside of the boundaries of existing categorizations. People need a place in social space, and the Korean adoptee identity is that placeholder, even if not all adoptees see themselves as a part of it.

5

Our Lives, Our Stories

"Have you seen *Twinsters*?" one of my mentors stopped me in the sociology department's hallway to ask. At the time, Netflix had recently released the documentary about the unbelievable reunification of twin Korean adoptees separated at birth and raised in different countries. Given the film's topic and my research interests, my mentor was right in her expectation that I had seen it. But, even a few years later, new acquaintances often referred to the film upon learning my personal background, reflecting not only Netflix's ubiquity but also the way viewers relied on this representation to connect with adopted people in their lives.

Twinsters takes a lighthearted, playful approach presenting Samantha Futerman and Anaïs Bordier's personal history of separation, deceptive adoption paperwork, and adoption as an incredible adventure. The twins' whirlwind reunion whisks them around the globe to Anaïs's home in France, to Sam's home in the US, and finally to their birth country, where they participate in the International Korean Adoptee Association (IKAA) Network's Gathering, an international meeting of hundreds of Korean adoptees from the US, Europe, and Australia. Toward the end of the film, Anaïs tearfully reflects on the impact of returning to Korea:

> Before I used to say that I wasn't born on the 19th of November. I was born on the 5th of March when I arrived in France. For me there was no life before, to me, because I was nothing without my parents. [cries] Yeah. Yeah. Yeah, now I see, I see that I existed before as well . . . and I just realized here coming to Korea, I realized that people loved me like the whole time before.

Anaïs's erasure of the first four months of her life reflects adoption discourse that produces adoptee personhood by expunging their personal history prior to adoption and making Korea into an unknowable place. The severance from their first families was necessary to make Korean children into adoptable orphans but it communicated that adoptees were unwanted. The assumption of being unloved prior to adoption made Anaïs fail to exist. Love as conveyed through adoption then became the mechanism that brought Anaïs into legibility. However, despite origin stories meant to craft a linear narrative of becoming, Anaïs's personal becoming happens through the realization "that people loved me like the whole time before."

What does it mean for Anaïs that she was someone before adoption? How does that change what she knows—and by extension what we, as an audience, know—to be true about adoptee personhood and belonging? Much of how adoptees have been understood is through cultural representations, immigration policy, adoption agency messaging, and adoptive parent perspectives portraying adoptees as children in need, who come into being through adoption by couples in the West.[1] Anaïs's reflection echoes these beliefs, locating her becoming once she arrives in France. Through this depiction, adoptive parents and receiving nations are positioned as benevolent rescuers, without which adoptees are nobody or at least no one desirable. This unequal relationship requires adoptees to discard their past in favor of being grateful for the better future adoption provided. Anaïs's revelation that she was loved and the resultant integration of her pre-adoption history disrupts the adoptee origin story with its expectations of a clean break and along with it the expectations of who Anaïs could be and how she should feel.

This chapter analyzes *Twinsters* (2015, Netflix) and *aka SEOUL* (2016, NBC Asian America),[2] two contemporary mainstream adoptee cultural productions created by adoptees, as sites of disidentification, where adoptees rework the normative meanings of adoptee, adoption, family, race, and citizenship. Whereas the previous chapter demonstrated how adoptees imbue meaning in the Korean adoptee identity among one another, this chapter shows how adoptee-centered media make this reworking visible to broader audiences, including adoptees, especially those who are not aware of the global adoptee community.

The chapter concludes with an examination of *Blue Bayou* (2021, Focus Features/Universal Pictures), another mainstream adoptee representation, though one created by a non-adopted Korean American.[3] Although *Blue Bayou* is a fictionalized account of an undocumented US Korean adoptee as he learns of his impending deportation, I argue this theatrical release contributes to adoptee subjectivity in similar ways as *Twinsters* and *aka SEOUL*. It, too, challenges traditional adoption discourse, namely expectations of adoptee gratitude, while simultaneously confronting the "model minority" framing of Asian Americans. In so doing, *Blue Bayou* forces viewers to confront their racialized assumptions about Asian American belonging. However, unlike *Twinsters* and *aka SEOUL*, which publicize adoptee stories on their own terms, because *Blue Bayou* is not adoptee-created media, it cannot operate as adoptee disidentificatory practice. Yet, in Korean adoptees' coordinated response to the appropriation of an adoptee story, adoptees reassert control over the narrative. Taken together, these media make the ways Korean adoptees transgress and travel between normative categories of identity visible for broader audiences, while transforming meanings for adoptees' own empowerment.

Korean Adoptee Auto-Ethnography

Twinsters and *aka SEOUL* join a long history of what Eleana Kim termed "Korean adoptee auto-ethnography."[4] These media emerged in the mid-1990s as the earliest cohorts of Korean adoptees entered adulthood. In these video memoirs, Korean adoptees take control over their adoption stories, reflecting on their experience as transnational transracial adoptees, questioning what their lives may have been like without adoption, and reflecting on the effects of being racially hyper-visible in their predominantly White families and communities. Instead of simply integrating into their new families and new nations by abandoning their connections to their lives prior to adoption as adoption discourse suggested, Korean adoptee auto-ethnography showed adoptees' search for identity through birth family and birth nation exploration.[5] Across the documentaries, one common theme is adoptees' feelings of not belonging in the US or Korea. Where early media depictions created by adoption stakeholders, such as government, mainstream media, and adoption agencies, sought to demonstrate adoptees' potential for being remade into American citizens,[6] adoptee-created media showed the limitations inherent in those assumptions.

Through the mid-1990s to the early 2000s, Asian American film festivals screened more than half a dozen Korean adoptee films.[7] In 2000, PBS aired Deann Borshay Liem's *First Person Plural* as part of their Point of View documentary series. Borshay Liem's film brought national attention to the complexity of transnational transracial adoption outside of feel-good success stories. Her documentary publicized the darker side of adoption—fraudulent paperwork, Korea's lack of social welfare services, and adoption as an industry. This brought a new perspective to the cultural narrative of Korean transnational adoption. Rather than the utility of adoption for adoption stakeholders, *First Person Plural* inserted an adoptee voice, one that was out of line with expectations for adoptees' quiet assimilation. Kim Park Nelson argues that adoptee memoirs function as dissent against the expectations for adoptee gratitude.[8] Within these memoirs, adoptees rail against the promise of a "better life" by showing the emotional, social, and mental vulnerability that resulted from denying their pre-adoption personhood.

Importantly, *First Person Plural* also presented a counter-story of adoption as loss—losses of birth country, birth culture, birth family, and personal history, among numerous other losses that adoption discourse erases and assimilation expectations devalue. By acknowledging these as losses, Korean adoptee auto-ethnographies contributed to a process of recognition. Adoptee personhood is relocated from originating at the point of adoption and re-placed within their nation and family of origin. Not only do these portrayals help adoptees grieve loss, they also unsettle beliefs about adoptees as blank slates that exist as objects of desire upon which adoptive parents can project their hopes and dreams. Kimberly McKee argues "adoptees *kill* joy when they fail to adhere to the adoption fantasy" (emphasis in original).[9] In challenging the adoptive parent savior narratives and the framing of adoption as humanitarianism, adoptee killjoys, like those presented within the counter-stories of Korean adoptee auto-ethnography, disrupt expectations of adoptee gratitude and intrude upon the happiness of those who are invested in transnational transracial adoption.

As some of the earliest and most widely circulated adoptee counter-stories, these films challenged traditional adoption discourse. Early Korean adoptee auto-ethnographies were groundbreaking in broadcasting an adoptee "journey of the self" with pointed critiques about adoption. *Twinsters* and *aka SEOUL* take a slightly different approach by situating the adoptee journey within general themes of self-actualization. The question of nature versus nurture is an organizing theme in *Twinsters* as Sam and Anaïs's similarities and differences are the focus of many of the documentary's scenes, notably traveling to the Twin Studies Center at California State University, where they take part in a series of mental, physical, and personality assessments. In *aka SEOUL*, five Korean adoptees—four from the US and one from Sweden—return to Korea for the 2016 IKAA Gathering. Through the vignettes of the featured adoptees, audiences are offered a glimpse into how adoptees navigate adoptee-specific issues within the context of universal experiences of personal discovery. *aka SEOUL* is the follow-up to *aka Dan*, which followed US Korean adoptee Dan Matthews as he learns he has a twin brother (not adopted) and travels to Korea to meet his biological family for the first time as an adult. In *aka SEOUL*, Dan's White adoptive mother travels to Korea with him, and the primary focus of his vignette is navigating family relationships post-reunion.

In *Twinsters* and *aka SEOUL*, the featured adoptees' process of searching—whether for biological connections through birth family search, details about their personal history in adoption file reviews, cultural heritage by returning to Korea, or a sense of belonging in one's homeland or among other adoptees—are represented as part of a natural process of self-discovery. Although the featured adoptees' journeys are largely presented as individual undertakings (except for Samantha and Anaïs in *Twinsters*), they also happen parallel to one another. Showing the similarities in their journeys conveys that the adoptee experience is, in fact, a shared experience, particularly as their individual self-discovery converges within the context of an organized Korean transnational adoptee community. The journey of the self portrayed in the documentaries, then, presents adoptee personhood as a self-determined collective subjectivity unconstrained by normative identity categories of race, family, and nation.

Although adoption is a necessary precondition for the journeys in *Twinsters* and *aka SEOUL*, adoption itself is not the explicit focus of the documentaries. Without the direct critiques of adoption as a practice or industry, the documentaries run the risk of being characterized as apolitical. However, I argue that the documentaries' critique happens outside of predictable routes. While McKee conducts a reading against the grain to explore how the silences, or absences, within *Twinsters* act as resistance,[10] I find that what is present offers a compelling criticism when examined through the lens of disidentificatory practice. In focusing on adoptee self-discovery, the documentaries disidentify with adoptee personhood that is predicated on discarding their birth country, culture, and family as well as the binary of the happy/angry adoptee. José Esteban Muñoz conceptualizes disidentification as "a remaking and rewriting of a dominant script."[11] Rather than an identification that is counter to the norm and thus beholden to it, disidentification exposes identity categories' dominant meanings and then reworks them in a way that empowers the minoritized subject. The process of exceptional belonging positions adoptees inside and outside multiple identity categories. Instead of showing adoptees as they attempt to adhere to the normative protocols of race, family, or national citizenship and how they should feel as adopted persons, *Twinsters* and *aka SEOUL* are representations of adoptee disidentification that rework the meaning of adoptee personhood.

"You're a Part of Something"

In *Twinsters* and *aka SEOUL*, the IKAA triennial Korean Gathering serves as a key setting for the featured adoptees' stories. This context itself works as a site of disidentification in showing the relevancy of a collective adoptee experience for adoptees rather than adoptees as special interest stories for general audiences. The return featured in the documentaries is not only to return to the adoptees' country of origin but also to return to other adoptees. The process of adoption removed Koreans from the collective with the expectation that they would remain separate from their homeland, biological family, and co-ethnics. Yet here we see adoptees returning en masse to their birth countries for an *adoptee* gathering. Although "adoptee" as a social identity was not a consideration previously, throughout the film viewers are privy to the shared identity and emotional repertoire borne out of transnational transracial adoptees' unique social position. Overall, the adoptee *group* experience showcased in the films transforms the meaning of adoption from a discrete past action that happened *to* adoptees to an ongoing process of becoming that happens in community with other adoptees.

Founded in 2004 in Europe and the US, IKAA serves as a centralized hub for the Korean adoptee community. Beginning in 2004, every three years IKAA hosts a multi-day international gathering of Korean adoptees in Seoul, South Korea.[12] In the years in between the Korea Gatherings, "mini-gatherings" are alternately held in Europe and the US. The Korea Gatherings typically attract a larger attendance, as they provide first-time attendees and first-time travelers to Korea a more structured way to visit their homeland. The Gatherings include a flexible schedule, so participants can attend as many of the pre-planned activities, or not, as they wish. Most of the activities are more social in nature, such as scavenger hunts, tourist attractions, sporting events, happy hours, karaoke, and family-oriented activities. There is one day of panel sessions, which include topics such as identity and race, LGBTQ experiences, birth family search, and, at the 2016 Gathering, adoptees and citizenship. One of the key sessions is the breakout sessions by age cohort, where same-age adoptees discuss issues relevant to their life stage. Importantly, in 2007, IKAA hosted the inaugural international symposium on Korean adoption studies. Here the world's foremost Korean adoption scholars present their research about Korean adoptees and Korean adoption. The day-long symposium continues to be held every three years at the Seoul Gatherings.

Attending an event created by and for a group you're a member of might seem unremarkable; however, adoptees typically did not feel as though "adoptee" was a shared group identity. It is not uncommon for adoptees' first encounter with another adoptee to be in adulthood;[13] for some it's in their early 20s, for others in their 40s or later. Because of the ways their birth country had been construed in their origin stories, many adoptees felt no emotional connection to Korea as a homeland, and some felt an active aversion. As a result, the decision to attend an adoptee event, especially one in Korea, is remarkable.

As Siri Szemenkar, a 21-year-old Korean Swedish adoptee, describes in her vignette in *aka SEOUL*, even though her parents traveled to Korea to pick her up with the express purpose of experiencing Korea so they could tell her about her birth country, their stories were all negative. According to her parents, Korea was "a weird culture, where nothing was 'right.'" While it is unlikely that her parents meant to convey that there was something wrong with her, their stories stopped Siri from wanting to connect with her birth culture and hindered the development of her Asian identity. To be "right," Siri describes a childhood of assimilating into Swedish culture and counter-identifying with Asianness by actively avoiding anything that might emphasize her Asian heritage or connection to other Asian people.[14] Her participation in IKAA in Korea, then, is out of alignment with who she is supposed to be and how she is expected to feel. We do not know what spurs her reconsideration of Korea, but through her vignette we see positive affect toward her birth country.

Among the adoptees I spoke with, a negative predisposition toward Korea often surfaced. Patricia (b. 1962) described it directly: "I never thought I would ever go back to Korea. I didn't think I would ever want to go to Korea. I viewed going to Korea would be like, 'Oh, they don't want me. They got rid of me, so why would I want to go back there?' That was my mentality all these years, but through volunteering [with a Korean culture camp], and then the Korean people who volunteered who were not adoptees, I realized, 'Oh, they do care about us adoptees from Korea.'" Part of the script defining adoptees was that they were discarded by their birth country and birth families. Without Patricia's proactive decision to volunteer at culture camp, which resulted from her initiative to seek out other adoptees, her previous disdain for Korea and Korean people would have remained unchallenged.

Patricia would eventually return to Korea on a homeland tour with other adoptees, and, like some of the featured adoptees in *Twinsters* and *aka SEOUL*, described the experience as life changing.[15] The return to Korea is transformational but not because it resolves the past. I find the transformation is not solely located in the physical return to Korea; rather, it begins with the change in perspective toward Korea precipitating adoptees' return. In considering the possibility of journeying to their birth country, adoptees adopted into White families break away from normative protocols for identifying as a family member predicated on difference from non-Whiteness and adherence to the nuclear family model. Thinking of oneself in such a way, whereby who you are and your sense of belonging expand beyond the confines of what you've been told it means to be adopted, Korean, and American, is transformative.

In *Twinsters*, it is Sam who suggests that she and Anaïs attend the upcoming IKAA Gathering. She sees it as a once-in-a-lifetime opportunity for them to go to Korea together and be with the "more than 600" Korean adoptees from around the world who will attend. For Sam, who primarily views adoption as a positive in her life, IKAA is one more fun adventure to enjoy with her newfound sister. For Anaïs, who mainly views adoption as something she had no choice in, IKAA and Korea are an unnecessary risk to the happiness she has experienced so far with her and Sam's relationship. Underlying her tentativeness is fear about the potential trauma of traveling to Korea and being rejected again. Eventually, she decides to attend, though we are not privy to why she changes her mind.

In one of the first scenes at the IKAA Gathering, Sam and Anaïs are seated in a large hotel ballroom with hundreds of Korean adoptees. At the front of the room are government officials and other VIPs. Korean President Park Geun-Hye appears on video screens throughout the ballroom, where she welcomes the adoptees back to "your mother country." Her address continues, "I humbly ask you to take pride in your mother country and love it as well, I also hope with all my heart that you achieve your dreams." The acceptance into their mother country from a mother figure visibly moves Anaïs and Sam.

Including the welcome back to their mother country in the documentary does significant disidentificatory work, as adoption origin stories often impressed upon adoptees that Korea did not accept them. Thus, adoptee becoming was predicated on Western intervention. Within Anaïs's storyline, this scene bridges her erasure of the first few months of her life in Korea to her reworking of what it means to be an adopted Korean person. She was not meant to have positive feelings toward Korea beyond what was acceptable to or filtered through the West's act of adoption. Yet this scene shows Anaïs's previous contempt for Korea turning into positive feelings of belonging through the president's warm welcome.

In highlighting adoptees' participation in a transnational adoptee event in their birth country, *Twinsters* and *aka SEOUL* demonstrate that adoptee personhood is not contingent upon separation from race, culture, nation, and community. Adoption discourse emphasizes this separation to create a linear narrative of becoming that moves adoptees from "there" (Korea) to "here" (Western nation). Being "here" requires adherence to a model of one nation, one family, one race. Instead, the featured adoptees are American *and* Korean, French *and* Korean, Swedish *and* Korean. As they move from "here" back "there," the early ruptures from family, nation, and race are acknowledged and then transformed through participation in IKAA. Anaïs describes attending IKAA stating, "You feel like you're a part of something." Sam reflects, "It's so cool to be part of something bigger than just us." Adoption shifts from individual personal history to a collective experience. The declaration of being part of something through adoption contrasts with how many adoptees felt like they were the "only one."

Anaïs continued, "You know you're going to have a lot of fun for a whole week with people that understand you completely. And you know that you're in Korea and that your birth country cares about you as well. It's really moving." Through this adoptee-mediated experience of Korea, Anaïs reframes her conception of Korea, from neglect to care, and of herself, from an individual, who was adopted, to a member of an adoptee community. Siri characterizes the IKAA Gathering similarly, describing the opportunity it provided to "connect with people on a different level." She goes on to explain that this did not mean explicitly talking about adoption, but rather the comfort of interacting with others who are assumed to have an unspoken shared familiarity. This "different level" of connection and the characterization of being "completely" understood is the sense of an alignment of affect, something that had previously been unavailable to adoptees because they did not meet the normativizing protocols of their other social groups (e.g., White family member, Asian peer, Korean co-ethnic).

Anaïs and Siri interpret the adoptee community through contingent essentialism, whereby being adopted provides an inherent shared way of relating to one another.[16] Beyond essentializing adoptee identity, I read disidentification in Anaïs's and Siri's reflections. Anaïs's initial wariness to attend the IKAA Gathering is retroactively replaced with the confidence that "You *know* you're going to have a lot of fun for a whole week with people that *understand you completely*" (emphasis added). This retrospective of "knowing" implies that shared adoptee understanding "always already" existed. It just had to be accessed. Being part of a community where one is "understood completely" is not restricted to those who embody normative identifications. The characterization of "adoptee" as having a shared emotional repertoire, understanding, and identity is a disidentification with "adoptee" as inherently deficient, unable to be whole, or a mimicry of legitimate forms of personhood.

As Anaïs continued to reflect on IKAA, she speculated, "Everyone who's here is happy, I think." This description is an affective disidentification with the "happy adoptee." "Happy adoptees" are those who adhere to dominant adoption discourse, assimilating into the normative nuclear family, White racial frame, and nation without critique. That is not the happiness Anaïs refers to, nor is it the affective disposition of gratitude required from being "saved" through adoption. Anaïs's assessment is not meant to convey that only "happy" adoptees attend IKAA. Rather, by being in Korea with other adoptees, adoptees are affected in a similar way. Just as Korea was made into an "unhappy place" because it was constructed as the site of rejection, it is remade into a "happy place" through connecting with other adoptees at IKAA. Finding happiness in Korea and among adoptees is in contradistinction to the White racial frame of many adoptees' upbringing that devalued non-Whiteness and of adoption discourse that expunged birth ties. Being moved by Korea as a "happy place," then, offers a new way of feeling. IKAA becomes an affective site whereby adoptees can make and be made by the adoptee social.

The portrayal of the gathering as a "happy place" resonated with Korean adoptee viewers. Although it is unclear the exact number of attendees who learned of the Gathering through *Twinsters*, in informal conversations with IKAA 2016 attendees, about half of the first-time attendees I spoke with mentioned *Twinsters* as the impetus for their attendance. *Twinsters* was a powerful activating event for adoptees, especially considering the mere nine-month timeline between *Twinsters'* Netflix release in November 2015 and the IKAA Gathering in August 2016.[17] Approximately 500 adult Korean adoptees plus their spouses and children traveled to Seoul for the 2016 Gathering. More than half of the sojourners were from the US, and for many, this was their first trip back to their ancestral homeland. The appeal of IKAA is a disidentificatory allure. Through their participation in IKAA, adoptees were represented in a self-affirming manner, not as objects but subjects, and as full of agency, not infantilized. Furthermore, *Twinsters* showed that adoptees with different dispositions toward their adoption, like Sam and Anaïs, could still experience being "part of something." Importantly, the "something" did not require adoptees to discard parts of who they are. Whereas adoption was predicated upon severance from birth family, culture, and nation in order to integrate adoptees into their new families, culture, and nation, IKAA allowed space for the coexistence of adoptees' lives pre- and post-adoption.

Similar to the 2013 IKAA opening ceremonies featured in *Twinsters*, at the 2016 opening ceremonies President Park Geun-Hye again welcomed attendees in a pre-recorded video message.[18] In her message, she referred to Korean adoptees as "overseas Koreans," a perspective popularized by the Korean government to tap into the Korean diaspora's resources for Korean economics, government, and business.[19] President Park promised that the Korean government would support adoptees in visiting Korea and learning Korean language and culture. She went on to remind the audience that Korea was once a poor country but is now advanced due to the hard work of Korean people.

The "Miracle on the Han," referring to South Korea's rapid economic advancement after the Korean War, is a point of pride among Koreans.[20] Former Korean President Park Chung-Hee, who was President from 1963 to 1979 and who was the father of President Park Geun-Hye, is most credited with Korea's economic recovery.[21] The "miracle" was due, in part, to exporting social welfare via international adoption of Korean children.[22] The irony of President Park's message is that Korean adoptees were part of the economic industry that transformed this once poor country into the developed country we see today, an economic "miracle" organized by her father. Yet, within her message, and the broader messaging of overseas Koreans, Korean adoptees are welcomed back as global Koreans who will serve as ambassadors to the world.[23] Earlier in the evening Mr. Roberto Powers, US Consul General in Korea, referred to adoptees as a "human bridge between our countries." In this way, Korean adoptees are deployed for their geopolitical labor at birth and now when they return.

While the Korean and US governments attempt to bring adoptees' return in line with their own political agendas, the featured adoptees' sojourn is not part of an intentional political movement. Nonetheless, their decision to return to Korea in the company of adoptees from across the West makes a statement. Adoption was centered around multi-layered separation and adoption stakeholders' desires. In the documentaries' portrayals, adoptees reconnect with their birth origins—nation, culture, and family—and with one another for themselves, not for anyone else's benefit.

The decision to return to Korea in the company of adoptees had a profound effect on the adoptee sojourners. *aka SEOUL* closes with each of the featured adoptees reflecting on the role this trip to Korea is playing in their individual journeys. The adoptees share that through the trip they learned "there's a space where I fit" (Min) and that they've found "more acceptance about myself. Something I didn't even know I was looking for when I came" (Siri). In both documentaries, it is the IKAA Gathering that allows their birth country to fulfill its role as a mythological homeland of acceptance. Even though family, nation, and the act of adoption have traditionally been positioned as the origins of adoptee personhood,[24] the documentaries make clear that it is the experience of being together with other adoptees that brings them into an adoptee subjectivity that defies the expectations of their exceptional belonging.

Of course, the promise of a community that understands one another "completely" is not always fulfilled. Being "part of something" is only available to adoptees who have the financial means and flexibility to access it. Even among those who can travel internationally for several days, not all adoptees experience the IKAA Gathering as a communal welcoming space. There are cleavages by class, sexuality, political leaning, and perspective on adoption. The return to Korea is itself not always experienced as a homecoming. For example, one of the adoptees I spoke to who had traveled to Korea confessed in a whispered tone, "I didn't love it." Likewise, Monica (b. 1973) described her two-week stay saying, "It was strange because I kept thinking like I should feel a sense of homecoming. I should feel a sense of community and I'm home but I don't feel home. I still am a stranger in a strange land. It was very clear to everybody that I didn't fit in . . . Again, it was that sense of like, 'Wait, I belong here. Wait, no. I don't belong here. I'm still not one with you.'" Adoptees who return to Korea in hopes of finding a sense of home, do not always find what they are looking for.

By focusing on the IKAA Gathering as a transformative, overwhelmingly positive event that brings together adoptees from around the world, *Twinsters* and *aka SEOUL* offer a snapshot into adoptees' lives within their current realities as adults. These are not the counter-stories of early Korean adoptee auto-ethnography with their explicit critiques of adoption. Instead, these are representations of adoptees as agentic adults navigating their belonging. In representing themselves in this way, the documentaries reject the limiting portrayals of adoptees that infantilize them as eternally dependent upon adoptive parents and leave their personhood confined within the act of adoption.

"Your Life, Your Story"

In rewriting the script of adoptee personhood, both *Twinsters* and *aka SEOUL* confront adoption stories that erased or minimized adoptees' birth origins. In traditional origin stories, adoptees are abandoned by their birth families because of their inability to care for them and their desire for a "better life" for their children in the West. The adoptees then emerge in their new country within their new families. It is at this point that adoptees' lives begin. However, these stories exclude one common detail in adoptees' life histories: their care by foster mothers.

In *Twinsters*, Sam connects with Kim Shin-Ja, her foster mother, for the second time post-adoption, and Anaïs meets her foster mother, Moon Eui-Soo, for the first time. The connection between the foster mothers and the adoptees they cared for is palpable. Shin-Ja expresses motherly affection throughout their time together, even feeding Sam and Anaïs when they go to lunch. Although Eui-Soo cared for Anaïs for only a few months many years ago, after their initial meeting Sam marvels, "she remembers you, like everything, she remembers."

While foster care is often stigmatized or seen as less important in comparison to the "forever family" that adoption is purported to bring, in the context of Korean adoptees' adoption stories, reinserting foster care serves as a correction to adoption stories of abandonment and neglect. Being cared for in Korea by Korean people contrasts traditional adoption discourse of birth country rejection and challenges the nuclear family as the only site of care. Most of my online survey respondents noted being in foster care and interviewees reported foster care on their demographic questionnaire, yet foster care was rarely included in their adoption stories. For Anaïs, meeting her foster mother completely alters how she thought of her own personal history. Rather than coming into existence through her adoptive parents' love, she now understands herself as being loved prior to adoption and therefore having existed before her immigration to France. Seeing the twins' reunion with their foster mothers provides adoptee viewers with a reframing of their own origin stories, challenging beliefs of adoptees as unwanted and unloved.

The reevaluation of adoption stories continues in the featured adoptees' birth family searches. As the featured adoptees reflect on their adoption files, it becomes clear how central, yet tenuous, adoption histories as conveyed through legal documentation are to adoptees' sense of self. In *aka SEOUL*, Min details the many ways that his Korean and US files were contradictory. In *Twinsters*, Anaïs reflects, "I knew that I didn't have a twin because it was written all over my papers that I was an only child." After Siri meets with her case worker at the Social Welfare Society office in Seoul, she reflects in frustration that there were "not much answers" and how it's "hard to get actual information." Although this is "your life, your story," Siri's meeting portrays the adoption agency as withholding personal information that adoptees have the right to know. During adoption file review meetings, adoptees can look through their Korean files, but they do not receive a copy. Because most adoptees cannot read Korean language, unless they bring their own Korean translator, they must rely upon what the case workers relay.

Muñoz argues, "Autoethnography is not interested in searching for some lost and essential experience, because it understands the relationship that subjects have with their own pasts as complicated yet necessary fictions."[25] Information about moments from the past—circumstances of relinquishment, for example—and even present details about birth family do not resolve adoptees' breach of normative categories of belonging, relocating them definitively within an identity of family or nation; rather, they further contribute to their in-between status. Even if adoptees learn more information about the circumstances of their relinquishment through adoption file reviews or being reunited with bio-logical family, there is no way of knowing if those new details are true. Moreover, even if they are accurate, it cannot change adoptees' previous experiences of their subjectivity as rendered through exceptional belonging. Adoptees inhabit yet traverse categories of citizenship, family, and race originating with legal documentation establishing their orphan status to produce their adoptability into Western nations.[26] Adoptees' reworking of identity at the inclusion of new information demonstrates the ongoing nature of identity formation and how identity categories are more porous than dominant depictions convey.

In these accounts, Korean adoptee personhood, though intimately entwined with their adoption history, is not solely beholden to the meanings created by the varied adoption stakeholders. The inclusion of reviews of adoption files moves adoptee becoming from originating at Western couples' desire or adoptees' entry into Western nations. Furthermore, adoptees' choice to undertake file reviews centers adoptee decision-making. This contrasts with traditional renderings of Korean adoptees as legible only through their service to the desires of others.

Centering adoptee desire, particularly a return to their birth country and searching for birth family, disrupts adoption discourse that privileges the sharp separation between pre- and post-adoption in creating adoptee personhood. In this way, the featured adoptees could be read as adoptee killjoys ruining adoptive parents' happiness; however, adoptees' choices to explore or reclaim birth culture and birth family are not acts of rebellion against adoption norms. They are decisions untethered to adoptive parents and the broader adoption industry, particularly in how they are presented in these documentaries.

I was chatting with Christine (b. 1978) when she shared her adoption story: "From the time that I could understand that I was adopted, they [her parents] were like, 'You're adopted,' and I'm like, 'Okay, I think I know what that is.' . . . They always told me that I was a police station child. That I was found in a basket at a police station. An abandoned child in the cold. 'Look, you were rescued,' blah blah blah." The "blah blah blah" as she relayed her adoption story signaled that she had come to question the standard adoption story she was told as a child. Abandoned at a police station, abandoned at a market, and born to an unwed mother were common relinquishment stories that adoptees heard growing up. Many never learn whether these stories are true or not, yet they often become central to how adoptees think about themselves and their place in the world.

In Christine's case, however, after traveling back to Korea and seeing her adoption agency file, she learned more. She shared, "I actually came to find out this past summer that that was not actually the case at all. I was actually born in a hospital. My mother had been in an unwed mothers' home. That was my origin story. It's actually been a complete flip-flop from being abandoned to actually there was foresight in terms of the story . . . Obviously that's what they were told by Holts [adoption agency]." It is not uncommon for adoption agencies to provide little information, misinformation, or selective backstories to make children more adoptable and desirable.[27] Rather than being abandoned at a police station, Christine was born in an unwed mothers' home[28] and "there was foresight in terms of the story." The newly discovered information surrounding her birth and relinquishment might seem minute, yet it made a big difference in how Christine thought about herself. While many question the veracity of the information in adoption files, Christine interpreted this information as certain details about her past. She then incorporated it into her retelling of her story, not as an essentialized history but as another piece of her identity narrative.[29] Adoptees' stories are continuously being reinterpreted as they gather more information from various versions of their adoption files, from other adoptee perspectives, and from learning the broader sociohistoric context of Korean adoption.

By including birth searches as key parts of both documentaries, the belief in biological family and ancestry as answers to an essentialized personal identity runs the risk of being affirmed.[30] In context of the documentaries as a whole, however, although birth search is a central component of the films, it is not the sole method of adoptee journey of the self. Instead, *aka SEOUL* revolves around the featured adoptees' "un-forgettable summer in Seoul" in the company of other adoptees, many of whom are experiencing Korea and Korean culture for the first time. Similarly, *Twinsters*'s focus is on adoptee reunion with one another moreso than with birth parents or extended biological family (though we can wonder how the framing of the twins' story would have changed had their birth mother been amenable to meeting). As a result, biological connections are not presented as the primary source of their personhood, even among the featured adoptees who had a successful birth family reunion.

By centering adoptees' experiences, both documentaries tell a story primarily about adoptees rather than adoptive parents, adoptive families, or adoption writ large. Moreover, *Twinsters* and *aka SEOUL* present these journeys of the self through the lens of universal desire for self-discovery similar to general ancestral exploration through DNA testing or curiosity about ancestral history popularized through shows like PBS's *Finding Your Roots*, which follows celebrities' searches.[31] In describing *aka SEOUL* in an NBC News interview, Dan shared, "That's the one thing I've discovered is that although this might be adoptee-oriented content, the themes of family, searching, and self discovery are universal."[32] By focusing on universal themes, transnational transracial adoption is less a unique form of family-making with distinct histories separating it from traditional ideas of family. As Dan described, adoptees navigating birth family and adoptive family as part of the search for self becomes relatable to "a lot of people" because they too "have a weird family situation."

Although the documentaries explore the featured adoptees' familial histories, they present their birth searches separate from the history of adoption. Doing so conceals the sociopolitical conditions that intentionally created the "weird family situation" of transnational transracial adoption. For example, neither provides a broad overview of international adoption's origins, the social or political contexts that facilitated Korean adoption in particular, the number of Korean adoptions that have taken place worldwide (though both allude to the hundreds of adoptees who attend the IKAA Gathering), or if and how Korean adoption has changed throughout the years. By presenting the featured adoptees' stories without situating Korean adoption within its sociohistorical context, the documentaries sidestep any critiques of Korean adoption. Absent are interrogations around why adoption continues to exist, the continued lack of social support for single Korean women, and the barriers to accessing adoption files—all topics that are focal points among adoptee activists in Korea.[33] Rather than interrogating the system that led to adoptees' dislocation from Korea, *Twinsters* and *aka SEOUL* simply portray the universalizing experiences of adoptees.

Through the presentation of the featured adoptees, the documentaries border on reifying the "better life" trope of adoption necessitating grateful adoptees. The featured adoptees are not angry; they are relatively well adjusted and generally grateful—the trifecta of expected adoptee affect. Even in cases that are more challenging, like Chelsea, whose adoptive family's strict religious beliefs strained their relationship when she came out as gay, or Anaïs, who seems quite troubled by her upbringing, the documentaries' portrayals mirror orphan redemption narratives. This belief is encapsulated by Chelsea's tattoo that she gets in Korea, which includes the quote "everything happens for a reason . . . things might fall apart but only to bring you back to something more positive." Samantha, too, emphasizes this but through the lens of divine orchestration. In reflecting on her journey and the happenstance reconnection to Anaïs, she muses, "when God closes a door, He opens a window."

However, as McKee notes, there is dissent within *Twinsters*, though it is distinct from the direct criticisms of early Korean adoptee ethnography.[34] She identifies adoptees' agency over how and how much of their stories they tell as "acts of refusal to maintain the status quo of the happy adoptee."[35] While adoptee narrative control is critical, these documentaries are also cultural texts of disidentification. The adoptee personhood presented in *Twinsters* and *aka SEOUL* is neither the absence of identifying with race, family, or citizenship nor the expressions of counter-identification whereby the norm remains centered. Instead, the portrayals acknowledge the expectations of transnational transracial adoptee assimilation while demonstrating how adoptees navigate that impossibility. The featured adoptees have discarded the nations or families neither of their origins nor of their adoption. Rather than present adoptee personhood as an either/or choice, the featured adoptees integrate both/and as they rework meanings of self, family, and belonging in ways that are messy and complex.

The adoptees I spoke with echoed this reworking of identity. Patrick (b. 1986) reflected on his own journey of self-discovery through finding community with other Korean adoptees:

> I don't have to fake it to make it. I just fit in, so that's always a good feeling . . . it gives me confidence wherever else I go or if somebody says, "Oh, you're Korean, but you're also adopted," I'll explain it however I need to explain it to that person. During my explanation, I feel 100 percent confident in myself, whereas I used to not. It was kind of, I'd explain and be ashamed. If it was with a Korean person, I'd be ashamed in some way. If it was a White person, I'd be ashamed in a different way. It's basically affected me negatively my whole life.

As with many other adoptees, it wasn't until Patrick moved to a larger city with more racial and ethnic diversity that he was able to connect with other adoptees. Through participating in Korean adoptee gatherings, exploring Korean culture, and traveling to Korea, Patrick's feelings of shame for not embodying the correct standards as a White or Korean person were replaced with confidence in his social position as a transnational transracial adoptee. Although adoptees experience these feelings of shame as individual, private feelings, they are a patterned response to the contradictory racialized emotions as transracial adoptees. *Twinsters* and *aka SEOUL* demonstrate that adoptees' emotional repertoires are shared among one another while presenting an alternative adoptee affect—one that is free from shame and not bound by others' expectations for how they should feel. Importantly, even for adoptees, who previously were unaware of adoptee groups and/or currently do not have adoptee groups in their vicinity, the documentaries introduce viewers to the global Korean adoptee community and provide a template for how to access it.

aka SEOUL further contributes to this reframing of the Korean adoptee experience by co-producing with NBC Asian America and distributing it through their digital video channel. Adoptees' lives are reinserted into the Asian American experience. As the adoptees in the films demonstrate, they experience the world as Asians regardless of their adoption or upbringing. For adoptee viewers, this acknowledges their previous exclusions from what it means to be Asian American. For non-adoptee and adoptee viewers alike, the films challenge monolithic portrayals of Asian Americans. Furthermore, adoptees' return to their birthplace mirrors how other Asian Americans may experience traveling to their ancestral homeland—as countries where they may have little familiarity despite lifelong assumptions of their foreignness.

Similar to other marginalized groups, Korean adoptees capitalize on the internet to create alternate programming where they are centered. Before *Twinsters* or *aka SEOUL*, both Samantha Futerman and Dan Matthews were actively creating YouTube content about their lives and connecting with other Asian American creatives. The ease and availability of technology and the normalization of vlogging as a type of public confessional laid the foundation for *Twinsters* and *aka SEOUL*. As a result, audiences and Korean adoptees specifically are offered a narrative normalizing Korean adoptee experiences as part of, yet unique within, the Asian American experience and providing a glimpse of a Korean adoptee transnational social space, something that would not have been possible in earlier decades. Importantly, this user-generated media facilitates a sense of place for a group that often feels in between places, spaces, and identities. Viewers not only can see themselves in the featured adoptees' journey of the self as it unfolds on screen, but can also participate in the Korean adoptee community in real life, such as the IKAA Gatherings. Through mainstream Korean adoptee-distributed media, IKAA Gatherings, and adoptees' reframing of their adoptee stories, symbolic and emotional ties are created generating a shared space of belonging traversing national boundaries. As Mike Mullen, a Korean adoptee and president of Also-Known-As, an international adoptee organization in New York City, proclaimed at the 2018 Chicago IKAA mini-gathering, "Our homeland is each other."

"The Dignity to Tell Their Story"

Despite the various ways *Twinsters* and *aka SEOUL* reworked the meaning of adoptee personhood, neither documentary included the role of legal citizenship in belonging. As *aka SEOUL* was filming, Adam Crapser's deportation case was underway and issues of adoptee citizenship were featured during the 2016 IKAA, though not in the docu-series.[36] To include adoptee stories of deportation would be in direct conflict with the overarching narrative of both documentaries, where adoption is the backdrop for adoptees' personal success. When adoptees are presented as undertaking an individual journey of the self divorced from the institutions and sociopolitical conditions enabling transnational transracial adoption, then the broader systems cannot be critiqued.

With the release of *Blue Bayou*, non-adoptee Korean American filmmaker Justin Chon attempted to bring awareness to the failures of the adoption system. The film illuminates the limits of adoption myths of a better life and forever family through a portrayal of one Korean adoptee's citizenship vulnerability. Chon wrote, directed, and starred in the film about the fictional account of Antonio LeBlanc, a Korean adoptee. After a run-in with local law enforcement that puts him on ICE's radar, Antonio learns that he is not an American citizen and now faces deportation. In an emotionally overwrought portrayal, Antonio confronts his past—his memories of his birth mother and his abusive foster family—and his limited options for a future with his wife and children in the US. The storyline ends with Antonio's deportation to Korea.

Blurring the lines between fact and fiction, the movie closes with a slide informing audiences that Antonio's fictional story is reflective of some adoptees' reality. The slide reads:

> No official statistics are available on how many adopted people face deportation.
>
> The Adoptee Rights Campaign estimates that 25,000 to 49,000 children who were legally adopted by US citizens between 1945 and 1998 may lack citizenship. That number is increasing to a new total of 32,000 to 64,000 adoptees without citizenship between 2015 and 2033, as children adopted between 1999 and 2016 reach their 18th birthdays.

Afterward, pictures of transnational adoptees who have been deported or are facing deportation flash across the screen along with their adoption date and deportation date, if applicable.

Similar to *Twinsters* and *aka SEOUL*, *Blue Bayou*'s fictional account emphasizes adoptees' experience of being the only one, disconnection from Korean American and Asian American communities, intrusive questioning, and cultural upbringing as (White) Americans. Overall, the movie interrogates the idea of home and belonging. Central to this exploration is the question of what it means to be American. In the opening scene, Antonio is interviewing for a mechanic job at an auto repair shop when the employer questions him about his name—LeBlanc—

and where he is from. In an exchange common among transnational transracial adoptees, his response of his Louisiana hometown is insufficient. The questioner asks again, "Where ya from, like born?" This scene sets the stage for who Antonio is grasped as as a non-White person in America—someone who could not be from "here."

The impossibility of Antonio's belonging continues as he learns that he does not have legal citizenship and is now facing deportation. Viewers watch as Barry, Antonio's immigration lawyer, explains the loophole left by the Child Citizenship Act of 2000, namely excluding adoptees who were already 18 years old at the time the law was passed.[37] Regardless of Antonio's adoption, how he dresses, or his English language proficiency and Louisiana drawl, Antonio is not legally a US citizen. Exasperated at the systemic failure and his impending deportation, Antonio yells in frustration, "Can't you just tell them I was adopted by White people!" In this moment, Antonio vocalizes the unique racial position created by transnational transracial adoption. Adoptees adopted by White families are raised to believe that they have access to the same rights and privileges as their family members, yet they learn throughout their lives in minor and major ways that they are not extended to them in the same way. Though Whiteness has historically been the measure of US inclusion,[38] adoption by White parents does not automatically guarantee citizenship rights. Similarly, cultural assimilation, no matter how complete, does not prevent one's formal exclusion from the US.

The revelation of Antonio's status completes his transition to a deportable immigrant. Early in the film, Antonio and his coworkers at the tattoo parlor joke with Merk, an ICE agent. In explaining his job to Antonio's stepdaughter, Merk describes it as finding and kicking out all the bad guys. As the film progresses, Antonio is no longer a good guy down on his luck who has overcome his criminal past, but one of the bad guys who must be expelled from the nation. In focusing on the undocumented status of an adult adoptee, *Blue Bayou* demonstrates what happens when adoptable orphans are no longer seen through the lens of their (White) adoptive families. Rather than being extended the benefits of honorary inclusion, Antonio is seen through the racialized lens of an undocumented, criminal immigrant. Despite previously satisfying White parents' desires for a child or currently sharing the bond of friendship with a White ICE agent, his class position, criminal background, and inalienable foreignness solidify his disposability.

Chon's depiction of an undocumented adoptee pushes against the adoptee success story and Asian American model minority framing. Antonio's adoption neither secured his "forever family" nor put him on a path to personal success, at least not as defined by socioeconomic or educational achievement. Not only has he failed to fully assimilate culturally and socioeconomically, as evidenced by his criminal background, his blended family fails to reproduce middle-class heteronormative nuclear family norms.

Throughout the film, viewers see an alternate portrayal of adoption, one that highlights adoptee abuse and neglect. Antonio's adoptive father is emotionally and physically abusive. As a particularly cruel example, Antonio reveals that his father threw away a letter from his birth mother. Antonio's father's intentional decision to withhold contact from his birth mother is a flagrant example of how transnational transracial adoptees' sense of self is mediated through adoptive parent choices. With his abusive upbringing and his current pending deportation, Antonio's story does not produce the "happy adoptee" of traditional adoption discourse. Instead, by showing the multiple failures of adoption in Antonio's story, the expectation of gratitude is rendered absurd.

Blue Bayou's challenge to traditional adoptee representations continues as it situates adoptees within the Asian American experience through the intertwined storyline of Antonio and Parker, a Vietnamese American woman. Parker and her family came to the US as refugees in search of a better life. As Parker's father comments to Antonio, "Korea and Vietnam have a lot in common, both had wars, a lot of sad stories. But we're strong. We're still here," a testament to the strength of

Asian Americans. Though the movie does not delve in depth into the US's military history that led to the displacement of Vietnamese families, like Parker's, or Korean children in the history of Korean adoption, this brief scene hints at the shared histories of US militarism throughout Asia. Similar to the opening scene that established Antonio's position as a foreigner in the US imaginary, here Antonio—and by extension other Asian transnational transracial adoptees—are realigned within Asian diasporas of displacement rather than portraying adoptees as exceptional immigrants.

While the conversation between Antonio, Parker, and Parker's father brings Antonio within a collective Asian American experience, the scene at Parker's family gathering also highlights Antonio's racial discomfort. Rather than feel at ease in this all-Asian family setting, Antonio is visibly uncomfortable, even seeking temporary refuge by hiding in the bathroom. The audience watches as he and his wife, Kathy, share an unfamiliarity with how to make spring rolls and must get a tutorial by one of the younger school-age family members. Even though Antonio is Korean and not Vietnamese like Parker's family, this scene highlights the Asian ethnic cultural socialization that has been lost in his upbringing.

In portraying how adoptee personal history is subject to public demands for divulging private details about their personal lives, during a meeting with Barry, Kathy learns that Antonio's adoptive mother, Susanne, is still alive despite him telling her that his parents were deceased. As Barry outlined the importance of demonstrating Antonio as a valuable member of the community, he emphasized Susanne's significance in presenting a strong case. Kathy feels blindsided by the news of Antonio's mother and his refusal to ask her to come to his deportation hearing. In a heated argument she says, "How are we married and I don't even know your mom's alive. I don't even know you." Antonio finally reveals why he has kept that part of his life private, a choice to not disclose childhood relinquishment, multiple foster care placements, and abuse. In this moment, *Blue Bayou* captures some adoptees' critiques of the film—that adoptees' stories are theirs to tell or not. As Adam Crapser stated in his public response to the film, "People who have experienced difficult things deserve the dignity to tell their story when and if they're ready. When that is taken away—when personal traumas are forcefully misappropriated for other people's purposes—it is hurtful."

"All of Our Stories"

Days after *Blue Bayou*'s theatrical release, adoptees took to social media, expressing their outrage at the depiction of adoptees, citing the exploitation of Adam Crapser's life story and the glaring lack of a call to action for adoptee citizenship rights. *Blue Bayou*'s portrayal of Antonio LeBlanc shares multiple similarities with the real-life story of Adam Crapser—run-ins with the law, an abusive adoptive family, leaving a wife and young children behind once deported. Adoptees also questioned Chon's intentions in making the film as a non-adoptee. As a filmmaker, Justin Chon has cited his goal to "bring empathy to my community, to Asian Americans."[39] His previous films, *Gook* and *Ms. Purple*, tell stories about the Korean American experience through contemporary social issues, while also striving to demonstrate how communities of different races and ethnicities can coexist. Upon learning about adoptee deportations, Chon felt "someone needs to shine light on this issue."[40] Chon reached out to Adam Crapser in 2017 asking to hear more about his story after seeing coverage of his case in *VICE* and the *New York Times*. Adam declined Chon's request for further communication, suggesting he contact Korean American actor Daniel Dae Kim, who had already visited him in Korea to discuss creating a documentary about his deportation. Chon never responded.[41]

In a press release, Adoptees for Justice (A4J) called for a boycott of the film due to its appropriation of Adam's story without his consent and asked for Justin Chon and Focus Features to halt distribution until consulting with Adam Crapser on restorative ways to move forward.[42]

The press release employed the idea of adoptee interchangeability when establishing that "the film exploits impacted members of our adoptee community by using their stories without their consent" and then detailing the commonalities between the character of Antonio LeBlanc and Adam Crapser. In describing the alleged use of *one* adoptee's story, A4J frames it as exploiting *the community's* "stories and lived experiences." Framing *Blue Bayou*'s storyline in this way is an attempt to activate a shared adoptee emotional response to motivate the community to join the boycott of the film.

Less than a week later, A4J issued another press release. The memo opened with A4J stating that they had been contacted by Focus Features a year prior to consult on the film. The release did not clarify whether they agreed to consult or not, though they did state that they "were fully aware that Adam Crapser had been approached by Justin Chon regarding *Blue Bayou* and had not given his consent to have his story told in or be connected to the film" and that they did not know the film's storyline until attending a pre-screening in 2021.[43] Acknowledging other undocumented adoptees' support for the film, A4J reiterated its call for a boycott and listed their demands for restoration. As of this writing, neither Focus Features nor Justin Chon has responded directly to A4J's calls. They have, however, reiterated their research for the film including consulting with undocumented adoptees and having their approval on each iteration of the script as well as consulting with a Korean American immigration lawyer. In their media responses, Justin Chon and Focus Features referred to Adoptee Advocacy, an organization created by adoptees who consulted on the film, and the associated *UnErased: The Deportation of Adoptees in America* podcast, co-produced by Focus Features and Treefort Media in support of the film,[44] as evidence of adoptee backing.

Shortly after the film aired and after A4J's initial press release, Adoptee Advocacy released a statement outlining their support for the film. In response to the accusations of appropriating Adam's story, they stated, "This movie isn't about only one person, it is about the whole community of deported adoptees. The script is all of our stories—we see strong similarities to many of our histories: abusive families, getting in trouble with the law, being deported while leaving behind small children." The statement detailed that deported adoptees were consulted, and deported and undocumented adoptees reviewed the script with changes being made based on their feedback. The undersigned adoptees also responded directly to the boycott, stating, "a boycott of this film by the adoptee community has been a devastating gut punch to us. We see *Blue Bayou* as a chance to shine a light on the injustice we have suffered, yet it is our own community that is now piling another injustice on us. We were abandoned by our country, and now we are being abandoned by people we thought were our brothers and sisters. Even worse than being abandoned, we feel we are being treated as the enemy."[45]

Similar to A4J, Adoptee Advocacy attempted to define the adoptee community to bring adoptees into a shared affect first by constructing the undocumented community as collectively in support of the film, and then by framing adoptee critics of the film as family who were rejecting their undocumented brothers and sisters. The deployment of the word "abandoned" to characterize the broader adoptee community is a deliberate attempt to trigger a common adoptee feeling. Adoptee origin stories are often characterized through themes of abandonment, rejection, and an absence of care. For Adoptee Advocacy to use such emotionally charged language against other adoptees was a purposeful choice in expressing the harm they felt and the harm of adoptees' boycott of the film.

Though the film was meant to "do justice to the adoptee community and their experience," the media responses effectively pitted adoptees against each other.[46] Focus Features used adoptees in support of the film to silence adoptee critiques. Adoptee Advocacy framed dissenters as ungrateful, a trope commonly used against adoptees who do not display the correct affect. Though adoptees have been vocal about not being a monolith, Adoptee Advocacy's press release sought to present adoptees as a unified front in support of the film, drawing on ideas of contingent essentialism, whereby shared adoption histories create fictive kinship and expectations of care, to do so.[47] Where Adoptee Advocacy members felt seen in an affirming way through *Blue Bayou*'s portrayal of an undocumented adoptee, they could not concede the fact that Adam, too, would feel seen—and exploited.

In a Gold House virtual Facebook panel about the film, panelist Kris Larsen, undocumented Vietnamese adoptee and Adoptee Advocacy member, scolded adoptees, stating that it was not Chon's responsibility to direct audiences to political action but rather for audiences to take it upon themselves to proactively learn more.[48] Continuing his paternalistic reprimand, he chastised adoptees who were commenting in the Facebook chat asking for Chon's response to A4J's boycott for their assumed inaction regarding adoptee citizenship rights advocacy, ignoring that many had been involved in advocacy since the earliest versions of the Adoptee Citizenship Act. In taking these approaches, undocumented adoptees adapted conventional adoption logics. Undocumented adoptees used the false dichotomy of grateful versus ungrateful adoptees to discipline adoptees who questioned the ethics of Chon's filmmaking and attempted to hold him accountable for the exploitation of a community member.

The intricacies of these debates were largely internal to adoptees who were already part of the Korean adoptee community and particularly those who had been involved in advocacy around Adam's case and the Adoptee Citizenship Act. However, Angry Asian Man and Reappropriate, two of the longest-running Asian American blogs, covered adoptees' call for a boycott of the film.[49] Amplifying adoptee voices situated Korean adoptees within Asian America and offered a corrective—or at least more well-rounded coverage—to the sites' previous promotion of the film.[50] For many other adoptees, who were not actively part of an adoptee community or were generally unaware of the boycott, *Blue Bayou* was a noteworthy adoptee representation, one that they enthusiastically welcomed. Although Chon created a sensationalized adoption story with layered trauma, the film also showcased nuance in the adoptee experience in ways that resonated with adoptee viewers. Thus, despite and even because of its approach to representing an undocumented adoptee story, *Blue Bayou* was a cultural moment for adoptees that bolstered shared meaning and emotions within different adoptee interest groups.

* * *

In taking control of the adoptee narrative, whether through adoptee-created media like *Twinsters* and *aka SEOUL* or by responding to mainstream portrayals of adoptees, Korean adoptees reclaim their sovereignty over their own story. *Twinsters*'s distribution via Netflix, *aka SEOUL*'s distribution via NBC Asian America, and Asian American media's amplification of adoptees' response to *Blue Bayou* emphasize the authority of the adoptee perspective. Adoptees present a narrative that highlights the patterned experiences among Korean transnational transracial adoptees because of their exceptional belonging, prioritizes adoptee desire to connect with their birth origins, centers their agency, and showcases an adoptee affect that is not beholden to oversimplified portrayals of adoptees as good/bad, grateful/ungrateful, or happy/angry.

Importantly, because *Twinsters* and *aka SEOUL* follow adoptees' journeys against the backdrop of traveling to Korea for an international Korean adoptee gathering, they act as a public artifact of a *collective* adoptee experience. Adoption may have previously been understood as an individual, past event, but being an adoptee now has shared meaning that is communally created in the present. These documentaries rewrite the dominant script of adoptee personhood by merging their lives pre- and post-adoption, and, in distributing the films through mainstream media outlets, publicize a template for adoptee becoming. Adoptee viewers are brought into an alternate adoptee affect, neither the acquiescence of gratitude nor the dissent of anger, but one that allows adoptees to feel the complex feelings of their adoptee racialized emotions. The effect of IKAA on the featured adoptees also presents an alternate type of citizenship, one that is not bound by national borders or conferring legal belonging. Instead, the transnational adoptee community offers a form of social citizenship that has been limited within adoptees' home nations.

Adoptees' shared identity is also activated in responding to *Blue Bayou*. While the film itself endeavors to offer a depiction of adoption contrasting traditional representations of adoptees as children, as necessarily happy or grateful, or as unquestionably benefiting from a better life in the US, all of which are important, it is adoptees' organized response to the film that provides a new way of understanding who adoptees are outside of limited, stigmatizing narratives.[51] Adoptees' outrage at the appropriation of an adoptee story positions adoptees as proprietors over their stories, and when their ownership is violated, adoptees have the right to be angry.

Conclusion

Staking Claims

During the summer of 2020, Kara Bos met her biological father. It was the first time they had seen each other since she was adopted to the US over 35 years prior.[1] Reunions are typically celebratory occasions; Kara, however, had no illusion of a happy meeting. Her father was compelled to meet after her lawsuit to establish paternity confirmed he was her biological father. Several years of searching, DNA testing that connected her with a nephew, refusal of acknowledgment by her half sisters, thousands of dollars in legal fees, and a paternity lawsuit in Korean courts culminated in a curt 10-minute meeting, where Kara's father offered no additional information about her origins.[2] Kara was legally established as his daughter in the eyes of the state—rewritten into the family registry and by extension Korean society—but to her father, she remained invisible.

Kara's lawsuit is another inflection point in Korean adoptee demands for recognition. Over two decades ago, Korean adoptees were included as "overseas Koreans" in the 1999 Act on the Immigration and Legal Status of Overseas Koreans. This categorization established adoptee access to the F-4 visa, a special visa for overseas Koreans that grants many privileges for work, reentry, and residency like that of native Koreans. The efforts of Global Overseas Adoptees' Link (G.O.A.'L.) in petitioning for Korean adoptees to be included in the Act was critical. Founded in 1998 by 12 Korean adoptees from Europe and the US, G.O.A.'L. has been instrumental in securing adoptees' legal position in Korean society, like through adoptees' inclusion for eligibility for the F-4 visa as well as dual citizenship.[3]

Adoptees petition to be legally recognized in Korean society, and they also demand acknowledgment for the reasons leading to their initial displacement. In the fall of 2022, the Danish Korean Rights Group (DKRG), led by adoptee attorney Peter Møller, submitted a request to Korea's Truth and Reconciliation Commission for an investigation into the circumstances of their adoptions.[4] Over 300 petitions from Korean adoptees in Europe and the US accompanied the request. Adoption agencies' inaccurate, incomplete, or falsified documentation of adoptees' origins contributed to the creation of adoptable orphans, and DKRG aims to hold them accountable.[5] As of this writing, the Commission has committed to investigating 34 of the adoptee cases of alleged human rights violations. These cases include adoptees who were adopted during the 1960s through the early 1990s to Denmark, Norway, the Netherlands, Germany, Belgium, and the US through Holt Children's Services and the Korea Social Service.[6] While it is up to the Commission to decide how many of the remaining applications for investigation they will consider, DKRG's coordinated efforts bring visibility to adoptees as adults, who refuse to accept the stories they've been told about who they are, where they come from, and where they belong.

Adoptee demands for recognition demonstrate the limits of exceptional belonging. Governmental policies, practices, and perspectives that crafted adoptable orphans failed to consider what would happen when these desirable children became adults. As adults, Korean adoptees are subsumed under racialized logics as deportable immigrants; however, adoptees themselves continue to stake claims to their own collectively defined personhood. Through individual lawsuits like Kara's or coordinated group efforts like DKRG's, adoptees engage in their own refusals of belonging—refusal to be grateful "happy adoptees" who accept the "better life" of adoption, refusal to adhere to the normative protocols of belonging linking race, kinship, and national membership, refusal to stay in the place assigned to them as adoptable orphans and deportable immigrants. Korean transnational transracial adoptees are not the only exceptionally crafted group who refuse to stay where they are placed.

Refusing to Stay in Place: Dreamers' Pathway to Citizenship

In 2001, Congress introduced the Development, Relief, and Education for Alien Minors (DREAM) Act.[7] This act would have created a pathway for citizenship for the then more than one million children and youth who had been brought to the US without legal authorization. Though the legislation did not pass, it brought mainstream, nationwide attention to the citizenship issues facing undocumented youth and their ongoing movement for citizenship rights. Over the next decade, almost a dozen versions of the DREAM Act were reintroduced to Congress unsuccessfully. The undocumented youth who would have benefited from the bill came to be known as "DREAMers," which proved to be a salient frame for generating sympathy for this class of undocumented immigrants because of how it reified existing investments in race, citizenship, and kinship.

Originally a label mobilized by immigrant rights activists to humanize undocumented youth, "DREAMer" advanced tropes around deserving, good immigrants versus undeserving, bad immigrants. Similar to framing of transnational transracial adoptees, this dichotomous oversimplification was tied to DREAMers' age, race, and familial (dis)connections. DREAMers, the majority hailing from Latin American countries, were portrayed as high-achieving youth with upstanding moral behavior, who would continue to contribute to the US economy and not pose a threat to the cultural identity of the US.[8] Even though the framing of bad immigrants, who are criminal, a threat to US culture, and/or a drain on resources, has contemporarily been linked to "illegal immigrants" from south of the border, these young DREAMers were presented as conceptually distinct. Through this lens, DREAMers were suspended in adolescence, separate from "criminal aliens" but also unable to be seen as adults.

By presenting DREAMers as young people who had undocumented status through no fault of their own, the concept of DREAMers resulted in effectively separating these youth from their adult counterparts. Their innocence and lack of culpability for their undocumented status made them deserving of legal protection. The action that brought them to the US, however, criminalized their parents, thereby making those adult undocumented immigrants undeserving of citizenship. Therefore, DREAMers' deservingness hinged on their individual relationship to the state rather than their family or community ties. Where DREAMers must be distinct from their parents to secure their citizenship rights, transnational transracial adoptees' citizenship rights rely on their predominantly White adoptive parents' legality. Both approaches are similar in how they require the undocumented population to remain seen through the lens of youth and innocence. When DREAMers and undocumented adoptees are seen as vulnerable, helpless children, supporters of pathways to citizenship can be viewed as contributing to the welfare of children, not criminal adults.

After the unsuccessful passage of the DREAM Act in 2010, DREAMers campaigned for administrative relief, and in 2012, the Obama administration instituted the Deferred Action for Childhood Arrivals (DACA) program.[9] Since then, more than 820,000 immigrants have enrolled in DACA.[10] The most recent proposal, as of this writing, adheres to the same criteria as the original 2012 memo, which included but is not limited to arriving in the country before age 16, continuously residing in the United States since arrival, no felony convictions, and being in the country on June 15, 2012, when the DACA policy was originally established. DACA uses prosecutorial discretion to defer removal action against an individual for two years, subject to renewal, and provides people who were brought to the US unlawfully as children the temporary protection to live, study, and work in the US. Deferred action does not provide lawful status, and DACA does not provide a pathway to citizenship.

News framing of those who have or will benefit from DACA continues to emphasize their economic contributions to the US, cultural assimilation, and upstanding moral character.[11] This portrayal positions DACA recipients within the conditional inclusions of exceptional belonging. Undocumented immigrants who do not contribute economically, have low levels of educational attainment, break the law, or do not demonstrate their patriotism through military service are not extended the conditional benefits of temporary and limited inclusion in the nation. Although DACA recipients, like transnational transracial adoptees, generally spent most of childhood and adolescence in the US and see themselves as members of the nation, they are seen as distinct from real Americans.

Immigration policy is guided by the welfare of the nation. Immigrants who provide a benefit to the nation, like those who are DACA eligible, are suitable for inclusion, albeit conditionally and temporarily. Those who do not, cannot, or no longer serve the material interests of or emotional investments in the nation are marked for exclusion. Although many of the DREAMers who benefit from DACA are adults with families of their own, current actions for preserving and fortifying DACA relies on their framing as innocent, young, full of hope and promise.

DREAMers, however, refuse to stay in place as rescuable children, whose personhood and belonging is determined by state recognition. Through coordinated campaigns to come out of the shadows and declare themselves undocumented, unafraid, and unapologetic, DREAMers reframe their position in the US. The US government's refusal to grant formal citizenship is met by their own refusal to be limited by their legal status. DREAMers continue to organize nationwide protests and engage in civil disobedience to bring attention to immigrant rights and the contradictions of citizenship policy.

* * *

As I was talking with Angela, I asked her if she felt there were any privileges to being an adoptee. She reflected:

> Privileges is just growing up in a White home and I feel like I did carry some of that privilege. I thought I had that privilege, yet maybe I never did because people might perceive me differently. I'd never really thought about it growing up and now looking back, maybe your perceived White privilege was what I thought I had, so it made me very confident. But I never had it to begin with in that way. I remember getting made fun of a lot like with your eyes being slanted. I grew up around mostly White people . . . I thought I was a part of it and that's the way it was. I didn't know any different.

The paradoxes of having immigrated to a country but often not thinking of oneself as an immigrant, of being racially foreign and honorarily White, and of being exceptional Americans but not accepted Americans expose the contradictions of belonging. As adoptees remake their belonging through cultural, political, collective, and affective channels, their everyday practices of refusal offer a critique of the dominant culture that made them out of place. In reworking adoptee personhood among one another, adoptees stake claims. For Angela, there was an assumption of belonging, a confidence of Whiteness, that she had come to question. This questioning is necessary to refusing the cultural logics that create adoptable orphans and deportable immigrants so that no one must be exceptional to belong.

ACKNOWLEDGMENTS

Even as a child I was an avid reader. I thought everything worth knowing and everything knowable could be found within the pages of a book. So I was devasted by the absence of writing by or about Korean adoptees. Of course, a lot has changed since then. Now there are books, anthologies, blogs, podcasts, movies, and other media by and for us, but the seeds for this book had already been planted, and my determination to contribute to writing us into existence remained unchanged. There are numerous people to thank for making this book into reality. First and foremost, thank you to the Korean adoptees who took the time to respond to my survey and share their stories with me. A special thank you to Anthony Ocampo for considering a book about Korean adoptees for this series on Asian American sociology. For many years, Asian adoptees were excluded from Asian America, so to have this book in this series is especially meaningful. Thank you to Ilene Kalish and the NYU editorial team for bringing this book to fruition.

The initial research for this book would not have been possible without the financial support from the Adoption Initiative's Pre-Doctoral Dissertation Award; the University of Maryland's Consortium on Race, Gender, and Ethnicity's Dissertation Research Grant, which paid for most of the interview transcriptions; and the University of Maryland's Dean's Research Initiative Grant and Travel Award, which allowed me to travel across the US and Korea to engage with Korean adoptee communities and present my work. Thank you to Philip N. Cohen, Feinian Chen, Patricia Hill Collins, and Rashawn Ray, who provided me the space to grow as a scholar and the support to pursue a topic that was my own. Thank you especially to Dr. Collins for reminding me that my work matters and to stay tethered to who I do the work for and why. Thank you also to the University of Memphis for the time to finish this manuscript.

This book would not be what it is without a writing community—in fact, many writing communities. From the beginning, the University of Maryland Department of Sociology's Critical Race Initiative (CRI) was crucial. Thank you to the members of our writing group for helping me think through earlier iterations of this work. Many of the ideas that began with our intellectual engagement so many years ago were refined and ultimately found their way into these pages. But, more than the exchange of ideas facilitated through our monthly writing workshops, I continue to be sustained by the relationships created through CRI. A special thank you to Jessica Peña and Jonathan Cox for their continued friendship and engagement with this work. Sometimes community comes from the most unexpected places. Thank you to Dana Miller-Cotto, a social media friend turned accountability partner, for our ambitious summer research plan. Thirteen weeks of having unbelievably high expectations and ridiculously long to-do lists turned into multiple journal articles and the book proposal that ultimately secured this book contract. Then, when it was time for book copyedits and proofs, it was our online co-working that created the space, accountability, and support to work through them. I am also grateful to the writing group that Saida Grundy started and that Zawadi Rucks-Ahidiana continued to host. Your accountability and camaraderie ushered me over the finish line when it seemed like the book would never find its stopping point.

Although I am a Korean adoptee, my entry into the Korean adoption community did not begin until this project and was graciously facilitated by Spencer Stevens. As he has done for many other adoptees, Spencer welcomed me into the adoptee community, introduced me to countless other adoptees, and provided insight into the inner workings of the transnational Korean adoptee community. Thank you to Aimee, Trish, Stephen, Letitia, and David for support throughout my dissertation research but most of all for welcoming me into Adoption Links DC. Thank you to Katelyn, Oh Myo, and Mike for their friendship and a memorable weekend at the Queen's College Research Center for Korean Community College. I don't know where I would be in my own Korean adoptee journey without you. And to Patrick Armstrong, thank you for listening to my ideas and encouraging me to write them into this book (even the unpopular ones).

There are countless friends and colleagues who have supported me throughout this book's journey, and I would be remiss if I did not take the time to acknowledge some by name. As with any big goal, you only need one "yes." Thank you to Rashawn Ray for your unyielding belief in me as a sociologist. After countless "no"s, yours was the "yes" that made all the difference. There are not enough words to tell you how important you are to me. I am honored to call you a mentor and friend. To Kati Barahona-Lopez, a brilliant scholar and an even better friend, who, when I thought I couldn't go any further, reminded me of the importance of this work. Jessica Peña, my cohort bff, your friendship has sustained me through many seasons of work and life, including the final drafts of this manuscript. Kim McKee and Kim Park Nelson, thank you for offering invaluable feedback on the manuscript. Amanda Assalone, our friendship, especially our vent sessions, has been priceless; thank you for all that you do for the adoptee community and taking the time to read chapter drafts in the midst of it all. A special thank you to Devon Goss for always being willing to read drafts of my work and for being an early collaborator. Carla Goar, thank you for all your encouragement and for extending the invitation to work on a project together. Joanna Pepin, you have truly been a gem; thank you for all of your feedback on my work and your friendship. Jenni Mueller, a kindred spirit, a gifted theorist and teacher, I am beyond grateful that our paths crossed. It had to be so. Dumi Lewis-McCoy, your friendship, mentorship, and countless laughs have kept me sane on many days. We need celebratory Chip City! Speaking of staying sane, thank you to Teri Del Rosso, a colleague turned friend and workout partner; where would I be without your encouragement and our weekly hill workouts. You are an inspiration. And to Darren Garcia, thank you for the reminders that I was doing a great job even on the days that it didn't feel like it. Most importantly, thank you for your active support for my own adoptee journey and Korean cultural reclamation. It has meant the world to me.

Because this book is not just a discrete academic endeavor but a lifetime in the making, I must thank the people who've been with me through many, many seasons of life. Michelle Marzette, we've walked together—quite literally—through many evolutions of our selves. It has truly been a beautiful journey. My Twin, Wayne Armstead, words can't quite capture our bond and it's not for folks to understand, but when I was at my absolute lowest, it was you that I called because I knew it was you who would understand me in that moment without judgment, with care, and with the support I needed. Thank you. Let's walk soon. Finally, it goes without saying, but I wouldn't have made it here without Connie Williamson and Cynthia Ray—who knew our days working at Checkers would turn into a lifelong friendship?

There are also many unnamed and unknown people who offered a word of support, encouragement, or sparked an insight that they will never know. Like the barista at my favorite coffee shop, who after seeing me countless days, sitting by the window staring at my computer for countless hours, asked me how my work was going—he didn't know what I was working on—and affirmed me with a "We believe in you!" It was what I needed to hear on that day. So, if you have made it this far in the acknowledgements or if, like me, you read the acknowledgments first, this is your sign to encourage someone. I have been uplifted by the words of a stranger too many times to count. Kindness makes all the difference. Of course, it is also the case that we often take it for granted that the people closest to us know that we believe in them, that we're proud of them, that they are important to us. Tell them.

Even though I do not know my biological family, it is not lost on me that regardless of whether we are known to each other, we are still known by each other. I am because they were. I am because they are. So, thank you to my Korean family, whoever and wherever you may be.

To the biggest supporter in my life, my father, who taught me some of the most important lessons worth knowing. Where would I be without you. Who would I be without you. While I do not believe "love is enough," I do believe that unconditional love is a great power. And I am constantly in awe of the way you have shown me what love is. As with anyone else, you have, are, and will continue to become many different people, many different lives, but in my life, it remains that you are my dad and I love you for that.

Finally, this book would not exist without my mom and dad, who instilled in me a love of reading and who made me believe that I could accomplish anything I set my mind to. This is proof.

NOTES

INTRODUCTION

1 Kim and Park Nelson, "Natural Born Aliens"; McKee, "(Un)documented Citizens, (Un)naturalized Americans," in *Disrupting Kinship*, 39.

2 Immigration and Naturalization Form N-402.

3 Application for Certificate of Citizenship Form N-600.

4 Jones, "Adam Crapser's Bizarre Deportation Odyssey."

5 Reappropriate, "Pending Deportation."

6 Shoichet, "Americans Adopted Him."

7 Associated Press, "Feds Targeted Adoptee."

8 Reappropriate, "Pending Deportation."

9 Perry, "Korean Adoptee."

10 Jones, "Adam Crapser's Bizarre Deportation Odyssey."

11 Child Citizenship Act of 2000, Pub. L. No. 106–395 (2000).

12 Internationally adopted children also immigrate under IR-4, IH-4, and IR-2 visas, each with specific steps that must be taken to ensure citizenship. See www.uscis. gov.

13 Hewitt, "International Adoptee Faces Deportation."

14 Adam was previously convicted of assault, burglary, and being a felon in possession of a weapon. Selsky, "Abuse, Crime Haunted Adoptee."

15 Jones, "Adam Crapser's Bizarre Deportation Odyssey."

16 US Department of Homeland Security, "Table 39. Aliens Removed or Returned."

17 With one caveat: international adoptees cannot be president.

18 Chung, *Adopting for God*; Oh, *To Save the Children of Korea*.

19 Wu, *The Color of Success*.

20 United States Congress, "An Act to Establish an Uniform Rule of Naturalization" (March 26, 1790).

21 The Expatriation Act of 1907; 59th Congress, 2nd session, chapter 2534, enacted March 2, 1907.

22 The Cable Act, also known as the Married Women's Citizenship Act or the Women's Citizenship Act; enacted September 22, 1922.

23 Haney López, *White by Law*.

24 Haney López, *White by Law*.

25 Erika Lee, *The Making of Asian America*; Lowe, *Immigrant Acts*; Mia Tuan, *Forever Foreigners or Honorary Whites?*

26 Chang, *Disoriented*; Tuan, *Forever Foreigners or Honorary Whites?*; Wu, *The Color of Success.*

27 Lowe, *Immigrant Acts*, 8.

28 Okihiro, *Margins & Mainstream.*

29 Erika Lee, *The Making of Asian America.*

30 Erika Lee, *The Making of Asian America.*

31 Kim, "The Racial Triangulation of Asian Americans."

32 Hill Collins, *Black Feminist Thought.*

33 Ahmed, *The Cultural Politics of Emotions.*

34 Cheng, *Citizens of Asian America*; Tuan, *Forever Foreigners or Honorary Whites?*

35 Ioanide, *The Emotional Politics of Racism.*

36 Bonilla-Silva, "Feeling Race."

37 Richard M. Lee, "The Transracial Adoption Paradox," 711.

38 Feagin, *The White Racial Frame*, xi.

39 Eleana J. Kim, *Adopted Territory*; Kim, Suyemoto, and Turner, "Sense of Belonging"; Park Nelson, *Invisible Asians.*

40 Hübinette, "Disembedded and Free-Floating Bodies"; Hübinette, "Adopted Koreans"; Eleana J. Kim, *Adopted Territory.*

41 Park Nelson, *Invisible Asians.*

42 Myers, "'REAL' FAMILIES."

43 McKee, *Disrupting Kinship.*

44 McKee, *Disrupting Kinship*, 11.

45 Eleana J. Kim, *Adopted Territory.*

46 Jerng, *Claiming Others.*

47 Oh, *To Save the Children of Korea.*

48 Herman, *Kinship by Design.*

49 Pate, *From Orphan to Adoptee.*

50 Graves, *A War Born Family.*

51 General Court of Massachusetts, "An Act to Provide for the Adoption of Children," *Acts and Resolves Passed by the General Court of Massachusetts* (Boston, 1851), chap. 324.

52 Briggs, "Mother, Child, Race, Nation."

53 Oh, "Making Families on a New Frontier," in *To Save the Children of Korea*, 112; Pate, "Marketing the Social Orphan," in *From Orphan to Adoptee*, 73.

54 Oh, "The Contradictions of Love and Commerce," in *From Orphan to Adoptee*, 145.

55 1924 Johnson-Reed Act; 1952 McCarran-Walter Act (also known as the Immigration and Nationality Act).

56 Kim and Park Nelson, "Natural Born Aliens."

57 Choy, *Global Families.*

58 Hübinette, "Comforting an Orphaned Nation."

59 Raleigh, *Selling Transracial Adoption.*

60 Eleana J. Kim, *Adopted Territory*.

61 Eleana J. Kim, *Adopted Territory*; McKee, *Disrupting Kinship*; Palmer, *The Dance of Identities*; Park Nelson, *Invisible Asians*.

62 Eleana Kim describes an adoptee kinship forged through "contingent essentialism." See Kim, *Adopted Territory*.

1. FEELING WHITE, FEELING RIGHT

1 Chin, Chan, Inada, and Wong, *Aiiieeeee!*

2 Chin, Chan, Inada, and Wong, *Aiiieeeee!*, xxvi.

3 Du Bois, "Strivings of the Negro People."

4 Du Bois, "The Souls of White Folk."

5 Lowe, *Immigrant Acts*.

6 Richard M. Lee, "The Transracial Adoption Paradox."

7 Feagin, *The White Racial Frame*.

8 Feagin, *Racist America*.

9 Picca and Feagin, *Two-Faced Racism*.

10 Espiritu, *Asian American Women and Men*.

11 Pyke and Johnson, "Asian American Women and Racialized Femininities."

12 Raleigh, *Selling Transracial Adoption*.

13 Goss, Byrd, and Hughey, "Racial Authenticity."

14 Du Bois, "The Souls of White Folk"; Roediger, *The Wages of Whiteness*.

15 Frankenberg, *White Women, Race Matters*; Lewis, "What Group?"; Lipsitz, "The Possessive Investment in Whiteness."

16 Ahmed, "Happy Objects," 39.

17 Brian, *Reframing Transracial Adoption*; Eleana J. Kim, *Adopted Territory*; Park Nelson, *Invisible Asians*.

18 McGinnis, Smith, Ryan, and Howard, *Beyond Culture Camp*.

19 McKee, "Monetary Flows."

20 For more on racialized logics in adoption from Asia, see Dorow, "Racialized Choices."

21 Brian, *Reframing Transracial Adoption*, 57.

22 National Association of Black Social Workers, "Position Statement on Trans-Racial Adoptions."

23 Graves, *A War Born Family*; Oh, *To Save the Children of Korea*.

24 Raleigh, *Selling Transracial Adoption*.

25 Frost, *Never One Nation*; Pinder, "Whiteness."

26 Erika Lee, "The Chinese Exclusion Example."

27 Erika Lee, "The Chinese Exclusion Example," 9.

28 Jacobson, *Culture Keeping*, 96.

29 Brian, *Reframing Transracial Adoption*, 57.

30 For a history of racial residential segregation, see: Rothstein, *The Color of Law*. For more on contemporary residential segregation, see Schuetza, Larrimore,

Merry, Robles, Tranfaglia, and Gonzalez, "Are Central Cities Poor and Non-White?"

31 Bonilla-Silva, Goar, and Embrick, "When Whites Flock Together."

32 Hagerman, "White Families and Race."

33 Berbery and O'Brien, "Predictors"; Vonk, Yun, Park, and Massatti, "Transracial Adoptive Parents' Thoughts."

34 Richard M. Lee, "The Transracial Adoption Paradox."

35 Lee, Grotevant, Hellerstedt, Gunnar, and The Minnesota International Adoption Project Team, "Cultural Socialization."

36 Quiroz, "Cultural Tourism in Transnational Adoption."

37 Jacobson, *Culture Keeping*.

38 Laybourn and Goar, "In My Heart, I Am Cambodian."

39 Gans, "Symbolic Ethnicity"; Waters, *Ethnic Options*.

40 Waters, *Ethnic Options*, 51.

41 Waters, *Ethnic Options*.

42 Kibria, "Race, Ethnic Options, and Ethnic Binds"; Tuan, *Forever Foreigners or Honorary Whites?*

43 Goss, Byrd, and Hughey, "Racial Authenticity."

44 Song, *Choosing Ethnic Identity*; Tuan, *Forever Foreigners or Honorary Whites?*

45 Tuan, *Forever Foreigners or Honorary Whites?*

46 Edmonds and Killen, "Do Adolescents' Perceptions."

47 Park Nelson, *Invisible Asians*.

48 Eaton and Rose, "Has Dating Become More Egalitarian?"

49 None of my male respondents mentioned explicit dating advice from their parents, and very few shared negative reflections about their dating experiences. This difference is likely a reflection of my own positionality as a woman and the gendered dynamics in my interviews with male respondents and should not be taken as indication that male Korean adoptees did not receive dating advice or have negative dating experiences.

50 For more on how immigration policy, miscegenation laws, and economic disenfranchisement have shaped Asian American emasculation, see Park, "Asian American Masculinity Eclipsed."

51 Balistreri, Joyner, and Kao, "Relationship Involvement among Young Adults"; Robnett and Feliciano, "Patterns of Racial-Ethnic Exclusion by Internet Daters."

2. REFUSALS OF BELONGING

1 Shah, "Race, Nation, and Citizenship."

2 Erika Lee, "The Chinese Exclusion Example"; Haney López, *White by Law*.

3 Tuan, *Forever Foreigners or Honorary Whites?*

4 United States v. Wong Kim Ark, 169 U.S. 649 (1898).

5 United States v. Wong Kim Ark, 169 U.S. 649 (1898).

6 Gustafsson, "Theorizing Korean Transracial Adoptee Experiences."

7 Claire Jean Kim, "The Racial Triangulation of Asian Americans."

8 Richard M. Lee, "The Transracial Adoption Paradox."

9 For more on recognition and intersubjectivity defined through what one is not, see Fanon, *Black Skin, White Masks*.

10 Eng and Han, *Racial Melancholia, Racial Dissociation*.

11 Eng, "Transnational Adoption and Queer Diasporas."

12 Eng and Han, *Racial Melancholia, Racial Dissociation*, 36.

13 Kim and Park Nelson, "Natural Born Aliens."

14 Although adoptive parents had lobbied for legislation that would ensure transnational adoptees' US citizenship and eliminate the separate naturalization process for adoptees, it would not be until 2000 with the passage of the Child Citizenship Act (CCA) that the adoption process and citizenship process for adoptees would be conjoined.

15 Graves, *A War Born Family*; Oh, *To Save the Children of Korea*; Pate, *From Orphan to Adoptee*.

16 The Page Act of 1875 (Sect. 141, 18 Stat. 477, 3 March 1875) prohibited the immigration of those deemed "undesirable," in particular Chinese "coolie" laborers and prostitutes. Chinese women were stereotyped as sexually promiscuous and disease-carrying, threats to white purity. The Act was used to prevent Chinese women from immigrating.

17 In practice, Chinese were generally not naturalized prior to the 1882 Act given that they did not fall under the category of "free white persons" as outlined in the Naturalization Act of 1790.

18 Mueller, "Racial Ideology or Racial Ignorance?"

19 Feagin, *The White Racial Frame*.

20 Mueller, "Racial Ideology or Racial Ignorance?"

21 Fausset, Bogel-Burroughs, and Fazio, "The Suspect in Spa Attacks."

22 Jeung, Yellow Horse, Popovic, and Lim, "Stop AAPI Hate National Report."

23 For many Asian adoptees, the Atlanta spa shooting spurred them to seek out Asian adoptee online groups.

24 Baumgaertner, "Atlanta-Area Spa Shootings"; Wong, "The Racist Misogyny."

25 Hayes, "Georgia Sheriff Spokesman."

26 Pérez, *The Souls of White Jokes*.

27 Pérez, *The Souls of White Jokes*, 18.

28 Conway, "Tony Baker."

29 Mueller, "Racial Ideology or Racial Ignorance?"

30 Presidential Proclamation No. 2525 (December 7, 1941); Executive Order 9066 (February 19, 1942).

31 *San Francisco Chronicle*, November 18, 1945.

32 Kiang, Yip, Gonzales-Backen, Witkow, and Fuligni, "Ethnic Identity"; Neblett, Rivas-Drake, and Umaña-Taylor, "The Promise"; Serrano-Villar and Calzada, "Ethnic Identity."

33 Eng and Han, *Racial Melancholia, Racial Dissociation.*

34 Perea, "The Black/White Binary Paradigm of Race."

35 Leading Asian American to Unite for Change (LAAUNCH), STAATUS Index 2022.

36 LAAUNCH, STAATUS Index 2022..

37 Yuen, Smith, Pieper, Choueiti, Yao, and Dinh, *The Prevalence and Portrayal.*

38 Yuen, Smith, Pieper, Choueiti, Yao, and Dinh, *The Prevalence and Portrayal*; McTaggart, Meyer, Conroy, Perez, Espinoza, Trinh, Campos, Burrows, Virgo, Brennan, Dolan, Ackel, and Christensen, *I Am Not a Fetish.*

39 An, "Asian Americans in American History."

40 Nadia Y. Kim. *Imperial Citizens*, 18.

41 Yang, "How Connecticut Became the First State."

42 Alcoff, "Latino/as, Asian Americans, and the Black-White Binary."

43 Ho, *Racial Ambiguity*, 12.

44 Ellen D. Wu, *The Color of Success.*

45 Lowe, *Immigrant Acts*, 42.

46 Espiritu, *Homebound*, 47.

47 Oh, *To Save the Children of Korea*; Woo, *Framed by War.*

48 Haney López, *White by Law*; Painter, *The History of White People.*

49 Nadia Y. Kim, *Imperial Citizens*; Erika Lee, *The Making of Asian America*; Tuan, *Forever Foreigners or Honorary Whites?*; Frank H. Wu, "Where Are You Really From?"

50 Choy, *Asian American Histories of the United States*; Hong, *Minor Feelings*; Nadia Y. Kim, *Imperial Citizens*; Erika Lee, *The Making of Asian America*; Tuan, *Forever Foreigners or Honorary Whites?*

51 Jo and Mast, "Changing Images of Asian Americans."

52 Mi Na's use of "colored" may seem archaic given the history of the term in the US. "Colored" is associated with slavery and Jim Crow and has largely fallen out of favor for everyday usage given its connotation with the US's racist, violent history. However, it is not uncommon for young people, whether people of color themselves who are US born or raised, or White youth, to use the term. While there has not been, to my knowledge, a systematic examination of when and where young people use "colored people" to refer to "people of color," I frequently see college instructors expressing frustration at students' continued use of the term each semester. This may reflect a general lack of education on different racial terminology, meanings, and change over time; the assumed interchangeability of "colored people" and "people of color" to refer to racially minoritized groups; a right-wing response to language associated with an alleged liberal "woke" agenda; or the use of the term within their families, particularly among older family members. Here Mi Na uses the term as an acceptable substitution for "people of color" to refer to the shared racialization of racially marginalized people in the US.

53 Hübinette, "Disembedded and Free-Floating," 145.

54 Bonilla-Silva, "We Are All Americans!"; Gans, "The Possibility of a New Racial Hierarchy"; Warren, and Twine, "White Americans, the New Minority?"; Yancey, *Who Is White?*.

3. ADOPTABLE ORPHAN, DEPORTABLE IMMIGRANT

1 Me & Korea, Inc., is an all-volunteer, non-profit organization that serves Korean adoptees and their families. Founded in 2013 by Minyoung Kim, the organization offers annual homeland tours for adult Korean adoptees and an educational program for young Korean adoptees and their families.

2 Snow and McAdam, "Identity Work Processes in the Context of Social Movements"; Snow and Oliver, "Social Movements and Collective Behavior."

3 Angry Asian Man, "#KeepAdamHome"; Reappropriate, "Petition"; Reappropriate, "Pending Deportation."

4 Briggs, "Mother, Child, Race, Nation."

5 Briggs, "Mother, Child, Race, Nation."

6 Angry Asian Man, "#KeepAdamHome."

7 The Crapsers had one biological son, three adopted children, including Adam, and several foster children. The Crapsers were charged with 34 counts of criminal mistreatment of five boys and three girls, ages 6–13. Ultimately Thomas served 90 days in prison and Dolly served three years of probation.

8 For an overview of the divergences between adoption policy and immigration legislation, see Kim and Park Nelson, "Transnational Adoptees and US Citizenship."

9 Kim and Park Nelson, "Transnational Adoptees and US Citizenship."

10 Gazillion Voices, "Adam Crapser."

11 Oh, *To Save the Children of Korea*.

12 Kim and Park Nelson. "Transnational Adoptees and US Citizenship," 258.

13 H.R. 3110, S. 1359, FACE Act, 111th Congress, 2009–2010.

14 S. Amdt. 1222 to S. 744, 113th Congress, 2013–2014.

15 S. 744, Border Security, Economic Opportunity, and Immigration Modernization Act, 113th Congress, 2013–2014.

16 DeLeith Duke Gossett, "[Take from Us Our] Wretched Refuse."

17 For more on the long-lasting effects of the War on Crime, see Alexander, *The New Jim Crow*.

18 For more on race and the War on Drugs, see Provine, *Unequal under Law*.

19 Motomura, *Americans in Waiting*.

20 Erika Lee, *American for Americans*.

21 Light and Miller, "Does Undocumented Immigration Increase Violent Crime?"; Light, Miller, and Kelly, "Undocumented Immigration, Drug Problems"; Bersani, Fine, Piquero, Steinberg, Frick, and Cauffman, "Investigating the Offending Histories."

22 Newton, *Illegal, Alien, or Immigrant.*

23 H.R. 4437, 109th Congress, § 220–25, 2006.

24 Garcia Hernández, "Creating Crimmigration."

25 Holper, "The Unreasonable Seizures of Shadow Deportations."

26 Wadhia, "The Rise of Speed Deportation."

27 Wadhia, *Banned.*

28 To my knowledge, a class action lawsuit of adoptees against the US has not been filed.

29 Jessa would be eligible for a waiver for the English portion under the "55/15" exception, which grants exemption if you are "age 55 or older at the time of filing for naturalization and have lived as a permanent resident in the United States for 15 years."

30 In many ways, Jessa is one of the lucky ones. Even though she is not a naturalized citizen, she has been able to maintain lawful permanent residence. Many children who migrated to the US do not have the necessary paperwork to maintain lawful residence. For more on how undocumented migrants who migrated as children attempt to make sense of their cultural, legal, and social citizenship, see Vargas, *Dear America.*

31 Molina, *How Race Is Made in America.*

32 AAPIData, "One Out of Every 7."

33 Jessa's reference to undocumented immigrants' unearned privileges is a common anti-immigration myth. Undocumented immigrants are ineligible for benefits such as Medicare, Supplemental Security Income, Children's Health Insurance Program, Supplemental Nutrition Assistance Program, unemployment benefits, and voting rights, as they require citizenship or lawful permanent residence. Undocumented immigrants are eligible for a driver's license in 16 states and the District of Columbia, though they are unable to obtain a REAL ID, as it requires proof of citizenship (see UnitedWeDream.org for updates on driver's license eligibility).

34 S. 2275, Broadband Transparency and Accountability Act of 2019, 116th Congress, 2019–2020.

35 H.R. 5454, Fairness for Landowners Facing Eminent Domain Act, 116th Congress, 2019–2020; S. 2275.

36 McKee, *Disrupting Kinship*, 41.

37 Kim and Park Nelson, "Transnational Adoptees and US Citizenship."

38 Kim and Park Nelson, "Transnational Adoptees and US Citizenship."

39 Perry, "After 37 Years in US."

40 March 8, 2018, bills dropped in the House, H.R. 5233 Adam Smith and 46 co-sponsors, and the Senate, S. 2522 Roy Blunt and 3 co-sponsors. With the caveat: Automatic citizenship may not be granted to an individual who was deported for an offense that involved the use of physical force against another person.

41 H.R. 5233, Adoptee Citizenship Act of 2018, 115th Congress, 2017–2018; S. 2522, Adoptee Citizenship Act of 2018, 115th Congress, 2017–2018.

42 The Adoptee Citizenship Act of 2021 was included in the COMPETES Act, which passed the House and Senate in early 2022. However, the final version of the bill did not include provisions for intercountry adoptees' citizenship. Throughout the last quarter of 2022, ACA co-sponsors tirelessly worked to have the ACA added to the omnibus bill but to no avail. In an emailed update about the ACA, Adoptees for Justice noted that although this was the last opportunity to pass the ACA this Congress, advocacy would continue. For more on ACA organizing, see adoptees-forjustice.org.

43 Adoptee Rights Campaign, "How ARC Came to Support the 2019 Adoptee Citizenship Act."

44 While ARC was originally formed under the leadership of NAKASEC, as of January 2018 it became part of the World Hug Foundation.

45 However, currently, both groups list citizenship for all intercountry adoptees as their goal.

46 H.R. 2731, Adoptee Citizenship Act of 2019, 116th Congress, 2019–2020; S. 1554, Adoptee Citizenship Act of 2019, 116th Congress, 2019–2020.

47 United States Senate, "Blunt, Hirono, Collins, Klobuchar."

48 United States House of Representatives, "Congressman Smith and Congressman Woodall."

49 Kim and Park Nelson, "Transnational Adoptees and US Citizenship."

50 United States House of Representatives, "Congressman Smith and Congressman Woodall."

51 Given Alex's age, she would have been covered under the Child Citizenship Act.

52 Dawson, *Behind the Mule*; Masuoka, "Together They Become One."

53 For more on the global Korean adoptee network, see Eleana J. Kim, *Adopted Territory*.

54 National Center for the Rights of the Child currently oversees pre- and post-adoption services in Korea.

55 International Korean Adoptee Association (IKAA) Network, 2017 mini-gathering in San Francisco.

56 2019 IKAA Gathering, Seoul.

57 Meier, "Cultural Identity and Place"; Tuan and Shiao, *Choosing Ethnicity, Negotiating Race*.

4. KOREAN PLUS SOMETHING ELSE

1 Stryker and Serpe, "Commitment, Identity Salience, and Role Behavior."

2 Hübinette, "Disembedded and Free-Floating Bodies"; Eleana J. Kim, *Adopted Territory*; Park Nelson, *Invisible Asians*.

3 Baden, "Do You Know Your Real Parents?"; Docan-Morgan, "Korean Adoptees' Retrospective Reports of Intrusive Interactions."

4 Eleanor Singer, "Reference Groups and Social Evaluations."

5 Eleana Kim's (*Adopted Territory*) ethnography of the beginnings of the global Korean adoptee network took place between 1999 and 2005 and included interviews with adoptees who were born or adopted between 1953 and 1986. Kim Park Nelson's (*Invisible Asians*) oral histories were taken from around 2003–2007 with Korean adoptees who were born between 1949 and 1983. Kristi Brian's (*Reframing Transracial Adoption*) work on Korean adoptive parents, adoptees, and practitioners was conducted from 2001 to 2003 and included adoptees adopted between 1958 and 1985.

6 Brian, *Reframing Transracial Adoption*; Kim, *Adopted Territory*; Park Nelson, *Invisible Asians*.

7 Kim, *Adopted Territory*, 85.

8 Park Nelson, *Invisible Asians*, 140.

9 Kim, Reichwald, and Lee, "Cultural Socialization."

10 Tuan, *Forever Foreigners or Honorary Whites?*; Nadia Y. Kim, *Imperial Citizens*.

11 Brian, *Reframing Transracial Adoption*; Palmer, *The Dance of Identities*; Park Nelson, *Invisible Asians*; Singer, "Reference Groups and Social Evaluations"; Tuan and Shiao, *Choosing Ethnicity, Negotiating Race*.

12 This mirrors research findings on multi-racial Asian Americans and the importance of phenotype and cultural exposure for reflected appraisals defining their self-concept. Nikki Khanna, "The Role of Reflected Appraisals in Racial Identity."

13 Prébin, "Three-Week Re-Education to Koreanness."

14 Eleana Kim, "Wedding Citizenship and Culture."

15 Gordon, *Assimilation in American Life*.

16 Mistry and Wu, "Navigating Cultural Worlds and Negotiating Identities."

17 Kim and Park Nelson, "Transnational Adoptees and US Citizenship."

18 Nguyen and Benet-Martínez, "Biculturalism Unpacked."

19 Stroink and Lalonde, "Bicultural Identity Conflict," 49.

20 Phinney and Devich-Navarro, "Variations in Bicultural Identification."

21 McAdams, "Narrative Identity."

22 Eleana J. Kim, *Adopted Territory*; Park Nelson, *Invisible Asians*.

23 Richardson and Schankweiler, "Affective Witnessing."

24 Baden, "Do You Know Your Real Parents?"

25 Amanda Baden identifies 13 different themes within common adoption microaggressions. According to Baden's framework, questions about birth family are a type of microinvalidation. Baden, "Do You Know Your Real Parents?"; Docan-Morgan, "Korean Adoptees' Retrospective Reports of Intrusive Interactions."

26 Chang, Feldman, and Easley, "I'm Learning Not to Tell You"; Sara Docan-Morgan, "They Don't Know What It's Like."

27 Ahmed, *The Cultural Politics of Emotion*, 156.

28 Park Nelson, "Loss Is More than Sadness."

29 Eleana J. Kim, *Adopted Territory*; Park Nelson, *Invisible Asians*.

30 McKee, *Disrupting Kinship*.

31 Tuan and Shiao, *Choosing Ethnicity, Negotiating Race*.

32 Smith and Mackie, "Dynamics of Group-Based Emotions."

33 Feagin, *The White Racial Frame*.

34 Park Nelson, *Invisible Asians*; Tuan and Shiao, *Choosing Ethnicity, Negotiating Race*.

35 Palmer, *The Dance of Identities*; Rigell, "I Guess Someone Forgot."

36 In her ethnography of Korean adoptees, Kim Park Nelson notes, "Travel to Korea also appeared to be almost a prerequisite for entry in to adoptee leadership circles." This speaks to socialization practices within adoptee communities— travel to Korea becomes a marker of group identity, defining the adoptee group culture. Park Nelson, *Invisible Asians*, 155.

37 Baden, Treweeke, and Ahluwalia, "Reclaiming Culture."

38 Baden, Treweeke, and Ahluwalia, "Reclaiming Culture."

39 Tuan, *Forever Foreigners or Honorary Whites?*

40 Tuan and Shiao, *Choosing Ethnicity, Negotiating Race*.

41 Kim, Reichwald, and Lee, "Cultural Socialization."

42 Although karaoke is enjoyed in many cultures, including the US, it takes on heightened cultural significance in Korea. Karaoke was introduced to Korea in the early 1980s but remained an adult form of entertainment (often linked with illicit behavior) until the 1990s. In the early 1990s, karaoke became a more family-friendly activity and quickly gained popularity across the country. Noraebang (translated "singing room") is the Korean word for karaoke and refers to how karaoke is performed in Korea. In Korean karaoke, groups of friends or business associates will rent a private karaoke room. There will also be snacks and often alcohol. It is not simply a sporadic leisure activity but integrated into Korean culture and business. Corporations will have noraebang as part of business retreats, and potential new business partners will karaoke as part of their business deals.

43 Waters, *Ethnic Options*.

44 The Janchi Show, Episode 21.

45 Snow and Anderson, "Identity Work among the Homeless."

5. OUR LIVES, OUR STORIES

1 Myers, "'REAL' FAMILIES."

2 Futerman and Miyamoto, *Twinsters*; Maxwell, *aka SEOUL*.

3 Chon, *Blue Bayou*.

4 Eleana Kim, "Korean Adoptee Auto-Ethnography."

5 Borshay Liem, *First Person Plural*; Adolfson, *Passing Through*; Tolle, *Searching for Go-Hyang*.

6 Oh, *To Save the Children of Korea.*

7 Arndt, *Crossing Chasms*; Theiler, *Great Girl*; Ahn, *living in half tones*; Tomes, *Looking for Wendy*; Adolfson, *Passing Through*; Tolle, *Searching for Go-Hyang.*

8 Park Nelson, "Loss Is More than Sadness."

9 McKee, *Disrupting Kinship*, 11.

10 McKee, "The Consumption of Adoption and Adoptees."

11 Muñoz, *Disidentifications*, 23.

12 COVID-19 disrupted the original plans for the 2022 IKAA Gathering. IKAA and the associated International Korean Adoption Studies Symposium were rescheduled for 2023.

13 Kim, *Adopted Territory*; Park Nelson, *Invisible Asians.*

14 As Richey Wyver argues, Sweden's national colorblind ideology and pro-adoption stance renders Swedish transnational transracial adoptees' racial difference "visible but disavowed." Adoptees are rendered as distinct from other immigrants and wholly Swedish, yet their racialized physical features makes their Swedish identity precarious. For more, see Wyver, "Too Brown to Be Swedish."

15 Many of the adoptee homeland tours are coordinated in conjunction with the Korean government and include cultural education, such as learning Korean history, traditional music, and cooking; visits to orphanages; and birth search. In her analysis of the Holt International Summer School, a three-week homeland program. Elise Prébin discusses how the program acts as a rite of passage, remaking Korean adoptees into members of the Korean diaspora. For more, see Prébin, "Three-Week Re-Education to Koreanness."

   Eleana Kim examines the Overseas Korea Foundation's homeland tour, a 10-day program, for how it attempts to make adoptees into "overseas Koreans" who will act as Korean ambassadors in their adoptive countries. Kim demonstrates how adoptee participants engaged in disidentification with normative constructions of what it means to be "Korean," thereby subverting the goals of the Korean government. Eleana Kim, "Wedding Citizenship and Culture."

16 Eleana J. Kim, *Adopted Territory.*

17 While *Twinsters* originally screened at SXSW in March 2015, it is likely that most adoptee viewers saw it once it was released via Netflix.

18 In December 2016, the South Korean National Assembly voted to impeach President Park due to a corruption scandal. In March of 2017, South Korea's Constitutional Court upheld the decision, and President Park was removed from office. Fifield, "South Korean President Removed."

19 Eleana Kim, "Our Adoptee, Our Alien"; Samuel S. Kim, *East Asia and Globalization.*

20 Eckert, *Park Chung Hee and Modern Korea.*

21 Eckert, *Park Chung Hee and Modern Korea.*

22 Oh, *To Save the Children of Korea.*
23 For an examination of how Korea attempts to leverage adoptees' return within its own state project and the limitations as experienced by Korean adoptees, see Eleana Kim, "Human Capital."
24 Myers, "'REAL' FAMILIES."
25 Muñoz, *Disidentifications*, 82–83.
26 Pate, *From Orphan to Adoptee*, 73; Oh, *To Save the Children of Korea*, 112.
27 Park Nelson, *Invisible Asians.*
28 Given Christine's age, it is likely that her biological mother had few options other than an unwed mothers' home. At that time, Korea had almost nonexistent social support services. This lack of social support was acute for single mothers. Unwed mothers' homes were primarily run by adoption agencies, and mothers who went to these homes but wanted to keep their child received less support than those who relinquished. For more, see Oh, *To Save the Children of Korea.*
29 At the time of our interview, Christine was developing a play about adoptees' stories. During the course of my remaining data collection, she completed the script for her play. The play premiered in the fall of 2017 and ran for one month. It was the topic of conversation among Korean adoptees and circulated among adoptee organizations. All shows sold out.
30 In fact, one of the prerequisites for being considered for *aka SEOUL* was to undertake a birth search.
31 Gates, *Finding Your Roots.*
32 NBC News, "NBC Asian America and ISAtv."
33 For example, Truth and Reconciliation for the Adoptee Community of Korea (TRACK) was key in the creation of the annual Single Moms' Day, a day to raise awareness about single motherhood in Korea and to encourage government support for single mothers; participated in revising the Special Adoption Law; and participated in National Assembly audits of the Ministry of Health and Welfare.
34 McKee, "The Consumption of Adoption and Adoptees."
35 McKee, "The Consumption of Adoption and Adoptees," 672.
36 Jones, "Adam Crapser's Bizarre Deportation Odyssey."
37 Child Citizenship Act of 2000, Pub. L. No. 106–395 (2000).
38 Haney López, *White by Law.*
39 Aguilar, "In 'Blue Bayou.'"
40 Nelson, "Someone Needs to Shed Light on This Issue."
41 In Gold House's virtual panel with Justin Chon, Jose Antonio Vargas (immigrant rights activist), and Kristopher Larsen (undocumented Vietnamese adoptee) on September 21, 2021, Chon stated that he had been locked out of his Facebook account and never saw Crapser's response.
42 NAKASEC, "Justin Chon's New Film."

43 NAKASEC, "Adoptees For Justice Demands a Response." In the Fall 2021 issue of *Korean Quarterly*, Becky Belcore, the executive director at NAKASEC, and a co-founder of A4J, explained, "Our understanding was that the film, per Crapser's request, would not be about his story and that it would include a call to action for the Adoptee Citizenship Act. After those initial discussions, we no longer received updates as to the content of the film. A screenplay was shared with us, but I did not read it, and, as far as I am aware, none of the other A4J board members at that time read it either. In August 2021, when I pre-screened the film shortly before its release, I was shocked to see that the agreements we made had been broken, as 1) the story was clearly based on Adam's life and 2) there was no call to action for the legislation." Adoptees For Justice, "The Right to His Own Story."

44 UnErased Podcast, "Introducing UnErased." The podcast included five episodes released from September to October 2021. While the five-episode format is similar to its previous topic on conversion therapy (four episodes), given the controversies around *Blue Bayou* it seems disingenuous to promote the podcast as evidence of adoptee support.

45 Adoptee Advocacy, "Statement from the Deported and Impacted Adoptee Community."

46 Kylie Cheung, "Justin Chon on His Heartbreaking 'Blue Bayou.'"

47 Eleana J. Kim, *Adopted Territory*.

48 Gold House Facebook panel, "Immigration, Adoption, & 'Blue Bayou,'" featuring Jose Antonio Vargas, Kristopher Larsen, Justin Chon, and Rebecca Sun, September 21, 2021.

49 Reappropriate, "Adoptees Call For Boycott."

50 Angry Asian Man, "They Call Us Bruce 134"; Reappropriate, "Bringing a Transnational Korean American Adoptee Story to Film"; Reappropriate, "Finding Peace in the End."

51 Kline, Karel, and Chatterjee, "Covering Adoption"; Myers, "'REAL' FAMILIES."

CONCLUSION

1 Choe, "Korean Adoptee Wins Landmark Case."

2 Vickery, "Her Father's Daughter."

3 In 2010 Korea's Nationality Law was amended to grant dual citizenship and adoptees were included as eligible.

4 Tong-Hyung Kim, "Nearly 300."

5 In January of 2019, Adam Crapser filed a similar lawsuit against the Korean government and the Korea office of Holt Children's Services for gross negligence. The amount of the civil suit, 200 million won (177,000 USD), was symbolic. Ultimately, it was the government's and adoption agency's acknowledgement of culpability that Adam sought. The first hearing for Adam's lawsuit was held in August of that same year. Over 60 South Korean–born international adoptees and adoptee rights advocates squeezed into the small district courtroom in support of

Adam and his lawsuit. After opening statements from Adam's lawyer, the Korean government, and Holt, the session adjourned without setting a date for the next hearing. See Hafner, "First Hearing in Holt Lawsuit."

6 Young-joon Ahn, "More South Korean Adoptees."

7 S. 1291, DREAM Act, 107th Congress, 2001–2002.

8 Haynes, Merolla, and Ramakrishnan, *Framing Immigrants*.

9 US Department of Homeland Security, "Memorandum to David V. Aguilar."

10 Bruno, "Deferred Action for Childhood Arrivals (DACA)."

11 Haynes, Merolla, and Ramakrishnan, *Framing Immigrants*.

BIBLIOGRAPHY

AAPIData. "One Out of Every 7 Asian Immigrants Is Undocumented." *AAPIData*. September 8, 2017. www.aapidata.com.

Adolfson, Nathan, dir. *Passing Through*. San Francisco: Center for Asia American Media, 1999.

Adoptees For Justice. "The Right to His Own Story." *Korean Quarterly*, 2021. www.koreanquarterly.org.

Adoptee Advocacy. "Statement from the Deported and Impacted Adoptee Community in Support of *Blue Bayou*." September 27, 2021. www.facebook.com/anissa.druese-dowdethelwell/posts/pfbid02pVhVytbr2d2uVx6fZaEVez51N5QWXHtHaWzbhX-mAoRZwD74PLWdLKKEzWNEgjejml.

Adoptee Rights Campaign. "How ARC Came to Support the 2019 Adoptee Citizenship Act." March 14, 2018. www.facebook.com/citizenshipforalladoptees/posts/pfbid-02NRaMfkYMpbbsGD7KSfydRpkBLNkdXtLNen31ghET3aVeGPbBaeEy2FN8bFt-BN3Gol.

Aguilar, Carlos. "In 'Blue Bayou,' Justin Chon Demands Justice for Adopted Immigrants Facing Deportation." *Los Angeles Times*, September 17, 2021. www.latimes.com.

Ahmed, Sara. *The Cultural Politics of Emotions*. New York: Routledge, 2004.

Ahmed, Sara. "Happy Objects." In the *The Affect Theory Reader*, edited by Melissa Gregg and Gregory J. Seigworth, 29–51. Durham, NC: Duke University Press, 2010.

Ahn, Me-K, dir. *living in half tones*. New York: Third World Newsreel, 1994.

Ahn, Young-joon. "More South Korean Adoptees Who were Sent Overseas Demand Probes into Their Cases." NPR, December 9, 2022. www.npr.org.

Alcoff, Linda Martín. "Latino/as, Asian Americans, and the Black-White Binary." *Journal of Ethics* 7, no. 1 (2003): 5–27.

Alexander, Michelle. *The New Jim Crow: Mass Incarceration in the Age of Colorblindness*. New York: The New Press, 2010.

An, Sohyun. "Asian Americans in American History: An AsianCrit Perspective on Asian American Inclusion in State U.S. History Curriculum Standards." *Theory and Research in Social Education* 44, no. 2 (2016): 244–276.

Angry Asian Man. "#KeepAdamHome: Stop Adam Crapser's Deportation Now." *Angry Asian Man*, March 3, 2015. http://blog.angryasianman.com.

Angry Asian Man. "They Call Us Bruce 134: They Call Us Justin Chon." *Angry Asian Man*, September 17, 2021. http://blog.angryasianman.com.

Arndt, Jennifer Christine Yang Hee, dir. *Crossing Chasms*. Neenah, WI: Rainbow World, 1998.

Associated Press. "Feds Targeted Adoptee without Citizenship Because of Crimes." *Associated Press*, November 1, 2016. www.nbcnews.com.

Baden, Amanda. "'Do You Know Your Real Parents?' and Other Adoption Microaggressions." *Adoption Quarterly* 19, no. 1 (2016): 1–25.

Baden, Amanda., Lisa M. Treweeke, and Muninder K. Ahluwalia. "Reclaiming Culture: Reculturation of Transracial and International Adoptees." *Journal of Counseling and Development* 90, no. 4 (2012): 387–399.

Balistreri, Kelly Stamper, Kara Joyner, and Grace Kao. "Relationship Involvement among Young Adults: Are Asian American Men an Exceptional Case?" *Population Research and Policy Review* 34, no. 5 (2015): 709–732.

Baumgaertner, Emily. "Atlanta-Area Spa Shootings Highlight Knotted Intersection of Sexism and Racism, Scholars Say." *Los Angeles Times*, March 19, 2021.www.latimes.com.

Berbery, Maria Luz, and Karen M. O'Brien. "Predictors of White Adoptive Parents' Cultural and Racial Socialization Behaviors with Their Asian Adopted Children." *Adoption Quarterly* 14 (2011): 284–304.

Bersani, Bianca E., Adam D. Fine, Alex R. Piquero, Laurence Steinberg, Paul J. Frick, and Elizabeth Cauffman. "Investigating the Offending Histories of Undocumented Immigrants." *Migration Letters* 15, no. 2 (2018): 147–166.

Bonilla-Silva, Eduardo. "Feeling Race: Theorizing the Racial Economy of Emotions." *American Sociological Review* 84, no. 1 (2019): 1–25.

Bonilla-Silva, Eduardo. "We Are All Americans!: The Latin Americanization of Racial Stratification in the USA." *Race and Society* 5, no. 1 (2002): 3–16.

Bonilla-Silva, Eduardo, Carla Goar, and David G. Embrick. "When Whites Flock Together: The Social Psychology of White Habitus." *Critical Sociology* 32, no. 2–3 (2005): 229–253.

Borshay Liem, Deann, dir. *First Person Plural*. Brooklyn, NY: PBS POV, 2000.

Brian, Kristi. *Reframing Transracial Adoption: Adopted Koreans, White Parents, and the Politics of Kinship*. Philadelphia: Temple University Press, 2012.

Briggs, Laura. "Mother, Child, Race, Nation: The Visual Iconography of Rescue and the Politics of Transnational and Transracial Adoption." *Gender and History* 15, no. 2 (2003): 179–200.

Bruno, Andorra. "Deferred Action for Childhood Arrivals (DACA): By the Numbers." April 14, 2021. R46764. https://crsreports.congress.gov.

Chang, Doris F., Kalli Feldman, and Hailey Easley. "'I'm Learning Not to Tell You': Korean Transracial Adoptees' Appraisals of Parental Racial Socialization Strategies and Perceived Effects." *Asian American Journal of Psychology* 8, no. 4 (2017): 308–322.

Chang, Robert S. *Disoriented: Asian Americans, Law, and the Nation-State*. New York: New York University Press, 1999.

Cheng, Cindy I-Fen. *Citizens of Asian America: Democracy and Race during the Cold War*. New York: New York University Press, 2013.

Cheung, Kylie. "Justin Chon on His Heartbreaking 'Blue Bayou': 'I Wanted to Do Justice to the Adoptee Community.'" *Salon*, September 18, 2021. www.salon.com.

Chin, Frank, Jeffrey Paul Chan, Lawson Fusao Inada, and Shawn Wong. *Aiiieeeee!: An Anthology of Asian American Writers*. 3rd ed. Seattle: University of Washington Press, 2019.

Choe, Sang-Hun. "Korean Adoptee Wins Landmark Case in Search for Birth Parents." *New York Times*, June 12, 2020. www.nytimes.com.

Chon, Justin, dir. *Blue Bayou*. Universal City, CA: Focus Features, 2022.

Choy, Catherine Ceniza. *Asian American Histories of the United States*. Boston: Beacon Press, 2022.

Choy, Catherine Ceniza. *Global Families: A History of Asian International Adoption in America*. New York: New York University Press, 2013.

Chung, Soojin. *Adopting for God: The Mission to Change America through Transnational Adoption*. New York: New York University Press, 2021.

Conway, Leana. "Tony Baker." *Enjoy Cherokee*, January 6, 2021. https://enjoycherokee.com.

Dawson, Michael C. *Behind the Mule: Race and Class in African-American Politics*. Princeton, NJ: Princeton University Press, 1994.

Docan-Morgan, Sara. "Korean Adoptees' Retrospective Reports of Intrusive Interactions: Exploring Boundary Management in Adoptive Families." *Journal of Family Communication* 10, no. 3 (2010): 137–157.

Docan-Morgan, Sara. "'They Don't Know What It's Like to Be in My Shoes': Topic Avoidance about Race in Transracially Adoptive Families." *Journal of Social and Personal Relationships* 28, no. 3 (2011): 336–355.

Dorow, Sara. "Racialized Choices: Chinese Adoption and the 'White Noise' of Blackness." *Critical Sociology* 32, no. 2 (2006): 357–279.

Du Bois, W. E. B. "Strivings of the Negro People." *The Atlantic*, August 1897. www.theatlantic.com.

Du Bois, W. E. B. "The Souls of White Folk." In *Darkwater: Voices from Within the Veil*, edited by Henry Louis Gates Jr. Oxford: Oxford University Press, 2007.

Eaton, Asia Anna, and Suzanna Rose. "Has Dating Become More Egalitarian? A 35 Year Review Using Sex Roles." *Sex Roles* 64 (2011): 843–862.

Eckert, Carter J. *Park Chung Hee and Modern Korea: The Roots of Militarism, 1866–1945*. Cambridge: The Belknap Press of Harvard University Press, 2016.

Edmonds, Christina, and Melanie Killen. "Do Adolescents' Perceptions of Parental Racial Attitudes Relate to Their Intergroup Contact and Cross-Race Relationships?" *Group Processes and Intergroup Relations* 12, no. 1 (2009): 5–21.

Eng, David L. "Transnational Adoption and Queer Diasporas." *Social Text* 21, no. 3 (2003): 1–37.

Eng, David L., and Shinhee Han. *Racial Melancholia, Racial Dissociation: On the Social and Psychic Lives of Asian Americans.* Durham, NC: Duke University Press, 2018.

Espiritu, Yen Le. *Asian American Women and Men: Labor, Laws, and Love.* Lanham, MD: Rowman & Littlefield Publishers, 2003.

Espiritu, Yen Le. *Homebound: Filipino American Lives across Culture, Communities, and Countries.* Berkeley: University of California Press, 2003.

Fanon, Frantz. *Black Skin, White Masks.* New York: Grove Press, 2008.

Fausset, Richard, Nicholas Bogel-Burroughs, and Marie Fazio. "The Suspect in the Spa Attacks Has Been Charged with Eight Counts of Murder." *New York Times,* July, 27, 2021. www.nytimes.com.

Feagin, Joe R. *Racist America.* 2nd ed. New York: Routledge, 2010.

Feagin, Joe R. *The White Racial Frame: Centuries of Racial Framing and Counter-Framing.* New York: Routledge, 2013.

Fifield, Anna. "South Korean President Removed from Office over Corruption Scandal." *Washington Post,* March 10, 2017. www.washingtonpost.com.

Frankenberg, Ruth. *White Women, Race Matters: The Social Construction of Whiteness.* Minneapolis: University of Minnesota Press, 1993.

Frost, Linda. *Never One Nation: Freaks, Savages, and Whiteness in U.S. Popular Culture, 1850–1877.* Minneapolis: University of Minnesota Press, 2005.

Futerman, Samantha, and Ryan Miyamoto, dir. *Twinsters.* Los Gatos, CA: Netflix, 2015.

Gans, Herbert. "The Possibility of a New Racial Hierarchy in the Twenty-first Century United States." In *The Cultural Territories of Race: Black and White Boundaries,* edited by Michèle Lamont, 371–390. Chicago: University of Chicago Press and Russell Sage Foundation, 1999.

Gans, Herbert. "Symbolic Ethnicity." *Ethnic and Racial Studies* 2 (1979): 1–20.

Garcia Hernández, Cesar Cuauhtémoc. "Creating Crimmigration." *Brigham Young University Law Review* 6 (2014): 1457–1515.

Gates, Henry Louis Jr., executive producer. *Finding Your Roots.* TV series. PBS, 2012.

Gazillion Voices. "Adam Crapser: Gazillion Voices Radio." *Soundcloud,* 2015. https://Soundcloud.Com/Gazillion-Voices/.

Goss, Devon R., W. Carson Byrd, and Matthew W. Hughey. "Racial Authenticity and Familial Acceptance among Transracial Adoptees: A Bothersome Bargain of Belonging." *Symbolic Interaction* 40, no. 2 (2017): 147–168.

Gordon, Milton M. *Assimilation in American Life: The Role of Race, Religion, and National Origins.* New York: Oxford University Press, 1964.

Gossett, DeLeith Duke. "'[Take from Us Our] Wretched Refuse': The Deportation of America's Adoptees." *University of Cincinnati Law Review* 85 (2017): 1–57.

Graves, Kori A. *A War Born Family: African American Adoption in the Wake of the Korean War.* New York: New York University Press, 2020.

Gustafsson, Ryan. "Theorizing Korean Transracial Adoptee Experiences: Ambiguity, Substitutability, and Racial Embodiment." *International Journal of Cultural Studies* 24, no. 2 (2021): 309–324.

Hafner, Liza. "First Hearing in Holt Lawsuit by Korean Adoptee Deported from US Highlights Fight for Transparency, Adoptee Rights." *Korea Herald*, August 18, 2019. www.koreaherald.com.

Haney López, Ian. *White by Law: The Legal Construction of Race.* 10th Anniversary ed. New York: New York University Press, 2006.

Hagerman, Margaret. "White Families and Race: Colour-Blind and Colour-Conscious Approaches to White Racial Socialization." *Ethnic and Racial Studies* 37, no. 14 (2014): 2598–2614.

Hayes, Christal. "Georgia Sheriff Spokesman in Spa Shootings Removed from Case after 'Bad Day' Comment, Controversial Anti-China Shirt." *USAToday*, March 18, 2021. www.usatoday.com.

Haynes, Chris, Jennifer Merolla, and S. Karthick Ramakrishnan. *Framing Immigrants: News Coverage, Public Opinion, and Policy.* New York: Russell Sage Foundation, 2016.

Herman, Ellen. *Kinship by Design: A History of Adoption in the Modern United State.* Chicago: University of Chicago Press, 2008.

Hewitt, Scott. "International Adoptee Faces Deportation." *Columbian*, March 29, 2015. www.columbian.com.

Hill Collins, Patricia. *Black Feminist Thought: Knowledge, Consciousness, and the Politics of Empowerment.* New York: Routledge, 2000.

Ho, Jennifer Ann. *Racial Ambiguity in Asian American Culture.* New Brunswick: Rutgers University Press, 2015.

Holper, Mary. "The Unreasonable Seizures of Shadow Deportations." *University of Cincinnati Law Review* 86, no. 3 (2018): 923–970.

Hong, Cathy Park. *Minor Feelings: An Asian American Reckoning.* New York: Penguin Random House, 2020.

Hübinette, Tobias. "Adopted Koreans and Development of Identity in the 'Third Space.'" *Adoption & Fostering* 28, no. 1 (2004): 16–24.

Hübinette, Tobias. "Comforting an Orphaned Nation: Representations of International Adoption and Adopted Koreans in Popular Culture." PhD dissertation, Stockholm University, 2005.

Hübinette, Tobias. "Disembedded and Free-Floating Bodies Out of Place and Out of Control: Examining the Borderline Existence of Adopted Koreans." *Adoption and Culture* 1, no. 1 (2007): 129–162.

Ioanide, Paula. *The Emotional Politics of Racism: How Feelings Trump Facts in an Era of Colorblindness.* Stanford, CA: Stanford University Press, 2015.

Jacobson, Heather. *Culture Keeping: White Mothers, International Adoption, and the Negotiation of Family Difference.* Nashville: Vanderbilt University Press, 2008.

Jeung, Russell, Aggie Yellow Horse, Tara Popovic, and Richard Lim. "Stop AAPI Hate National Report 3/19/20–2/28/21." Stop AAPI Hate, 2021.

Jo, Moon H. and Daniel D. Mast. "Changing Images of Asian Americans." *International Journal of Politics, Culture and Society* 6, no. 3 (1993): 417–441.

Jones, Maggie. "Adam Crapser's Bizarre Deportation Odyssey." *New York Times Magazine*, April 1, 2015. www.nytimes.com.

Mark C. Jerng. *Claiming Others: Transracial Adoption and National Belonging*. Minneapolis: University of Minnesota Press, 2010.

Khanna, Nikki. "The Role of Reflected Appraisals in Racial Identity: The Case of Multiracial Asians." *Social Psychology Quarterly* 67, no. 2 (2004): 115–131.

Kiang, Lisa, Tiffany Yip, Melinda Gonzales-Backen, Melissa Witkow, and Andrew J. Fuligni. "Ethnic Identity and the Daily Psychological Well-Being of Adolescents From Mexican and Chinese Backgrounds." *Child Development* 77, no. 5 (2006): 1338–1350.

Kibria, Nazli. "Race, Ethnic Options, and Ethnic Binds: Identity Negotiations of Second-Generation Chinese and Korean Americans." *Sociological Perspectives* 43, no. 1 (2000): 77–95.

Kim, Claire Jean. "The Racial Triangulation of Asian Americans." *Politics & Society* 27, no. 1 (1999): 105–138.

Kim, Eleana J. *Adopted Territory: Transnational Korean Adoptees and the Politics of Belonging*. Durham, NC: Duke University Press, 2010.

Kim, Eleana. "Human Capital: Transnational Korean Adoptees and the Neoliberal Logic of Return." *Journal of Korean Studies* 17, no. 2 (2012): 299–327.

Kim, Eleana. "Korean Adoptee Auto-Ethnography: Refashioning Self, Family, and Finding Community." *Visual Anthropology Review* 16, no. 1 (2000): 43–70.

Kim, Eleana. "Our Adoptee, Our Alien: Transnational Adoptees as Specters of Foreignness and Family in South Korea." *Anthropological Quarterly* 80, no. 2 (2007): 497–531.

Kim, Eleana. "Wedding Citizenship and Culture: Korean Adoptees and the Global Family of Korea." *Social Text* 21, no. 1 (2003): 57–81.

Kim, Eleana, and Kim Park Nelson. "'Natural Born Aliens': Transnational Adoptees and US Citizenship." *Adoption and Culture* 7, no. 2 (2019): 257–279.

Kim, Grace S., Karen L. Suyemoto, and Castellano B. Turner. "Sense of Belonging, Sense of Exclusion, and Racial and Ethnic Identities in Korean Transracial Adoptees." *Cultural Diversity and Ethnic Minority Psychology* 16, no. 2 (2010): 179–190.

Kim, Nadia Y. *Imperial Citizens: Koreans and Race from Seoul to LA*. Stanford, CA: Stanford University Press, 2008.

Kim, Oh Myo, Reed Reichwald, and Richard Lee. "Cultural Socialization in Families with Adopted South Korean Adolescents: A Mixed-Method, Multi-Informant Study." *Journal of Adolescent Research* 28, no. 1 (2013): 69–95.

Kim, Samuel S. *East Asia and Globalization*. Lanham, MD: Rowman and Littlefield, 2000.

Kim Tong-Hyung. "Nearly 300 Demand South Korea Probe Their Adoptions Abroad." *AP News*, September 13, 2022. https://apnews.com.

Kline, Susan L., Amanda I. Karel, and Karishma Chatterjee. "Covering Adoption: General Depictions in Broadcast News." *Family Relations* 55, no. 4 (2006): 487–498.

Laybourn, SunAh M, and Carla Goar. "'In My Heart, I Am Cambodian': Symbolic Ethnicity among Parents Who Adopt Transracially." *Sociology of Race and Ethnicity* 8, no. 1 (2022): 145–159.

Leading Asian Americans to Unite for Change (LAAUNCH). STAATUS Index 2022. www.staatus-index.org.

Lee, Erika. *American for Americans: The History of Xenophobia in the United States.* New York: Basic Books, 2019.

Lee, Erika. "The Chinese Exclusion Example: Race, Immigration, and American Gatekeeping, 1882–1924." *Journal of American Ethnic History* 21, no. 3 (2002): 36–62.

Lee, Erika. *The Making of Asian America: A History.* New York: Simon & Schuster, 2015.

Lee, Richard M. "The Transracial Adoption Paradox: History, Research, and Counseling Implications of Cultural Socialization." *Counseling Psychologist* 31, no. (2003): 711–744.

Lee, Richard M., Harold D. Grotevant, Wendy L. Hellerstedt, Megan R. Gunnar, and The Minnesota International Adoption Project Team. "Cultural Socialization in Families with Internationally Adopted Children." *Journal of Family Psychology* 20, no. 4 (2006): 571–580.

Lewis, Amanda E. "'What Group?' Studying White and Whiteness in The Era of Color-Blindness." *Sociological Theory* 22, no. 4 (2004): 623–646.

Light, Michael T., and Ty Miller. "Does Undocumented Immigration Increase Violent Crime?" *Criminology* 56, no. 2 (2018): 7–401.

Light, Michael T., Ty Miller, and Brian C. Kelly. "Undocumented Immigration, Drug Problems, and Driving Under Influence in the United States, 1990–2014." *American Journal of Public Health* 107, no. 9 (2017): 1448–1454.

Lipsitz, George. "The Possessive Investment in Whiteness: Racialized Social Democracy and the 'White' Problem in American Studies." *American Quarterly* 47, no. 3 (1995): 369–387.

Lowe, Lisa. *Immigrant Acts: On Asian American Cultural Politics.* Durham, NC: Duke University Press, 1996.

Masuoka, Natalie. "Together They Become One: Examining the Predictors of Panethnic Group Consciousness Among Asian Americans and Latinos." *Social Science Quarterly* 87, no. 5 (2006): 993–1011.

Mawell, Jon, dir. *aka SEOUL.* New York: NBC Asian America, 2016.

Meier, Daniel. "Cultural Identity and Place in Adult Korean American Intercountry Adoptees." *Adoption Quarterly* 3 (1999): 15–48.

McAdams, Dan P. "Narrative Identity." In *Handbook of Identity Theory and Research,* edited by Seth J. Schwartz, Koen Luyckx, and Vivian L. Vignoles, 99–115. New York: Springer, 2011.

McGinnis, Hollee, Susan Livingston Smith, Scott D. Ryan, and Jeannne A. Howard. *Beyond Culture Camp: Promoting Healthy Identity Formation in Adoption.* New York: Evan B. Donaldson Adoption Institute, 2009.

McKee, Kimberly. "The Consumption of Adoption and Adoptees in American Middle-brow Culture." *Biography* 42, no. 3 (2019): 669–692.

McKee, Kimberly. *Disrupting Kinship: Transnational Politics of Korean Adoption in the United States.* Champaign: University of Illinois Press, 2019.

McKee, Kimberly D. "Monetary Flows and the Movements of Children: The Trans-national Adoption Industrial Complex." *Journal of Korean Studies* 21, no. 1 (2016): 137–178.

McTaggart, Ninochka, Michele Meyer, Meredith Conroy, Romeo Perez, Cameron Espinoza, Sarah Trinh, Pamela Campos, Emma Burrows, Jenna Virgo, Camryn Brennan, Isabel Dolan, Cris Ackel, and Sofie Christensen. *I Am Not a Fetish or Model Minority: Redefining What It Means to Be API in the Entertainment Industry.* Los Angeles: Geena Davis Institute on Gender in Media, 2021.

Mistry, Jayanthi, and Jean Wu. "Navigating Cultural Worlds and Negotiating Identities: A Conceptual Model." *Human Development* 53 (2010): 1–21.

Molina, Natalia. *How Race Is Made in America: Immigration, Citizenship, and the Historical Power of Racial Scrips.* Berkeley: University of California Press, 2014.

Motomura, Hiroshi. *Americans in Waiting: The Lost Story of Immigration and Citizenship in the United States.* Oxford: Oxford University Press, 2007.

Mueller, Jennifer C. "Racial Ideology or Racial Ignorance? An Alternative Theory of Racial Cognition." *Sociological Theory* 38, no. 2 (2020): 142–169.

Muñoz, José Esteban. *Disidentifications: Queers of Color and the Performance of Politics.* Minneapolis: University of Minnesota Press, 1999.

Myers, Kit. "'REAL' FAMILIES: The Violence of Love in New Media Adoption Discourse." *Critical Discourse Studies* 11, no. 2 (2014): 175–193.

NAKASEC. "Adoptees For Justice Demands a Response from Justin Chon and Focus Features." September 28, 2021. https://adopteesforjustics.org.

NAKASEC. "Justin Chon's New Film Blue Bayou Exploits Impacted Members of Our Community." September 21, 2021. https://adopteesforjustics.org.

National Association of Black Social Workers. "Position Statement on Trans-Racial Adoptions." New York, 1972.

NBC News. "NBC Asian America and ISAtv to Present First Feature Film in San Diego." *NBC News,* October 24, 2016. www.nbcnews.com.

Neblett, Enrique W., Deborah Rivas-Drake, and Adriana J. Umaña-Taylor. "The Promise of Racial and Ethnic Protective Factors in Promoting Ethnic Minority Youth Development." *Child Development Perspectives* 6, no. 3 (2012): 295–303.

Nelson, Kim. "'Someone Needs to Shed Light on This Issue': Justin Chon on His Adoptee Deportation Melodrama, Blue Bayou." *Filmmaker Magazine.* September 16, 2021. www.filmmakermagazine.com.

Newton, Lina. *Illegal, Alien, or Immigrant: The Politics of Immigration Reform.* New York: New York University Press, 2008.

Nguyen, Angela-MinhTu D., and Veronica Benet-Martínez. "Biculturalism Unpacked: Components, Individual Differences, Measurement, and Outcomes." *Social and Personality Psychology Compass* 1 (2007): 101–114.

Oh, Arissa H. *To Save the Children of Korea: The Cold War Origins of International Adoption.* Stanford, CA: Stanford University Press, 2015.

Okihiro, Gary Y. *Margins & Mainstream: Asians in American History and Culture.* Seattle: University of Washington Press, 2014.

Painter, Nell. *The History of White People.* New York: W. W. Norton & Company, Inc., 2010.

Palmer, John D. *The Dance of Identities: Korean Adoptees and Their Journey Toward Empowerment.* Honolulu: University of Hawaii Press, 2010.

Pate, SooJin. *From Orphan to Adoptee: U.S. Empire and Genealogies of Korean Adoption.* Minneapolis: University of Minnesota Press, 2014.

Perea, Juan F. "The Black/White Binary Paradigm of Race: The Normal Science of American Racial Thought." *California Law Review* 85, no. 5 (1997): 127–171.

Pérez, Raúl. *The Souls of White Jokes: How Racist Humor Fuels White Supremacy.* Stanford, CA: Stanford University Press, 2022.

Park, Michael. "Asian American Masculinity Eclipsed: A Legal and Historical Perspective of Emasculation through U.S. Immigration Practices." *Modern American* 8, no. 1 (2013): 5–17.

Park Nelson, Kim. *Invisible Asians: Korean American Adoptees, Asian American Experiences, and Racial Exceptionalism.* New Brunswick, NJ: Rutgers University Press, 2016.

Park Nelson, Kim. "'Loss Is More than Sadness': Reading Dissent in Transracial Adoption Melodrama in *The Language of Blood* and *First Person Plural*." *Adoption and Culture* 1, no. 1 (2017): 101–128.

Perry, Alyssa Jeong. "After 37 Years in US, Korean Adoptee Speaks out about Imminent Deportation." *Guardian*, October 28, 2016. www.theguardian.com.

Perry, Alyssa Jeong. "Korean Adoptee in Immigration Battle Fights to Remain in His Country—The US." *Guardian*, April 3, 2015. www.theguardian.com.

Phinney, Jean, and Mona Devich-Navarro. "Variations in Bicultural Identification among African American and Mexican American adolescents." *Journal of Research on Adolescence* 7 (1997): 3–32.

Picca, Leslie Houts, and Joe R. Feagin. *Two-Faced Racism: Whites in the Backstage and Frontstage.* New York: Routledge, 2007.

Pinder, Sherrow O. "Whiteness: The Definitive Conceptualization of an American Identity." In *The Politics of Race and Ethnicity in the United States*, 39–65. New York: Palgrave Macmillan, 2010.

Prébin, Elise. "Three-Week Re-Education to Koreanness." *European Journal of East Asian Studies* 7, no. 2 (2008): 323–355.

Provine, Doris Marie. *Unequal under Law: Race in the War on Drugs.* Chicago: University of Chicago Press, 2007.

Pyke, Karen. D. and Denise L. Johnson. "Asian American Women and Racialized Femininities: 'Doing' Gender across Cultural Worlds." *Gender and Society* 17, no. 1 (2003): 3–49.

Quiroz, Pamela Anne. "Cultural Tourism in Transnational Adoption: 'Staged Authenticity' and Its Implications for Adopted Children." *Journal of Family Issues* 33, no. 4 (2012): 527–555.

Raleigh, Elizabeth. *Selling Transracial Adoption: Families, Markets, and the Color Line.* Philadelphia: Temple University Press, 2018.

Reappropriate. "Adoptees Call For Boycott of 'Blue Bayou.'" *Reappropriate*, September 21, 2021. http://reappropriate.co.

Reappropriate. "Bringing a Transnational Korean American Adoptee Story to Film: In Conversation with 'Blue Bayou' Filmmaker Justin Chon." *Reappropriate*, September 17, 2021. http://reappropriate.co.

Reappropriate. "Finding Peace in the End: In Conversation with Blue Bayou's Linh-Dan Pham." *Reappropriate*, September 17, 2021. http://reappropriate.co.

Reappropriate. "Pending Deportation of Korean American Adoptee Highlights Major Loophole in Immigration Law." *Reappropriate*, March 3, 2015. http://reappropriate.co.

Reappropriate. "Petition: Stop Deportation of Adult Adoptees and #KeepAdamHome." *Reappropriate*, March 12, 2015. http://reappropriate.co.

Richardson, Michael, and Kerstin Schankweiler. "Affective Witnessing." In *Affective Societies: Key Concepts*, edited by Jan Slaby and Christian von Scheve, 166–177. New York: Routledge, 2019.

Rigell, Molly Jin Ah. "'I Guess Someone Forgot to Ask Us if We Wanted to Be America's Diversity Mascots': The Identity Journey of Transracial, Transnational, Korean Adoptees." Master's thesis, University of Tennessee, 2015.

Robnett, Belinda, and Cynthia Feliciano. "Patterns of Racial-Ethnic Exclusion by Internet Daters." *Social Forces* 89, no. 3 (2011): 807–828.

Roediger, David R. *The Wages of Whiteness: Race and the Making of the American Working Class.* Brooklyn: Verso Books, 2007.

Rothstein, Richard. *The Color of Law: A Forgotten History of How Our Government Segregated America.* New York: Norton, 2017.

Santa Ana, Jeffrey. *Racial Feelings: Asian America in a Capitalist Culture of Emotion.* Philadelphia: Temple University Press, 2015.

Schuetza, Jenny, Jeff Larrimore, Ellen A. Merry, Barbara J. Robles, Anna Tranfaglia, Arturo Gonzalez. "Are Central Cities Poor and Non-White?" *Journal of Housing Economics* 40 (2018): 83–94.

Selsky, Adam. "Abuse, Crime Haunted Adoptee from South Korea Who Is Set to be Deported." *Seattle Times*, November 1, 2016. www.seattletimes.com.

Serrano-Villar, Maria and Esther J. Calzada. "Ethnic Identity: Evidence of Protective Effects for Young, Latino Children." *Journal of Applied Developmental Psychology* 42 (2016): 21–30.

Shah, Hemant. "Race, Nation, and Citizenship: Asian Indians and the Idea of Whiteness in the U.S. Press, 1906–1923." *Howard Journal of Communications* 10, no. 4 (1999): 249–267.

Shoichet, Catherine E. "Americans Adopted Him; Now He's Facing Deportation." *CNN News*, November 7, 2016. www.cnn.com.

Singer, Eleanor. "Reference Groups and Social Evaluations." In *Social Psychology: Sociological Perspectives*, edited by Morris Rosenberg and Ralph H. Turner, 66–93. New York: BasicBooks, 1981.

Smith, Eliot R., and Diane M. Mackie. "Dynamics of Group-Based Emotions: Insights from Intergroup Emotions Theory." *Emotion Review* 7, no. 4 (2015): 349–354.

Snow, David A., and Leon Anderson. "Identity Work among the Homeless: The Verbal Construction and Avowal of Personal Identities." *American Journal of Sociology* 92, no. 6 (1987): 1136–1371.

Snow, David A., and Doug McAdam. "Identity Work Processes in the Context of Social Movements: Clarifying the Identity/Movement Nexus." In *Self, Identity, and Social Movements*, edited by Sheldon Stryker, Timothy J. Owens, and Robert W White, 41–67. Minneapolis: University of Minnesota Press, 2000.

Snow, David A., and Pamela E. Oliver. "Social Movements and Collective Behavior: Social Psychological Dimensions and Considerations" In *Sociological Perspectives on Social Psychology*, edited by Karen Cook, Gary A. Fine, and James S. House, 571–600. Boston: Allyn and Bacon, 1995.

Song, Miri. *Choosing Ethnic Identity*. Cambridge: Polity Press, 2003.

Stroink, Mirella. L., and Richard N. Lalonde. "Bicultural Identity Conflict in Second-Generation Asian Canadians." *Journal of Social Psychology* 149 (2009): 44–65.

Stryker, Sheldon, and Richard T. Serpe. "Commitment, Identity Salience, and Role Behavior: Theory and Research Example." In *Personality, Roles, and Social Behavior*, edited by William Ickes and Eric S. Knowles, 199–218. New York: Springer, 1982.

The Janchi Show. Episode 21, "Adoptee Advocacy + Munch Addict!" January 12, 2021. https://janchishow.com.

Theiler, Kim Su, dir. *Great Girl*. New York: Women Make Movies, 1994.

Tolle, Tammy, dir. *Searching for Go-Hyang*. New York: Women Make Movies, 1998.

Tomes, Kimberly SaRee, dir. *Looking for Wendy*. New York: Third World Newsreel, 1997.

Tuan, Mia. *Forever Foreigners or Honorary Whites?: The Asian Ethnic Experience Today*. New Brunswick, NJ: Rutgers University Press, 1998.

Tuan, Mia, and Jiannbin Lee Shiao. *Choosing Ethnicity, Negotiating Race: Korean Adoptees in America*. New York: Russell Sage Foundation, 2011.

UnErased Podcast. "Introducing UnErased: The Deportation of Adoptees in America." Episode 1 description. September 16, 2021. http://open.spotify.com; http://podcast.apple.com.

US Department of Homeland Security. "Memorandum to David V. Aguilar, Acting Commissioner, U.S. Customs and Border Protection, Alejandro Mayorkas, Director, U.S. Citizenship and Immigration Services, John Morton, Director, U.S. Immigration and Customs Enforcement, from Janet Napolitano, Secretary of Homeland Security, Exercising Prosecutorial Discretion with Respect to Individuals Who Came to the United States as Children." June 15, 2012. www.dhs.gov.

US Department of Homeland Security. "Table 39. Aliens Removed or Returned: Fiscal Years 1892 to 2019." 2019. www.dhs.gov.

United States House of Representatives. "Congressman Smith and Congressman Woodall Introduce Adoptee Citizenship Act of 2019." Press Release. May 14, 2019. www.adamsmith.house.gov.

United States Senate. "Blunt, Hirono, Collins, Klobuchar Introduce Adoptee Citizenship Act of 2019." Press Release. May 22, 2019. www.blunt.senate.gov.

Vargas, Jose Antonio. *Dear America: Notes of an Undocumented Citizen*. New York: HarperCollins, 2018.

Vickery, Martha. "Her Father's Daughter." *Korean Quarterly*, Summer 2020 issue. www.koreanquarterly.org.

Vonk, M. Elizabeth, Sung Hyun Yun, Wansoo Park, and Richard R. Massatti. "Transracial Adoptive Parents' Thoughts about The Importance of Race and Culture in Parenting." In *International Korean Adoption: A Fifty-Year History of Policy and Practice*, edited by Kathleen Ja Sook Bergquist, M. Elizabeth Vonk, Dong Soo Kim, and Marvin D. Feit, 99–112. Binghamton, NY: Haworth Press, 2007.

Warren, Jonathan W., and France W. Twine. "White Americans, the New Minority? Non-blacks and the Ever-expanding Boundaries of Whiteness." *Journal of Black Studies* 28, no. 2 (1997): 200–218.

Waters, Mary C. *Ethnic Options: Choosing Identities in America*. Berkeley: University of California Press, 1990.

Wadhia, Shoba S. *Banned: Immigration Enforcement in the Time of Trump*. New York: New York University Press, 2019.

Wadhia, Shoba S. "The Rise of Speed Deportation and the Role of Discretion." *Columbia Journal of Race and Law* 5, no. 1 (2015): 1–27.

Wong, Brittany. "The Racist Misogyny of the Atlanta Spa Shootings." *HuffPost*, March 18, 2021. www.huffpost.com.

Woo, Susie. *Framed by War: Korean Children and Women at the Crossroads of US Empire*. New York: New York University Press, 2019.

Wu, Ellen D. *The Color of Success: Asian Americans and the Origins of the Model Minority*. Princeton, NJ: Princeton University Press, 2014.

Wu, Frank H. "Where Are You Really From? Asian Americans and the Perpetual Foreigner Syndrome." *Civil Rights Journal* 6, no. 1 (2002): 16–22.

Wyver, Richey. "'Too Brown to Be Swedish, Too Swedish to Be Anything Else': Mimicry and Menace in Swedish Transracial Adoption Narratives." *Social Identities* 27, no. 3 (2021): 394–409.

Yancey, George. *Who Is White?: Latinos, Asians, and the New Black/Nonblack Divide.* Boulder, CO: Lynne Rienner Publishers, 2003.

Yang, Angela. "How Connecticut Became the First State to Require—and Fund—Teaching Asian American History." *NBCNews*, June 6, 2022. www.nbcnews.com.

Yuen, Nancy Wang, Stacy L. Smith, Katherine Pieper, Marc Choueiti, Kevin Yao, and Dana Dinh. *The Prevalence and Portrayal of Asian and Pacific Islanders across 1,300 Popular Films.* Anneberg: USC Anneberg Inclusion Initiative, 2021.

INDEX

A4J. *See* Adoptees for Justice

AAAW. *See* Asian Adult Adoptees of Washington

ACA. *See* Adoptee Citizenship Act

Act on the Immigration and Legal Status of Overseas Koreans (1999), 173

"Adam Crapser's Bizarre Deportation Odyssey" (article), 3

adoptable orphans, 91–100; adoption agencies creating, 157, 174; deportable immigrants contrasted with, 4–5, 9, 19, 21, 174–75; differential inclusion extended by, 70; exceptional belonging of, 75; Korean children portrayed as, 14

adoptedness, Koreanness modified by, 116

Adopted Territory (Kim, E.), 194n5

Adoptee Advocacy (organization), 168–70

Adoptee Citizenship Act (ACA), 77, 92, 101, 104–5, 107, 198n43; adoptive parents prioritized by, 93, 109; in COM-PETES Act, 193n42; latest version of, 100; Smith introducing, 98–99; 2018 version of, 93–94; without deportable offense clause, 96–97

adoptee counter-public, 10, 15–16, 113

adoptee memoirs, 142

adoptee personhood, 154, 178; adoption discourse producing, 140, 149, 156; *aka SEOUL* presenting, 160; disidentification and, 20, 144–45, 160; Korean adoptee identity contrasted with, 123, 138; relocating of, 143; *Twinsters* rewriting, 154, 162

Adoptee Rights Campaign (ARC), 92–93, 95, 104, 163, 193n44; adoptees leading, 92; immigrant groups distanced from by, 95–96

adoptees, 38; ARC led by, 92; bitterness of, 135; deportation of, 100–101, 108; immigrant communities identified with by, 106; immigrants contrasted with, 83, 94, 196n14; as killjoys, 12, 143, 156; microaggressions internalized by, 134; White domestic, 38. *See also* Asian adoptees; gratitude, expectations of; Korean adoptees; transnational adoptees; transnational transracial adoptees; undocumented adoptees

Adoptees for Justice (A4J), 96, 167–70, 193n42, 198n43

adoptees without citizenship, 1, 82–83, 87–89, 104; ARC estimating, 163; gratitude contrasted with, 105; undocumented migrants distinguished from, 93–94; Woodall on, 99–100. *See also* Crapser, Adam

adoption: birth search separated from, 158–59; citizenship not guaranteed by, 81, 189n14; forever family trope and, 81; loss associated with, 142–43; naturalization not corresponding with, 58; racialized logics and, 35–36; rescue narrative framing, 11, 14, 35, 82, 105; undocumented adoptees revealing, 101–2. *See also* international adoption; Korean adoption; transnational transracial adoption

ABOUT THE AUTHOR

SunAh M Laybourn is Assistant Professor of Sociology at the University of Memphis. She is the co-author of *Diversity in Black Greek Letter Organizations: Breaking the Line*. She earned her PhD in sociology from the University of Maryland.